W9-BZX-475

WITHDRAWN
MARY RILEY STYLES PUBLIC LIBRARY
120 NORTH VIRGINIA AVENUE
FALLS CHURCH, VA 22046
(703) 248-5030

blue
rider
press

DEMOCRAZY

★ ★ ★

DEMOCRAZY

★ ★ ★

A TRUE STORY OF WEIRD POLITICS, MONEY, MADNESS, AND FINGER FOOD

TREY RADEL

Blue Rider Press ★ New York

blue
rider
press

An imprint of Penguin Random House LLC
375 Hudson Street
New York, New York 10014

Copyright © 2017 by Trey Radel
Penguin supports copyright. Copyright fuels creativity, encourages diverse voices,
promotes free speech, and creates a vibrant culture. Thank you for buying an authorized
edition of this book and for complying with copyright laws by not reproducing, scanning,
or distributing any part of it in any form without permission. You are supporting writers
and allowing Penguin to continue to publish books for every reader.

Blue Rider Press is a registered trademark and its colophon is a trademark of
Penguin Random House LLC

Library of Congress Cataloging-in-Publication Data

Names: Radel, Trey, 1976- author.
Title: Democrazy : a true story of weird politics, money, madness, and finger food /
Trey Radel.
Description: New York : Blue Rider Press, 2017.
Identifiers: LCCN 2016058525 (print) | LCCN 2016059542 (ebook) |
ISBN 9780735210721 (hardcover) | ISBN 9780735210738 (epub)
Subjects: LCSH: Radel, Trey, date. | Legislators—United States—Biography. |
United States. Congress. House—Biography. | Republican Party
(U.S.: 1854-)—Biography. | United States—Politics and government—2009- |
Political culture—United States—History—21st century.|
Journalists—United States—Biography. | BISAC: POLITICAL SCIENCE /
Government / National. | BIOGRAPHY & AUTOBIOGRAPHY / Political. |
HUMOR / Topic / Political.
Classification: LCC E901.1.R33 A3 2017 (print) | LCC E901.1.R33 (ebook) |
DDC 328.73/092 [B] —dc23
LC record available at https://lccn.loc.gov/2016058525

Printed in the United States of America
1   3   5   7   9   10   8   6   4   2

Book design by Lauren Kolm

Penguin is committed to publishing works of quality and integrity. In that spirit, we
are proud to offer this book to our readers; however, the story, the experiences,
and the words are the author's alone.

To my family.
While geography and time may separate us,
you remain close to my heart.

★

CONTENTS

=★1★=
WELCOME TO THE
TERRORDOME

This is happening.

Those were the only three words I could think of as I sat in the backseat of an SUV owned by one of the most powerful criminal defense attorneys in Washington, D.C. As his driver negotiated the streets around the federal courthouse, my lawyer, David Schertler, who looked straight out of central casting in a perfectly tailored suit and blow-dried hair, rode shotgun and peered out the window searching for the best entrance to avoid the media shitstorm outside.

Damn. This is happening.

The driver cautiously, slowly, and deliberately drove, making lefts and rights, then hitting bursts of gas. *Am I in* Boyz n the Hood? *Are we doing a drive-by here?* The driver turned left, then right, fast and slow. "There! Right there!" David shouted, pointing to a side entrance that appeared to be a reporter-free zone. The SUV darted forward, and the driver slammed on the brakes.

No! This is happening.

"Let's go!" David shouted. We jumped out, but immediately, from around corners, from across the street, and from parked vans, a mob of reporters wielding microphones as if they were knives and cameramen aiming shoulder-fired missiles rushed toward us like a pack of wild dogs.

My attorney hopped out of the car and became an NFL lineman. As if he were protecting Peyton Manning, David threw himself directly at a Fox News producer I knew well, Chad Pergram. Chad had started to say "Congress—"but was cut off before he could get out "man Radel"; had he been able to continue, he probably would have followed with "What the hell were you thinking?"

Even though I felt numb, I thought to myself, *God bless David Schertler.* He was doing what is ingrained in the DNA of criminal defense attorneys—protect the client, deflect as much as possible. I whispered to him, "Calm down. It's okay."

Okay? Far from it. I was the first United States representative in the history of Congress to have been arrested for cocaine possession. And my day in court was quickly becoming the kind of circus you see only on bad Lifetime movies. Then, as if it couldn't get any more bizarre, enter TMZ.

First, a little background. Soon after entering Congress, I became known in the press as the Hip-Hop Conservative. I do not rap. I did not call myself this, and I didn't get the nickname because of a love for money, gangs, pimping, or any other ignorant stereotype you may place on hip-hop. I earned this label because I made it a point to do whatever I could to reach out and spread a conservative message to people from all walks of life. I always believed the best way to connect with people and have engaging conversations was to find common ground, so I never shied away from sharing my love of movies, sports, and music, and especially my love of hip-hop. Plus, I was sick and tired of Republicans playing almost exclusively to one demographic—angry old white dudes.

Yes, I'm a white guy, but I'm certainly not angry. And even though I was one of the youngest members of Congress at thirty-six, I thought I had quite a bit of experience under my belt, culturally and professionally. I made every effort to bond with Democrats in the House. And when it came to sharing a conservative message with the public, I did it in atypical ways. I utilized social media like no other member. Once, on a flight from Florida to Washington, I reviewed a new Jay Z album in its entirety live on Twitter. This was some really out-of-the-box stuff, and it received playful and positive recognition from the media and Republican party leaders. The majority whip then, Kevin McCarthy, who understood the importance of breaking out of our small, narrow world and appealing to a diverse crowd, was one of the most supportive. He shared my style with others, hoping more Republicans would go beyond our dying GOP demographic—somewhere between "I just retired" and "It's time for me to leave this planet now."

But, yo! Today, outside the federal courthouse, the Hip-Hop Conservative moniker was coming back to bite me in the ass.

"Whassup, Hip-Hop Conservative?" yelled some guy, who I figured had to be from TMZ, the infamous tabloid website, which I'd heard was trying to make a name for itself in Washington. Among the dozens of reporters, photographers, and random gawkers, this guy got smack in my face with a camera and began drilling me. "You get a shipment in from Hova?" (Let me translate: Hova is a nickname for rap artist and business mogul Jay Z, who used to sell drugs. Allegedly.) Then he shouted, "Yo, TreyDawg, you hooking up with Lamar Odom?" (Translation: Are you hanging out with the NBA star who has had very public struggles with illicit substances.) "He hook you up, dawg? You runnin' stuff through da House?" (Translation: Capital *H* as in House of Representatives, not the old-school hip-hop "in da house.") To this day, I don't know if those questions ever made it on air or if I cracked a smile during one of the most terrible moments of my life. What an asshole. But a really funny asshole.

More barking continued. "Congressman Radel! Congressman Radel!" We bolted into the courthouse. My attorney stood shoulder to shoulder with me as security led us to a holding room. With my heart racing, I had a minute to sit down, catch my breath, and collect my thoughts.

That happened. This is happening.

David Schertler put his hand on my shoulder and slid into the seat next to me. "Would you like some water?" he asked. I managed to get out "please" with a mouth drier than the Sahara. "Here's what's going to happen," he said. In the way only an attorney can, he explained step-by-step what would go down in the next hour and somehow managed to balance his tone between "Get your head out of your ass and pay attention" and "I'm here for you and you're going to be okay."

As sick and narcissistic as it sounds, I was thinking about my image—*literally,* my image on video—as we walked into the packed courtroom. Physically, I looked fine. That wasn't the issue. Heck, I looked better than I had a month before. Shortly after my bust, I had stopped drinking, so I was less bloated. But with all the stress, I'd also stopped eating, so I'd dropped quite a few pounds fast. Now I was thinking, *Sure, I might look a little better than a few weeks ago, but I do* not, not, not *want video of me hanging my head in court to run all over the world.* Right there, facing drug charges in federal frigging court, I asked, "David, there will be no cameras in the courtroom, right?"

Striking an empathetic tone, he replied, "That's right, Trey. It's federal, so no cameras, not from reporters or the courtroom itself."

"Does that mean I'll get one of those weird court sketches?"

"Yes, but you'll look much more handsome," he said with a smile.

It's awful to have these kinds of thoughts, but when you live your life in the public spotlight, it's part of the deal; concern over image, brand, and appearance become instinctive. Any politician who tells you that he doesn't think about brand and image has thought out precisely how to say he doesn't think about brand and image in a way that makes this part of his *brand and image.*

Superior Court Judge Robert Tignor knew he had a high-profile case and that the sentence he handed down would be scrutinized by the public and the press. Too heavy? "C'mon, you're just making an example out of someone who wouldn't have hurt anyone but himself!" Too light? "Off with your head! Ya let him off cuz he's a congressman!"

The courtroom was small, carpeted, and had fluorescent

panel lights. If not for the raised judge's bench, it could have passed for a drab '70s-style corporate office. As we walked toward the well where the lawyers, defendant, and judge are, I kept my head down and my chin tucked into my chest—the position I had used everywhere since I had blown up my life.

The courtroom formalities began. The charge I faced was a misdemeanor with a potential sentence of 180 days in jail and a $1,000 fine. David asked the judge for six months of probation. As they talked, I managed to take a peek at the people seated throughout the courtroom. There was only one face I recognized. I randomly and uncomfortably locked eyes with Pete Williams, the prominent NBC correspondent I had watched on TV since I was a kid. *Keep your head down!* I screamed in my mind. I quickly buried my chin back into my chest.

The judge and attorneys swapped more formalities. "Charged with possession of a controlled substance . . . Your Honor, the statute I'm referring to . . . Your honor, my client suffers . . . Your Honor, what we're asking . . ." Finally the judge called on me to speak. "Mr. Radel?"

Earlier, David had told me that I might be asked to make a statement in court. I could make the call on whether or not I wanted to say anything. I had nothing written or prepared. "Your Honor, I apologize for what I've done. I am sorry to be here. I have a problem and will do whatever is necessary to overcome it. I hope I will set an example for others struggling with this disease. I know I let my constituents down, my country down, and, most important, my family, my wife, and my two-year-old, who doesn't know it yet."

My voice cracked slightly throughout my impromptu speech.

Thoughts and emotions were fighting for space in my head and heart—sadness, disappointment, disbelief, and anger. I was having loud arguments in my mind. *Who was I to talk about setting an example? Why did I even talk about my family? I have dragged their name through enough mud and put them through hell already!*

Yet another sick reality of living in the spotlight is that many public moments are designed to look and sound genuine. Now, there is no doubt I was in a terrible, awful, dark place, furious with myself and overwhelmed with what was happening, but my use of the word "disease" was deliberate.

Shortly after my bust, while working with David and a close family friend who was also an attorney, we discussed plans and strategies. They included talking points: "Trey, you have a problem. You have a disease, and you're going to get help."

The judge cut off my desperate, pathetic thoughts and sentenced me to a full year of probation and ordered me to pay $250 into a victims' compensation fund. David gently put his hand on my back to indicate that it was time for us to leave the room.

As soon as we stepped out of the courtroom, I could feel David tense. He picked up the pace. "Trey, we're heading down these steps here." I followed without saying a word.

We quickly climbed down a dark stairwell, as if training for a track-and-field event. At the bottom I could hear the buzz of a huge crowd that sounded like an audience awaiting a concert just before the lights go down. The doors swung open. It was complete chaos. "Let's go!" David screamed. We bolted smack through the middle of the massive media scrum. Each reporter tried to shout louder and more forcefully than the last. "Congressman Radel, will you resign?" I didn't say a damn thing. I just kept walking as fast as I could in my now-permanent head-down position as we desperately made our way back to the SUV.

It was intense, but I wasn't freaking out. I was totally, completely numb. I put one foot in front of the other, as I had been taught as a kid. The SUV was only a few feet away when I heard a woman yell, "Ouch!" The crowd gasped.

Only a few feet away from the peace and serenity of the SUV, I stopped and turned out of instinct. One of the reporters had been knocked over by the pack of rabid dogs armed with microphones and cameras. I walked back to help her up. As I got to her, she picked herself up and dusted herself off.

How symbolic.

CALL ME

My phone rang, jarring me out of falling asleep while pretending to watch whatever crazy *Housewives* show my wife had on with Andy Cohen from Bravo.

The caller ID read "Connie," as in Connie Mack, the congressman who represented my district. Known as Southwest Florida, the district included Sanibel, Naples, Marco Island, and my current hometown of Fort Myers. Connie had once tried to hire me, and through a long and sometimes complicated relationship, he'd become a close friend.

This call from Connie Mack—we'll call it *this call* to stress its importance—would be one that would drastically alter my life. Whatever Connie wanted, *this call* would have consequences in more ways than I could ever imagine.

It was October of 2011 when I answered *this call*. As Connie laid out his intentions, I hung on to every word the congressman had to say.

The Mack family has a rich history in American sports and politics. Connie's great-grandfather, also Connie Mack, was a Major League baseball player, a legendary manager of the Philadelphia Athletics, a team owner, and a Hall of Famer. Over the years, some of the family made their way to Florida, where Connie's father served as a congressman representing Southwest Florida before becoming a senator.

"Connie's calling me," I said to my wife, Amy, who was sitting on the couch next to me. "Wanna bet he asks me to work for his campaign and *not* run for his seat?" Rumors had been circulating for months that Connie, a Republican, was going to run for the Senate seat held by Democrat Bill Nelson, who was up for reelection. If so, it meant a rare opportunity. Congressional seats don't open up often, especially ones held by someone like Connie, who was young, well-liked, and could have held the seat for decades. Connie and I had met in 2004 when I was a Naples-based TV reporter covering Mack's first congressional campaign. Initially, we were professionally distant, but after he was elected and I started doing more stories about him, we both began to let our guard down.

Our conversations usually started with superficial stuff like sports, but they quickly turned to politics. Eventually, I told him, "I'm libertarian at heart, but a few years ago, I registered Republican. I wanted my vote to count." He, too, opened up, sharing everything from his path to getting elected to the harsh realities of Washington.

With time, we bonded, and the walls of our reporter-politician relationship came down. So much so that several years later, when I decided it was time to leave TV news, he offered me a job as his communications director.

The daily grind of the not-so-glamorous life of a TV journalist in Southwest Florida had run its course for me. Murders. Car accidents. Bad weather. County commission snooze fests. Repeat. I was exhausted and done with covering the same crap every week. Don't get me wrong. It was really fun while it lasted, but I had always been on the move throughout my life, constantly searching for something new.

My path to news and eventually politics was one hell of a wild ride.

> Sometimes it's the journey that teaches you a lot about your destination.
>
> ★ Drake

In 1994, when I was eighteen, I left my hometown of Cincinnati to go to Loyola University in Chicago. I immediately fell in love with the action of the city, especially the energy emanating from the different cultures.

Even as a child, I loved seeing, tasting, and absorbing the people, flavors, and scenery that were different from the suburbs where I grew up. When our family made the two-day drive in our trusty Chevy Suburban from Ohio to South Florida for a vacation, I was fascinated by the people speaking different languages and in awe of the palm trees dotting every road; the pink and teal colors on the art deco buildings reminded me of my favorite show, *Miami Vice*, which I had to watch secretly because my parents told me it was for adults only. I fantasized that I'd live there one day, feather my hair back like Don Johnson, wear white suits and loafers, and be a detective.

Over a decade later, I lived in Rogers Park, a diverse neighborhood on the north side of Chicago. It had some tough areas, with the people to match. I witnessed a drive-by shooting and a targeted shooting outside a nearby theater, and one night in my last year of living there, I almost stabbed someone trying to rob my apartment. It was a far cry from the finely manicured lawns where I grew up, *and I loved it*. The city never got old. I walked the streets every day as wide-eyed and amazed as a kid on Christmas morning.

In just a few blocks, I could be in a Spanish-speaking area dominated by Mexican immigrants, with the aroma of *tacos al pastor* in the air and *elotes* for sale on the street corner. Two blocks south, in the Pakistani and Indian community, the exotic smells of curry made my mouth water, and since I came from a place where most people wore khakis from Kmart, I was fascinated to see women dressed in saris. In the windows of the Chinese restaurants farther south, whole cooked ducks hung on display and buckets of fish lined the sidewalk.

At Loyola I did what any student with no real skills does: I majored in communications. In high school I had done some on-camera work that aired on the local public broadcast station. It's hilarious now to look at my huge wave of parted Zack Morris, *Saved by the Bell* hair, and totally awesome '90s clothes and hear my Westside Cincinnati accent that was so thick that Chicagoans would ask me, "Are you from the South?"

In my senior year of college, I hosted a show and reported the local news on Loyola's own radio station, which broadcast throughout the Chicago market.

Chicago is a hard-core Democratic city, but it's run like a ruthless Rudy Giuliani Republican regime. But instead of being transparent and honest like Giuliani, who would boldly announce that he was going to clean up New York and bust even the smallest petty criminals, Chicago Democrats were full of crap. They spouted the rhetoric of equality, justice, and "fair share" while uprooting entire minority communities that were too close to the white people on the Magnificent Mile to make way for expensive condos. And when a deal was struck, everyone got a handout—a sweet contract for the developer, easy permits for the connected builders, and kickbacks for local elected officials.

In my newfound role of cub reporter, I was always on the lookout for stories, even when I was out having beers.

On Tuesday nights, my buddy Ryan Anderson and I would go see freestyle rap battles at the Morseland, a short walk from where we lived. Ryan, better known as Ando, is of Scandinavian descent and has thin blond hair and bright blue eyes. We were the only two white dudes in the place. While artists were laying down lyrics over beats, I'd lean over and say stuff like "Now I know what it feels like to be the only black guy at the party." These events, with the rappers going at one another with cut-throat rhymes, words, and poetry, were some of the most amazing displays of artistry I have ever seen in my life.

The Morseland was also a favorite spot for local left-wing

political groups, and I began to hang out with them. They were involved in everything from local environmental issues to national causes like the case of Mumia Abu-Jamal, a convicted cop killer in Philadelphia who was on death row.

One night a random guy told me his group was "working with Pam Africa to free Mumia." Beer in hand with Biggie bumping in the background, I acted like I knew who the hell he was talking about.

The next day on my radio show, I did a phone interview with Pam Africa, who in certain circles is pretty damn famous. She was an original member of MOVE, the black-liberation group active in Philadelphia in the '70s and '80s, and now headed up the cause for Abu-Jamal, who many felt had been railroaded by the justice system.

Looking for stories, I attended more and more meetings with these liberal and Democratic political groups. The groups consisted mostly of white people, old hippies, and young educated liberals. They were good people with big hearts.

What dismayed me, though, was that the theme dominating many of the meetings was victimhood. It was especially disturbing to watch the older white hippies single out young men and women of color, talk down to them, and tell them to their faces that they were victims. "You're victims of a society biased against you from birth. You're victims of a political system set up to fail you." It was as if they were trying to instill hopelessness.

Worse, right in the middle of talking about political corruption, the conversation would end up in "if only" scenarios. "If only Mayor Daley would get more money for our schools." "If only Alderman [insert Irish last name] would get some more block grants for us." "If only the city could get some more funding for [insert nonprofit]." *They demanded action from the same politicians they damned.*

From the political corruption I reported on in Chicago to the shortcomings I observed while I was studying politics and current events in Washington, I began to develop something I believe our country's Founding Fathers had—a healthy distrust of government. While some of the liberal political groups I interacted with undoubtedly helped me to see issues from a broader perspective and with more depth, I quickly realized that no politician was going to step in and be anyone's savior.

My disillusionment wasn't only with Democrats. I was also frustrated with Republicans, especially those Bible-thumping, holier-than-thou Republicans who pissed on the American public for everything from divorce to drugs to a lack of religion—specifically Christianity, of course, the only religion they'd accept.

Remember, this was the '90s, the decade in which Vice President Dan Quayle scolded the fictional TV character Murphy Brown for being a single mother. I knew a few single mothers in college, some of whom had decided not to have an abortion. Of course, Quayle would have damned them to hell for that, too. But they chose to keep the child. And between raising a child, working a full-time job, and going to school, they didn't need to be lectured. They needed to be understood. The whole judgmental, self-righteous tone turned me off.

An occasional pot smoker in college, I also strengthened my belief that individuals should be able to make personal choices for themselves especially when they're not affecting or harming anyone else in society.

It was in the liberal bastion of Chicago that I began to cement my early conservative views as a libertarian.

The most basic, ridiculously oversimplified way of describing my philosophy of government is this: I'm happy to pay taxes for valuable investments and national security, from infrastructure to our military, but don't throw my money away. I'm happy to support society through government, but give people a hand up, not a handout. Other than that, stay outta my life.

At Loyola my love of news and politics took me from being a rookie radio reporter in Chicago to Atlanta, where I landed an internship at CNN headquarters. The only open spot was in their public relations department, but once I got a whiff of the action and intensity in the newsroom, I was hooked. I had to find a way to get in.

The year before, I had done a study-abroad program in Rome for a full year and had learned fluent Italian. With a knack for languages and a love of culture, I started to study Spanish when I returned. My grasp of foreign languages and politics helped me land on CNN's international news desk, where I helped coordinate news coverage while making coffee for overworked producers, reporters, and anchors. Even if I was just fetching an anchor team some candy they could nibble on during a rare pause in covering breaking news, I did it as if the entire goddamn network would blow up unless they had their M&M's. News was about passion and adrenaline. Chock-full of both, I fit right in.

After my internship in Atlanta, I returned to Chicago to finish school. I soon landed a job on the news desk of WBBM-TV, the CBS affiliate, doing everything from helping organize the stories of the day to handing the anchors their scripts to read on the newscast. I worked with amazing journalists who still loom large in the industry, including Lester Holt, who now anchors *NBC Nightly News*. I quickly learned that if you showed a real interest in news and worked hard, even the most high-profile players were more than willing to take you under their wing. I ate it up, learning as much as I could—how to interview, how to write for TV, how to use sound bites, even how to apply makeup and how to pull off those ridiculous, ill-fitting, oversize, late-'90's suits in shades of turd brown and swamp-ass green.

My last year at Loyola wrapped up in 1999. It was time to go. After my time studying abroad and my internship in Atlanta, the urge to keep moving struck again. This time I would throw on a backpack and see the world.

While journalism was my passion, I understood two things very clearly at twenty-three. The first was that I had the rest of my damn life to work. With my résumé, I could easily take a break from "real life" and return to another job later. The second was more existential. *I understood my place in life.* I was young, loved to travel, and might never again have this kind of time to break away.

My insane work ethic also made things easier. I had saved up a ton of cash. My tendency to push working hours to the extreme started at an early age, although I never let it take away from a healthy social life. Instead, I blended it all together.

At one point I was working as a bartender at an upscale Latin American restaurant called Nacional 27, and when Celia Cruz yelled *"¡Azúcar!"* on the weekends, it became Chicago's premier salsa club. As a gringo with an affinity for Latin culture, I was in heaven slinging cervezas, pouring stiff cocktails, and making mojitos a decade before they were a douchey drink at Applebee's. At the same time, I worked in liquor promotions, where I was literally paid to throw parties. "Yeah, Trey, we'd like to pay you several hundred dollars to head to Spy, buy everyone drinks, and teach them about sophisticated drinking. Does that work for you?"

"Uh . . . yeah."

I would throw a party to promote Johnnie Walker at some high-end happy-hour bar in the Loop, and then at night I would head over to Nacional to tend bar until two in the morning. After that, I often volunteered to work the overnight shift at WBBM, where I walked into a newsroom full of zombielike producers writing the news for the early-morning shows. The news wrapped up late morning, and when it did, I'd head home, sleep all day, get up, and do it over again.

During that time, I also managed to play guitar in a band and fit in some improv comedy classes at Chicago's famed Second City, which was the launching pad for comedians and actors like Chris Farley, Tina Fey, and John Belushi. Many nights I dreamed I'd be on *Saturday Night Live* one day.

These were some fun and wild years, but I wanted more. It was time to go.

Y porque gitano soy, como lo pienso voy.
And because I am a gypsy, how I think, I go.
★ The Gipsy Kings, "Soy"

With a yearning to learn fluent Spanish, I decided I needed to absorb the culture of our neighbor down south, swill tequila, and surely meet some girl named Maria. That November of 1999 I threw on a backpack and bought a one-way plane ticket to Mexico. I had no idea when I would return to the States. But I did know that if all technology failed on Y2K and the world blew up I'd be in the perfect spot, lying on a beach in some seaside village.

Trying to explain to my family that I was heading to deep south Mexico with nothing but a one-way ticket and no time frame wasn't exactly easy. But after my five intense years of school and work, my parents knew traveling, moving, seeing, and soaking in life was kinda my thing.

My mom was especially worried. We wouldn't be talking for weeks at a time as I wandered around remote beaches, jungles, and mountains. This was the '90s—no personal GPS tracker, no Google Maps, and no iPhone. I used these amazing pieces of folding paper called maps and called home from phone booths.

Ultimately, my parents were supportive. I tried to convince them that the "highly practical" reason I was traveling through Mexico was to become fluent in Spanish.

Friends and family questioned me. "Aren't you worried about your safety? That place is dangerous!" I was described and questioned in ways that I would hear throughout my life—"Total disregard. Cavalier. What the hell are you thinking?"

Screw it. I'm going to Mexico. I'm going to get to know an amazing country and have fun doing it.

I grew a beard and lived on as little as ten bucks most days. My main source of transportation was a *camioneta de pollos*, a "chicken bus," and some did have chickens on top. I made my way from Quintana Roo in the Yucatán to a backpacker's paradise called Caye Caulker in Belize. After a week or so of snorkeling and catching lobsters for dinner, I split for Guatemala.

There I spent most of my time in the colonial-style city of Antigua in the mountains, where I sharpened my Spanish. Antigua hosts many language schools for gringos, but I didn't have money to pay for lessons so I went to every school in the area and *asked* about lessons. I talked at length with teachers about studying Spanish while improving my Spanish. *Dick move, right?* At night I'd find a bar to belly up to and chat with the bartender or other locals and learn more. It was street Spanish, loaded with colorful words, but it was Spanish.

Tired of the mountains, I needed to get to a beach. From Antigua, I headed to Guatemala City to catch a bus for the coast of Oaxaca, a majestic, spectacularly beautiful state in southwest Mexico. But to get there, I'd have to travel through Chiapas, an area where rebels were fighting the Mexican army.

It was in Chiapas that I lost my fear of death.

From Guatemala City, I had an almost twenty-hour chicken-bus ride ahead of me, so I headed toward the back of the bus, where a window seat was open. There I could rest my head against the wall to sleep.

Whenever I took a long ride like this, I had a routine. I'd eat a big meal before and wash it down with a couple of beers, just enough to make me tired. I also had to have my music. I had a huge, awkward compact-disc player and a massive book of discs.

The CD case weighed more than my clothes. Finally, on top of my head sat some big ol' headphones like you see DJs wear. I looked like some sort of futuristic, robotic Mickey Mouse with cords coming from my head.

I pressed play and zoned out to Stone Temple Pilots' *Tiny Music . . . Songs from the Vatican Gift Shop* album. Songs like "Adhesive," with its smooth sax and Scott Weiland's trippy lyrics, were perfect for this long haul.

Before drifting off to sleep, the last thing I saw was a kid about ten years old sit down next to me.

Hours later, in a deep sleep, I felt something bump against my shoulder. Instinctively, I shooed it away, then that something grabbed my shoulder. I opened my eyes.

"Oh, no," I whispered. The tallest Mexican I had ever seen in my life was towering over me. He had a chiseled face, a clenched jaw, and was staring down at me. Adrenaline burst out of my glands and cleared my foggy head. As it did, I registered more worrisome details. He was in some sort of military garb and had a rifle slung over his shoulder.

"Por favor, blah blah blah," is all I heard. He was speaking so fast, I could barely understand. I just sat there, stunned, with a blank look on my face and those big-ass headphones making me look like I was about to sing "M-I-C-*see ya real soon!*" I snapped out of it, took Mickey's headphones off my head, and in a gringo accent, said, *"¿Disculpe?"* He motioned toward the front of the bus and stepped back to open the way for me to get up and walk off.

I looked out the windows; it was pitch-black. Then I looked around. Every passenger was wide-awake and staring at me.

Every single one of them. The kid next to me was staring at me. His eyes were bulging wide open, so much so that with his dark hair and dark skin he looked like a cartoon character. The kid's expression made me nervous, and the giant Mexican military guy was freaking me out. It was time for me to follow his gesture and get off the bus. As I stood up, he slowly began to remove the large rifle from his shoulder. Nervousness was now becoming raw, unadulterated fear.

Once I was standing, I looked him in the eyes and said, in a terrible accent, *"Sí, sí. No hablo español muy bien, pero sí."* Yes, yes. I don't speak Spanish well, but yes.

As I walked to the front of the bus, something steel made its way from just above my tailbone to the middle of my back. It was the barrel of his rifle. I was petrified.

I noticed the driver was not in his seat. As I exited, set foot on the road, and slowly looked up, I saw the bus driver sitting on the curb with his head buried in his hands, twitching his foot and shaking his head no. Seven men, all armed and in military fatigues, stood along the curb. The only things illuminating the area were flashlights and flares in the road.

These armed men had stopped the bus, *and I was the only passenger being dragged off at gunpoint.*

At that moment I knew I was going to die. *Well, this is it*, I thought. *Fun while it lasted.*

Then my fear completely vanished. My mouth didn't get dry. I didn't panic or even break out in a sweat. A feeling of peace and serenity rolled over me like a gentle ocean wave on the beach. The only touch of sadness I had was for my family, who would probably never know what had happened to me.

I figured the best possibility was immediate death. Execution. The worst was some sort of jail cell on a remote mountain in deep south Mexico coupled with torture.

Then I saw that someone had pulled my backpack from the baggage compartment, and three of the men were looking through it. Numb to everything and in complete peace, I headed toward them. I didn't even need to walk; I floated over.

I knew I didn't have anything illegal in my backpack. While I may have made a few poor decisions in life, carrying contraband in foreign countries wasn't one of them. My backpack did not contain even a can of beer, just my stanky clothes.

But I figured they had planted something. The questions now: Did they want money? Or did they need an excuse to kidnap or kill me?

One of the men gestured for me to come closer. He poked his rifle around the top of the bag, indicating he wanted to open and search it. *"Claro que sí,"* I said, barely rolling my *r*. Yes, of course. Another one joined him, and they tore the backpack apart. One even picked up my tube of toothpaste and squirted it out in case I had used it to smuggle something.

But as they continued digging, I sensed a slight chance that maybe they were legit men of the law and were simply suspicious. I thought maybe, just maybe, I'd get out of this. Still anticipating that they might pull out a massive brick of planted marijuana and cock their weapons, I kept watching. Suddenly, the main spelunker crouched over my bag stopped his search as if he had found something. *No!* With his hand still inside my pack, he looked me in the eyes and slowly stood up. There was nothing in his hands.

Then he smiled.

"*Gracias,*" he said, which was followed by a bunch of stuff I didn't understand. I let out a deep breath of relief. He and the others seemed relieved, too. They even packed the bag back up for me and returned it to the storage area. Then they motioned for me to get back on the bus, which I did pretty damn fast. The bus driver followed.

I was expecting a standing ovation from the passengers with big bear hugs. There was nothing. Only suspicious eyes.

But by then I didn't need any reassurance. At that moment I'd completely lost any fear of death.

The next day I finally made it to the beach at Zipolite. I walked the hot sand trying to find the best and cheapest place to stay. "*Oh Madonna! Ma che cazzo fai?*" I heard in the distance. *Is that Italian?* I asked myself incredulously. I walked up to an open-air restaurant where loads of Italians were hanging out. I felt weirdly, strangely at home. "*Buon giorno,*" I said loudly.

I had intended to stay only a few days in Zipolite, but I stayed two weeks with the Italian expats, eating homemade pasta and seafood caught right off the beach that day. The time in Oaxaca took a toll on my savings, though. After running out of money and yearning in some ways to get back to the professional side of life, I started checking in with my family and listening to voice mails from home. A friend told me about a job in TV news in Houston. *Maybe it's time for me to go,* I thought.

In retrospect I can see that even then it was difficult for me to accept the complete peace of the paradise I was in. There I was, on one of the most desolate beaches in Mexico with only a few dozen other people. The routine was amazing: wake up early when the sun cracked over the Sierra Madre, eat breakfast, swim, surf, smoke and drink, eat seafood, watch the sun disappear behind the Pacific Ocean, lie in the sand to gaze at more stars than I had ever seen in my life, go to sleep, wake up, and do it again.

Even in complete tranquility, I could not fight off the urge to go to work, to do, to create, to have action and movement. It was a love-hate relationship.

Eventually, I made my way north to Mexico City and caught a flight home to the States. I landed a job on the news desk of KHOU, the CBS affiliate in Houston, the (insert Texan twang here) "Spirit of Texas!" There I would handle many of the same duties I had had in Chicago and at CNN in Atlanta.

My job at the station entailed coordinating daily coverage, listening to police scanners, and dispatching crews to breaking news. While working, I always kept an eye out for good stories because I was making the TV version of a paper résumé. It's often called a reel, a collection of on-camera news stories that I could use to apply for on-air jobs in smaller media markets.

When reporters returned from the field, I would take their B-roll and write my own stories. Then, on my days off, I'd get some poor photographer to put up with my green ass while I stood in front of his camera and did pretend news.

Seasoned reporters and photographers taught me the importance of "walking and talking" and "putting motion into standups." Standups are the footage of the reporter standing in front of the camera during a prerecorded story. They're usually standing in a foot of water to show you how "terrible and dangerous" the weather is while everybody off-camera is walking around normally and avoiding that puddle.

When I first started to apply for on-air jobs, some of the reporters at KHOU warned me, "Don't aim for too high of a market, you'll never get a job. You're too green."

I fought back. "But I have major market experience! I know news. I'm not a college kid! Plus, I'm fluent in Spanish. That has to be worth something here in Texas or California or Florida."

In late 2001 I spotted an opening for a reporter at WINK-TV, the CBS station in Fort Myers/Naples. While working on the news desk at KHOU, I searched the WINK website for a list of managers and employees. I yelled out to the newsroom, "Does anyone know anyone at this station called W-I-N-K in Florida?" A reporter shot back, "It's too big of a market. What the hell are you thinking?"

The main anchor, Lisa Foronda, blurted out, "Shappy!" with a big smile on her face. Mike "Shappy" Shapiro was the assistant news director at WINK. She made a call, and Mike pulled out my reel, *my pretend news stories on DVD*, for a closer look.

After a year and a half in Houston, I landed a job as a general assignment reporter at WINK and became an actual, real, on-air TV news reporter. My experiences and résumé landed me the job I was warned not to even think about because it was too big of a market. Cavalier.

Working as a reporter is a front-row seat to life. You meet, see, and witness some of the most amazing, kind, big-hearted people and acts of life. You also see the most depressing, horrifying, and utterly senseless shit no human being should be subjected to.

The highs and lows of TV news are intense; the highs keep you going. There were the moments of scoring an exclusive interview or breaking a massive story that unlike 99 percent of the garbage—car accidents or black lights aimed at bodily-fluid-stained hotel bedsheets—actually affected people's lives.

Or . . .

Murder!

The producer would shout, "Woo-hoo! Someone got shot! Drop the black light you have aimed at the bedsheets to expose what people really sleep in when they visit Florida! No more covering semen, Trey! We have blood, bro! Get your ass moving!"

Of course, in Florida, we also have every reporter's dream—hurricanes! Massive storms destroying everything in their path make for great television! Any reporter can be the Weather Channel's Jim Cantore for a day, and I was *that guy* often. When you tune in and ask, "What's that idiot doing standing in the hurricane?" I was that idiot!

Those were the exceptions, though. Day after day there were accidents. Just swap out the name of the road. Even murders got boring. Just swap out the name of the victim and street; keep the same neighborhood. (Jaded, I know.) County commission meetings about tax rates and new construction permits dominated coverage. If you weren't jacked up on a few Cuban *cafecitos*, those meetings would put even the most serious insomniac to sleep fast.

After five intense years of being a general assignment reporter, I began to lose the rush and urgency to "inform the public" about something that had no effect on them. While I was proud of quite a few of the stories I did that genuinely touched and changed lives, I was done with TV news. I had hit the ceiling for job growth, and no anchor position was open. And with every news story blending in to become the same one, I needed something more. When I left, though, I took away great memories, life lessons, and something else—a relationship.

In my last year at the station, I met the love of my life, Amy, who I would later marry. She was also an employee at WINK, working as an editor. While editor might sound like a fancy title, it was a low-level position that put her in a dark room all day editing video and recording satellite feeds. She was beyond it. Amy was smart, full of energy, and, yes, stunningly beautiful. Way outta my league. I loved her confidence. As a "lowly editor," making maybe a dime over minimum wage, she would tell me, "You watch. I'm going to be a reporter in this market soon! I don't know where, but I will! And then I'll be an anchor!" She was confident but not cocky, tenacious but not overly ambitious. She was amazing. I fell hard for her. Soon we were a couple. And before she knew it, many of those goals she set for herself came true. Personally and professionally, Amy and I had a long, sometimes wild, journey ahead.

In 2006 I was looking to get out of TV news, and several years before *this call* from Connie Mack, he offered me the position of communications director in his congressional office. The comms director position, as it's often referred to, crafts press releases, manages media inquiries, and even helps with the overall brand of the member of Congress. I was well suited for it with my experience in TV news.

While I considered his job offer, I also looked for jobs in other industries and contemplated launching some sort of a business based on my own ideas. Laughably, I didn't know what or how. I just knew I wanted to do something entrepreneurial. Soon enough, I zoned in, and once again I heard the same words and questions I had heard earlier when I was planning a new venture.

One night, after a long day of covering breaking news all over Collier County, I bellied up to a favorite local bar in Naples, Bistro 821, and got into a conversation with a local entrepreneur I knew named Dan. He was a couple decades older than I was, but we got along well and occasionally had a drink together. I knew he had been highly successful, but what I did not know was that he owned a small local direct-mail newspaper, the *Naples Journal*, that targeted the ultrawealthy areas of Naples. And, by the way, Naples is loaded. It has the highest concentration of retired Fortune 500 CEOs in the nation. Half-acre plots of land in some neighborhoods start at $5 million. And that's just for the dirt.

After Dan and I finished a couple of "pops," as he called them, our conversation cut to the chase. He was tired of running the *Journal* and wanted to sell it. I became determined to find a way to buy it, with the goal of expanding it to challenge the local corporate papers and give it a digital presence.

Ha! I had no clue what I was doing! I had never worked in print. Heck, when you write for TV, you're taught to write "conversational style," which means writing at a fifth-grade level so viewers can understand what you are saying. And I didn't know a damn thing about publishing newspapers. Some friends and family members advised me not to do it. "Oh, now you're going to be a 'publisher.' Kinda cavalier, huh? What the hell are you thinking?"

I figured I had a few things going for me, though. I knew the Naples-area news, politics, and landscape really well. I had worked hard to build relationships and gotten close to some of the people I interviewed and did stories with, like Congressman Mack, as well as CEOs and restaurant owners. I knew I'd be able to come up with compelling news, but the real question was: Could I get these businesses to advertise in my paper?

Online publishing was starting to take shape in 2006, and people I consulted told me over and over, "Print is dead." But I knew that the demographic in the area was old. People in Naples clung to and loved print, and I didn't see that changing overnight. I also believed—and still do—that if there's any future for printed news it must be hyperlocal. So I focused strictly on the people, personalities, and news affecting Naples neighborhoods. Finally, for the future health of the paper, I developed long-term plans to take it digital and make it a powerful player online.

Amy, who'd been my girlfriend for a few months, was tremendously supportive, almost blindly believing in me. My dad, who was practical, but also knew the value of a potential gamble, helped me assess it. As always, he said, "You've gotta do what you believe in. If you think you can make this work, follow your dreams." I did. This was before the economic collapse, so money was easy to borrow—in retrospect, insanely, stupidly, idiotically *easy*. So I quit WINK, took out a loan, and, without really having a clue, bought a small community newspaper.

At that time I told Connie I wasn't going to take the communications director position but would instead publish a newspaper in Naples, which happened to be one of the major cities of his district. I gave Connie a space to write about whatever he wanted every month. It was a move he and his team appreciated.

I owned the *Naples Journal* for less than a year. After rebranding, reformatting, and expanding it, and before I even had the chance to pursue my plans of going digital, the E. W. Scripps Company, the corporate owner of the local Naples newspaper, made me a huge offer and bought me out. My gamble paid off big. I quintupled my investment.

I found myself wondering how words like "cavalier" and questions like "What the hell are you thinking?" once again had brought me success.

After selling the paper, I had two things I didn't have much of before—money and time. I had just turned thirty and figured this time in life was like my early twenties, so once again I decided to strap on a backpack and travel for a few months.

Amy, who also loved exploring and had backpacked a few places with me, couldn't make time for a long trip. She had done exactly what she said she'd do: She got a job on air as a reporter for the local Fox affiliate. Now she was the one dealing with murders, car wrecks, and county commission meetings.

Pushing the opportunity to the limit as usual, I told Amy, "I'm going to be gone for a few months." After all, the only things I'd miss back home were her and maybe a greasy cheeseburger from time to time. While she knew travel was my passion and was totally supportive, Amy reined me in. "Trey, how about one month." I agreed, although, like my trip to Mexico years before, I had no return ticket. I'd just have to find a city to depart from after a month.

I started in Colombia, then headed to Thailand. The weeks in Southeast Asia were an emotional rollercoaster and flat-out insane at times. My close friend Ando, the same guy I used to go to rap battles with when I was at Loyola, had settled there. Like many of my close friends, Ando was eccentric, extremely driven, and did things his own way.

After Chicago's cold winters, Ando had gone to Thailand as a student and made it his mission to eventually open a restaurant there. He did; it was Mexican. That's right, a Mexican restaurant in Thailand.

"Dude, it makes perfect sense," he convinced me. "People get sick of eating Thai food all day. This is something different! European and American travelers will love it!" When I got to the island of Koh Phangan, I saw his restaurant and gazed at the sign bearing the place's name, ANDO LOCO. "Great name," I told him with a huge smile. Ando, dressed in flip-flops, a T-shirt, and shorts, as usual, began in his loud, energetic voice, "We got tacos. We got burritos. And we got tequila. Oh, and this!" He pointed to his Ping-Pong tables, where we would have battles late into the night with people from all over the world.

But Ando wanted more in his life than partying, drinking, and eating. In his early visits to Thailand, he took it upon himself to raise money to help build an orphanage in neighboring

Cambodia, where many children had been left without parents after decades of war.

After a couple weeks in Thailand, we headed to Cambodia. In Phnom Penh, Ando took me to Stung Meanchey, the infamous garbage dump. It was horrifying.

As we drove up a long dirt road and glimpsed the dump in the distance, it looked scenic—rolling hills with a serene fog hovering over them. But when we got closer, I realized the hills were massive piles of trash and the fog was smoke. Acres of garbage stretched as far as I could see, and the smell was so intense and fierce, I gagged. The putrid stench was like nothing I had smelled before—a toxic mix of chemicals dumped from God knows where, bodily waste due to lack of plumbing, and rotting animal carcasses.

A sea of men, women, and children worked their way in and out and over the piles. Even toddlers begin their lives by scavenging for recyclable metal in terribly dangerous conditions. The people are barely paid pennies for metals they collect, and many die young, either through malnutrition or in accidents from the dump trucks zooming in and out at high speeds.

When we got there, the children flocked to us. Incredibly, they were giggling and smiling. Many of the kids had runny noses and were constantly coughing. Others had severe physical deformities or stunted growth from malnutrition. The kids were desperately hungry. The only thing they wanted from us was a little attention and care.

It was heartbreaking. I smiled as best as I could.

Food vendors occasionally came through selling plastic

sandwich bags of some sort of thick flavored protein drink for a few cents per bag. Ando and I gave a vendor the equivalent of twenty dollars and fed every kid we met. Their smiles got even bigger. I did my best to stay upbeat, but their brief happiness at the rare treat of nutritious food (or some liquid form of it) was tragic and agonizing to me. This level of poverty is something we simply cannot fathom in the United States.

It was a heavy, depressing trip. But after Stung Meanchey, Ando took me to the orphanage he had helped build. There the teachers and kids performed traditional folk dances and sang, and we all played instruments together. These kids were the lucky ones who would have a future. It was a touching moment, the complete opposite of what I had just witnessed.

After seeing the worst and best of humanity, I split off from Ando to go to Angkor Wat, the elaborate twelfth-century Cambodian temple complex built by the Khmer Empire. I hiked around the surrounding jungle and visited the nearby infamous Killing Fields, where dictator Pol Pot's Khmer Rouge regime murdered more than a million people in the late 1970s.

After the abandoned kids in Stung Meanchey and the display of five thousand victims' skulls in a huge glass tower at the Killing Fields, I needed to clear my foggy head, thick with the haze of death. I needed something more than a stiff drink. I needed to unload.

So I visited a nearby shooting range.

I had heard about the gun ranges of Cambodia from Ando but had no idea what I was getting into. I grabbed a ride in what's called a *tuk-tuk*, a gas-powered three-wheel vehicle with no doors that looks like someone put a roof on top of a large motor-cycle. In Thailand and Cambodia, it's what you use as a taxi.

The *tuk-tuk* took me deep into the jungle. As we pulled up to our destination, two young armed Cambodians stood out-side an open-air café. Their arms were folded, pistols holstered on their hips. They had hard looks on their faces. Cambodians are normally rather skinny, but these guys were rock solid. They both wore red muscle shirts and black cargo pants, and looked like a cross between local militiamen and '80s aerobics instruc-tors. Badasses, but I bet they could Jazzercise like nobody's business.

I stepped out of the *tuk-tuk* and looked around, noticing a nearby pond. As soon as I did—*boom!*—an explosion! "Whoa!" I yelled, and stepped back to take cover. Water shot up hundreds of feet into the air. I ducked down next to the *tuk-tuk* as if a mo-torcycle with a roof were going to protect me. The two young Cambodians didn't even react, not to my ducking or to the explosion. I peered around the *tuk-tuk* toward the water. Two guys in their twenties were laughing, pointing at the pond, and loudly speaking German to each other. One of them was hold-ing a grenade. He then chucked it into the water. *Boom!*

One of the Cambodians approached me and, in his limited English, invited me into the café. "You come." He gestured toward the structure. I walked to a table; he pushed my shoulder down to instruct me to sit and handed me a piece of paper with a clear plastic cover that looked like a menu.

I took a long look around. Massive displays of shotguns, rifles, and machine guns hung on two walls. But beyond the pond that they were using for grenade practice, there was only jungle as far as I could see. *Could probably get rid of a body pretty easily here*, I thought.

Then I started to read the menu. I could not believe my eyes! It read: "All prices in U.S. dollars. Fully automatic M16—$25 (one magazine). Fully automatic AK-47—$25 (one magazine). Grenade—$50 (per throw). M60 machine gun—$100 (one feed)."

"Whoa! That's the *Rambo* gun!" I said out loud, and pointed. The young Cambodian, who couldn't have been born when *Rambo* came out, finally cracked a smile. He laughed and repeated, "Yes! Rambo!" Then he uncrossed his arms and gave me two thumbs up. Smiling, I awkwardly sent two thumbs up right back at him.

At the very bottom of the menu, it read: "Angkor beer—$2. Heineken beer—$3."

"No friggin' way." I quietly laughed to myself. Weapons and beers were the only two things on the menu.

As I grabbed my camera, I noticed another line, "No pictures of menu." I may break rules from time to time but not with two armed Cambodians nearby. I put the camera back in my pocket.

I then motioned the Cambodian over to me as if I were at a five-star restaurant about to place an order for a medium-rare steak complemented by a bottle of fine wine.

"Um, yes, I'll have a Heineken and an AK-47," I said.

Of course I would! Made perfect sense!

I wanted the Heineken because I had been knocking down Angkor beers the entire trip. It was time to step up in quality,

especially to complement my tasty killing machine of a meal—
a fully automatic rifle probably left over from Pol Pot's regime.

Why the AK-47? Since the M16 is made in America, I was
sure I could get my hands on one back home if I really wanted
to. But when would I ever get another chance to rip a mag from
a fully automatic AK *while enjoying a cold beer*?

The Cambodian asked, "You fire grenade?" and pointed to
the two Germans who were coming into the café drenched
in water.

I was confident that even though the guns were probably old
they would be safe enough to fire without blowing up in my
face. But I wasn't so certain about the grenades.

"No, thanks, I'll let a German lose an arm today," I said with
a smile. The only thing the Cambodian understood was no
so he guided me to the concrete tunnels that served as the shooting range.

Unloading a full magazine of ammunition with a fully automatic machine gun takes all of about five seconds. *"Rat-tat-tat!"*
I pulled the AK's trigger for a short burst. Then I pulled again,
this time unleashing all of its fury. *"Rat-tat-tat-tat-tat!"* The gun
was smoking! "Hell, yeah!" I yelled, alpha-male testosterone
flying out of my mouth.

I shot a total of two magazines and handed the Cambodians
fifty-six dollars on my way out. The extra three bucks was for
another Heineken, a roadie.

My travels continued.

Somewhere in Hong Kong, I got back in touch with Amy,
calling every few days and swapping e-mails regularly. I missed
her dearly. One afternoon I got an e-mail from the WINK

news director asking me to come back and anchor the evening news at the station in Fort Myers. It was an easy decision. I was a bit burned out on traveling and this opportunity would keep me home in Southwest Florida, which I loved and where Amy continued to live and work. "I'm in," I wrote back.

Swapping out the palm trees of Southeast Asia for Southwest Florida, I moved in with Amy. I soon married her, my love, my best friend, and my biggest supporter. By this time, she had quickly made her way from reporter to morning anchor. Then, in a crazy turn of events, Amy was promoted to anchor the evening newscasts just after I launched a new evening newscast with WINK. We were competing head-to-head! (No need to ask. I lost.)

I signed a three-year contract and settled into the anchor spot, but it wasn't long before I felt frustrated on the job.

If anchoring the news had been like being Ron Burgundy in *Anchorman*, maybe I would have enjoyed it. But I was bored. Anchoring was like being a reporter except there was no action. Nothing was ad-libbed; you read what was scripted, stayed in a dungeon of a newsroom all damn day, and drank really crappy coffee. It wasn't like Ron Burgundy's newsroom. No scotch and no three-martini dinner breaks in between the six and eleven p.m. newscasts. We didn't even have time to leave the station. We were too busy following car accidents, murders, and county commission meetings.

Despite my frustrations, the three years passed quickly. They passed so fast because I had become consumed with finding another line of work or creating another business—something more, something new. I realized that after years of being on the sidelines reporting the news as a neutral journalist with no opinion, I wanted to get involved and shape current events, specifically in politics. Just before my contract was up, I let management know that I would be leaving to start a media-relations company focused on conservative candidates, politicians, and causes.

But here's the kicker.

Right after leaving the anchor position at WINK to start my company in late 2009, I received another job offer that would set up *this call* from Connie two years later.

It just so happened that when I left TV news to launch my political consulting company WINK had a position open up on one of their radio stations. Their longtime conservative radio show host, Mandy Connell, was leaving. Since I had worked many years for the company as both an anchor and reporter, they gave me the chance to sub for a few shows. Soon after, I was offered the job.

Next thing I know, I'm a radio-show host. Uh, okay.

I ran my company from home in the afternoons. Every weekday morning I woke up at the god-awful hour of three a.m. to host my radio show, *Daybreak with Trey Radel*. My focus was overwhelmingly on fiscal issues, foreign affairs, and national security and its abuses. I hosted guests from all walks of life, including Democrats, some of whom I thoroughly disagreed with. I always remained polite but never held back, and I often vented my own frustrations and allowed callers to do the same.

It was early 2010, and Republicans were pissed. I mean really pissed. Now, I'm not the doom-and-gloom guy on the radio telling you to "get yer guns, yer gold, 'n' get 'er done." Far from it. But after Democrats rammed Obamacare through Congress in the tone and style they did, people were angry, even the independents. I was no exception.

My radio gig put me in the political spotlight in Southwest Florida as if I were doing a solo Broadway show, and it began to plug me into political circles. I quickly became a quasi celebrity, and as the dominant political voice of Southwest Florida, I hosted more political events and town halls that year than any of the most seasoned politicians in the area. I can't even begin to count how many times I stood side by side with the Republican Party's newest, biggest, youngest, most popular rock star—Marco Rubio.

A few months before taking the radio gig, I had interviewed him for my newscast on WINK after he had announced his campaign for U.S. Senate.

Republicans and Democrats were gunning for the wide-open Senate seat, and Marco was hosting a lunch in Fort Myers in support of his fledgling campaign. Having known a little about Marco's impressive history and rise in the Florida Republican Party, I convinced my news director to let me interview "this young guy insane enough to take on Charlie Crist."

Marco was running in the Republican primary against Charlie, who at the time had sky-high approval ratings and was the country's most popular governor. Many insiders thought Marco was committing political suicide. They were convinced he would lose to Charlie and be shunned by the Republican Party forever. The lunch barely drew ten people.

As the first few people began to filter in, I pulled Marco aside for an interview. Instantly, I saw what made him different.

He spoke with conviction, and with his youth and energy, he had a unique spark and presence. Even as a jaded journalist, I could see he had the elusive "it" factor, that undefinable but undeniable quality few politicians have. After the interview, we talked a little about his hometown of Miami, its culture and people, and our mutual love for football.

Only a few weeks later, Marco quickly began to climb in the polls. As antiestablishment sentiment hit a fever pitch, Crist was attacked by grassroots groups and powerful D.C. political action committees, known as PACs, for supporting the Obama stimulus program.

When President Obama came to visit Fort Myers, Governor Crist gave him a "man hug" on stage. You know how it goes: Shake the right hand and embrace but keep your hand there so your chests don't touch. *Yeah, smooth.*

That image spread faster over the Internet than Republicans blame terrorism for everything and Democrats blame climate change for everything. That man hug, that fleeting public display of affection, was one of the major factors that led to Charlie's loss. It was not seen as Charlie welcoming the commander in chief to Florida; it was seen as an embrace of Obama policy and therefore a nail in Crist's political coffin.

In the Republican gubernatorial primary, Rick Scott was a candidate. I had met Rick a few times through mutual friends. He was a nice guy with a quiet intensity. He had never run for elected office, but when he did, he was all in, as in $72-million-of-his-own-money in. Like Marco, he destroyed the institutional Republican in the primary.

During this time, I was emceeing just about every local and

national political event in the area, all while I was live on the radio four hours a day, five days a week, talking politics to almost exclusively primary-voting, hard-core, conservative Republicans. Every day, every hour, I shared my beliefs, questions, and concerns.

President Obama's policy frustrated me deeply, but I also felt the man himself had let me down. Shortly after he was sworn in, it seemed to me that he took the hope and optimism he ran on and threw it right out the window. Regardless of how you feel today about the Affordable Care Act, known as Obamacare, the way he, along with Nancy Pelosi, then Speaker of the House, and Harry Reid, Senate majority leader, passed it set the tone for so much else in the years to come.

More than half the country wanted the president and the Democratic-controlled Congress simply to slow down. That's not asking much. After all, no one even knew what was in the legislation. Don't forget Nancy Pelosi's infamous words, "We have to pass the bill so that you can find out what is in it." That's no way to run government.

As for President Obama, I wanted more of the senator who had opposed raising the debt ceiling. I wanted more of the senator who had spoken out against the war in Iraq. I wanted the presidential candidate who was going to "reach out with an open hand instead of clenched fist" because so much of what he was doing was far from it.

If you're a Democrat, you might not like reading these sentiments, but understand that this was how more than half the country felt. Sure, that half may have been mostly Republican or conservative-leaning independents, but they are Americans, too.

However, as an equal opportunity shot taker, I was still frustrated with parts of the Republican Party. During President Obama's earliest days, Mitch McConnell, the top Republican in the Senate, set the tone by saying, "The most important thing we want to achieve is for President Obama to be a one-term president." *How kind! I'm sure he'll be excited to work with you!*

I also had a tough time understanding some conservatives who railed against "big government" but voted for bailouts. Conservatism to me was about minimal government and allowing people to make choices and take responsibility for their decision—win or lose. And that included corporate bailouts. I still find it hypocritical that some Republicans railed against the Big Auto bailouts yet embraced the Wall Street bailouts and vice versa for some Democrats.

Something else that drove me absolutely mad was the unfortunate but common theme emanating from the Republican Party during these years—hate. The attitude of "screw you" toward anyone "not conservative enough" was nothing like the party of Ronald Reagan I had studied as a young adult or remembered as a boy.

As I got more deeply involved in politics, I wanted to be more than a young adult in the Republican Party; I wanted to be an adult with youth and energy and an inclusive message rooted in my libertarian leanings.

These issues, coupled with the heightened emotion of the 2010 primary, drove me. I found as many ways to get involved in the party as I could. Along with my radio gig, my media-relations work segued into networking with and learning directly from candidates' campaigns.

From Marco Rubio's team, I learned the intricacies of building grassroots support while simultaneously, intentionally or not, building my own fund-raising network when I attended his fund-raising events.

From Rick Scott's team, I learned how to stay on message. Rick would be the first to admit he's not the best public speaker, but his team kept him on message like no other candidate had been. Watching his campaign, I learned the importance of not deviating from what's important to the voters. In his case, it was all about jobs. Rick never got through a sentence without using the word "job" as either a subject or object. If he could have made "job" a verb, he would have. "As the jobinator of our great state, I will grab Florida by the job and balls, and make sure jobs are jobbing coming to Florida. May Job bless America."

So when *this call* came from Connie in October of 2011 about his potential run for Senate and my run for the House, I had been doing radio and had been active in the political scene for almost two years. In that flashing moment of the phone ringing, it was like everything I had done had led up to this moment, *right here, right now.*

I don't know who "they" are, but *they* say luck is when preparation and opportunity meet. Both were meeting now, right in my lap.

Connie's call presented the opportunity, and I was prepared. Everything I learned from the Rubio and Scott campaigns and my deep involvement in the local political community was about to be put to real-world use.

Before raising a dime for our campaign, I realized I already owned some of the most critical components that a candidate needs. One of the biggest is name identification. Another is gaining the trust of voters by sharing their experience and beliefs. That's why candidates have to raise so much damn money! You see, politicians are products and products need to be advertised. They need to tell you about themselves, why you need them, why you just gotta have 'em! Candidates advertise to say "Pick me! Pick me!" Of course, they also use some of the money to tell you that their opponent is keeping a dead hooker in the trunk of their Chevy.

Name ID? Check! For years people woke up with me on the radio, and before that, when I anchored the late news, they went to bed with me. I even got to tell them good night with a smile. Sexy, right?

Public knowledge of my political beliefs? Check! I had some hard-core radio listeners who tuned in every day for the entire four-hour broadcast.

Of course, along with name ID and politics, there are the aesthetics, so it helps to be decent looking. After all, like the old Nirvana T-shirt says, we're talking American-style, superficial, flower-sniffin', kitty-pettin', baby-kissin' politics here!

Presentable candidate and family? Check. Aside from my four chins, odd watermelon-shaped head, and a gut that gets worse with age, I am presentable. But Amy's a different story. I married the most beautiful woman I've ever laid my eyes on, and she's smart! Amy made up for what I lacked.

I was ready when *this call* arrived!

This was it!

The phone rang a second time. "Hey, Connie!" I said, trying to sound energetic while still foggy from watching that

Housewives show, which had just featured two grown women with a net worth of $100 million in a fistfight.

"Hey, Trey. How are you? How's Amy?"

"All is well here," I said.

We dispensed with the formalities quickly.

"Trey, I want you to know that tomorrow I'm going to announce I'm running for Senate. I think you should seriously consider running for Congress."

I didn't say a thing. I tried to remain calm while I shook my head up and down as if Connie were watching me absorb his words. Then I broke the silence. "Wow! Well, first, congrats, man. This is one hell of a leap for you. I know it must be intense taking on Nelson." Connie was challenging Bill Nelson, the popular and beloved incumbent Democratic senator. "And . . . I'm really flattered you'd call me and let me know." I paused again to look over at my wife, who was staring directly at me. "And to even encourage me to run. Wow. Connie, thank you. Thank you so much. This means a lot."

Connie also took an important issue off the table right away. "Trey, I know we are friends, but for now, for many reasons, I can't endorse you in this race. For now, I am not endorsing anyone and don't know if I will."

Even though we were close and he was incredibly supportive, Connie had to hedge his bets. He had his own campaign to run, and he had to see how my campaign shaped up. After all, the last elected position I ran for was high school class president. I did win, though! So I had that going for me as I headed into the race for the United States Congress.

He didn't have to say these things out loud; I understood

completely and let him know. "Connie, c'mon, you kidding? I get it. Why piss in your own backyard when you have your own race to run?" I, uh, sometimes have a way with words, even with the congressman. I added, "No problem. And, yeah, it's also reassuring to know you won't be hopping on anyone's side." I wished him luck, and we hung up.

I stopped pacing and looked over in amazement at my wife. Amy was concerned about what this would entail, but she was totally supportive.

I walked back over to her, sat down, and rubbed her belly. She was eight months pregnant. Our son was due to enter this world in December, only one month before our January 2012 campaign would be launched.

As this journey begins, you may be wondering how I, a sitting U.S. congressman, husband, and father, ended up on the wrong side of a cocaine bust. My story is anything but a tragedy. I have my family, my friends, and my health. And though my story is pretty damn funny and utterly ridiculous at times, it isn't a comedy. It just is.

Life has ups. Life has downs. Hang on tight, especially to your sense of humor.

★3★
REBEL WITHOUT A PAUSE

The campaign was moving fast and so was life. I could barely keep up. Amy and I celebrated two years of marriage in December of 2011. Our son, Jude, was born that same month. Less than thirty days after that, in January 2012, I officially kicked off my campaign for the United States Congress.

In June of 2012 we were six months into the campaign and only months away from the August primary election, which is the only election that matters in this part of Florida. This District 19 seat in Southwest Florida is what's commonly referred to as a "Republican safe seat."

In many Republican and Democratic districts around the United States, all you have to win is the primary. The general election is a joke. It's one of the many reasons Congress is so deadlocked so often. Our state legislatures have gerrymandered districts to suit whichever party is in control. There's no balance. So, typically, whichever candidate is the most right or left, conservative or liberal, wins. Then, when they get to Congress, it's like locking Kim Jong-Il and George W. Bush in a room and telling them, "Have fun, boys! Play nice, compromise, and get some work done!"

Deep into an insane campaign, I was a completely insane person.

On the outside, I looked and acted normal. In fact, I was a pretty damn good candidate who could give rousing speeches, speak to and touch people from different walks of life, stay on message, and handle the media really well.

On the inside, though, I became what every candidate becomes—paranoid and irritable. Physically, I was a damn mess, too.

When a candidate kicks off a campaign, they typically look fresh, well rested, and in fairly good shape. By the end, most suffer the same symptoms: baggy eyes from no sleep, a constant robot-like smile, flashes of psychotic looks from dodgy eyes that move so quickly most people don't see them, and weight gain. Tons of weight. Big fat pouches around the gut appear that didn't exist months before because of a constant stream of fast food eaten in a car on the way to the next event.

This was the new me!

Just before I launched the campaign, I had been in pretty good shape from boxing three days a week and eating right. But when I officially became a candidate, I called my trainer, Marcus, and shared the news. "Trey!" he shouted loudly when he picked up.

Marcus, a professional boxer and close friend, always had a smile on his face, and when I called him, I could see it through the phone. But I was about to let him down. "Marcus, man, I got good news and bad news. The good, I'm running for Congress. The bad, I'm gonna have to take a break from hitting for a while. This is gonna be intense." Even though he was losing me as his client, he was totally supportive.

Marcus and I had grown tight. I had been boxing on and off with him and his brother, Quinton, for a few years. They had a gym in the not-so-nice part of town, an area they occasionally referred to as the "hood." I didn't have the balls to use that term with them, though. The gym itself was rough, too, offering no amenities, not a shower or even a water fountain. It was also crazy loud. Hip-hop blared every minute of the day through a really old '90s stereo that had both doors of its high-tech dual-deck cassette player ripped off. I loved the place cuz it wasn't full of muscle heads wearing Tom Hardy shirts who constantly talked about protein intake and supplements. I went there to get my butt in shape and occasionally work out some aggression by beating the hell out of a bag. On occasion, Marcus would beat the hell outta me when we sparred.

And now, months into the election, with a new gut and far removed from the boxing ring, the only sparring I did was in debates with opponents and occasionally with my campaign team when we didn't agree on things or when my actions—past or present—got us into a mess.

Like right now.

A news story was breaking. It was about me.

Not good.

We were leading in our internal polls, and our opponents must have had the same information because they were all com-

ing after us, *no one else*. When you're on top, both your opponents and the press set their sights on you, ready to assassinate.
The Republican Party of Florida was also against us, supporting
another institutional, more traditional candidate. Both local
newspapers, the Fort Myers *News-Press* and the *Naples Daily
News*, constantly zeroed in on us for mundane crap, like missing
a debate, which others had done without receiving any scrutiny
whatsoever.

And now the press cocked their weapons and set their sights
on us again with some serious breaking news.

The showstopper? *Record scratch, stop the music.* Domains.

Years ago I had a company that bought dozens of domain
names. By the way, does that term mean anything to you—
"domain names"? It's the words you type in your web browser to
go to a specific website, such as "Trey Radel dot com" to go to
our campaign website or "Delta dot com" to make a flight reservation. I wish the names I bought were that mundane. They were
not. They were very adult words, even in different languages. And
let's not forget, I'm a Republican!

Certain I was dead in the water, I frantically paced the same
living room Connie had called me in months before. Loudly, I
repeated over and over, "We're done! This is it!" while Matt
Pusateri, my close friend and campaign manager, tried to calm
me down. "We'll be fine, just relax, man," he insisted. "You're
not done." With his thick southern accent, he somehow sounded
laid-back. In the storm of crazy thoughts and arguments in my
head, Matt was a calm port.

To better understand my campaign, meet Matt Pusateri.
With his hard-core Italian last name, you might conjure up

someone with jet-black hair and dark brown eyes, maybe even a slight New York accent. But Matt Pusateri is a blond-haired, blue-eyed, heavily tatted, gun-toting, shit-kickin' North Florida Cracker. And in Florida, the farther north you go, the farther south you get.

Matt never got his bachelor's degree, yet he was highly self-educated and worldly. Never studied business, but ran his own successful company. Never formally learned graphic design or coding, yet did them all really well. Never spoke much in front of crowds, but crafted powerful, persuasive speeches.

Pusateri would never survive in a corporate environment. Like me, he doesn't like to be told what to do. He often looks at rules and norms, understands them, and then tosses them out the window. Not because he's angry. He's just determined to live the way he wants. He always found ways to use his artistic side to make a living as a professional graphic artist and musician. In his downtime, he camps out in the Florida swamps, drinks beer, and strums his guitar with his brother. And Matt always makes time to do what he loves most: spend time with his wife and two beautiful daughters.

Pusateri had absolutely no campaign experience and neither did I. Perfect! We were a helluva team—equals who had fallen into an incredible opportunity. And whether it was opportunities or problems, we faced them together.

If the highs and lows in TV news are measured in minutes, they are measured in seconds in a campaign. The pressure and intensity were like nothing I had ever experienced. Running for office has more drama than a Jerry Springer set with free meth and no Steve Wilkos.

Slowly enunciating each word, Matt said, "Cojible dot com. Dude, what in the hell does *cojible* mean?" It was no time to joke around, but his speaking Spanish with a southern accent was hilarious to me. I shot back in my best southern drawl. "Well, *coh-HEE-blay* means a girl who isn't that good looking but you'd still take her home."

"Oh. That ain't good."

"Yep," I said loudly, certain this was the end of my candidacy. Then he asked something I had become all too familiar with: "Man, what the hell were you thinking?"

Southwest Florida has one of the oldest demographics in the country, and in 2012 words like "domain" and "URL" didn't mean much. But the word "thief" does. And that's where my domain problem originated.

Let's go back.

While I was a reporter with WINK in 2001, I had another business on the side, and seeing myself as the consummate entrepreneur, I got, let's say, a little too aggressive. I set up an LLC to buy and sell domain names, but I never developed any websites or posted any content.

It was the early 2000s and the domain business was lucrative. A bit of a tech nerd, I had been reading about people making serious money from buying and selling domains, so I decided to get in on the action. I purchased a large portfolio of domain names; some of them I sold and made substantial profits. For example, I bought Internship Guide dot com for ten bucks and sold it a year later for a thousand. Nice, right? You just go online to a domain registrar, GoDaddy or whatever, and buy them. It's not rocket science.

Even before Connie called me, I was monitoring who might run for Congress. As potential candidates flirted with the idea publicly, they forgot one of the most basic things a candidate needs today—their name followed by "dot com." I had owned Trey Radel dot com for years. But these potential candidates who were talking about running for office didn't own their own names. Unbelievable! I mean, how old-school Republican is that? Out-of-touch politicians talking in their echo chambers about running for Congress, and they didn't even own their own domain names. I snatched them up for a few bucks.

If I decided to run, I'd own my competitors' names to post content about them or redirect them to our own website. If I didn't run, I could lease them out or resell them.

Great idea!

Boom! Blew up in our face.

Before I set up an official campaign, I bought those potential opponents' names with my personal GoDaddy account. But just in case one of the candidates threatened legal action, we transferred the names from my personal account to our campaign, which was called Friends of Trey Radel, Inc., so we would be better protected legally. And, yes, "Friends of [insert candidate name here]" is a standard cheesy name for a campaign although it sounds more like an '80s cartoon with superheroes.

In our GoDaddy campaign account, we also owned Trey Radel dot org and dot net, Vets For Trey Radel, Radel For Congress, and others. In the transfer, the domain privacy was lifted for one day, and that's all it took. In that twenty-four-hour period, someone searched and grabbed screenshots of all the domains owned by Friends of Trey Radel, which also included the name of a Naples City councilman who ended up not running and supporting us. Explaining that to him sucked.

When Matt called, it wasn't Matt's usual "Hey, man!" It was just "man." I could always judge the severity of the situation by his use of "man." Matt continued. "The *News-Press* somehow found out we own Chauncey's and Paige's domain names." Chauncey Goss and Paige Kreegel were two of our opponents, and they were pissed!

Paige Kreegel was a Florida state representative and physician. Being a doctor played well for him politically with Obamacare being a huge issue. He, like most Republicans, was dead set against it.

Chauncey Goss came from an Ivy League, überwealthy family that lived in the fantastically rich and beautiful island community of Sanibel. The Goss family was a force in Southwest Florida. You might recognize the name Goss because Chauncey's father is Porter Goss, the former director of the CIA under George W. Bush. Before that, Porter was Connie's predecessor in Congress and prior to that, mayor of Sanibel. Chauncey had just moved back to Southwest Florida from Washington, where he had been deputy staff director for the House Committee on the Budget and worked directly under the powerful and well-respected representative from Wisconsin, Paul Ryan, who would later become Speaker.

What really lit up both candidates was that our campaign posted content on the sites with their names. On Chauncey's, who worked on the federal budget, we posted his résumé next to a giant debt clock. On Paige's, we listed all the crappy votes he took while working as a state representative.

We thought it was hilarious!

When it hit the press, it was awful!

Chauncey and Paige were smart to avoid phrases like "purchased our domain names." Instead, they used words like "thief."

In many areas of the United States that have aggressive campaigns and bare-knuckle politics, what I did would be seen as a brilliant move. Shrewd? Yep. Cunning? Maybe. But as Republicans were getting their asses handed to them by Obama's tech-savvy Democrats, we tried to portray our technology skills as a strength. We were young and understood the digital age like no other candidate. Our team (meaning Matt and I) put out official statements saying, "We are running a cutting-edge, aggressive campaign."

Unfortunately, some of the older constituents didn't give a rat's ass about "domains" or "Twit-book" or a "goddamn Google." The way they saw it, we straight up stole our opponents' names. Calls poured in to our campaign office and our own supporters started questioning our tactics. And the retirees put pen to pad and wrote. Letters to the editor were flooding the local paper about that "bad man," Trey Radel—all because of domains.

Eventually, I broke. I went on the local conservative radio show (yes, the same one I used to host) and announced that I was giving up the domains.

"Drew," I said to the host. "This is just too much of a

distraction, so I'm done. They can have them. We got aggressive and bought them in order to expose our opponents' liberal records!"

You see the delicate choice of words there, right? Wink, wink! Sorry. Not sorry!

Sigh of relief. It blew over.

Until . . .

A reporter from *Mother Jones* magazine was ready to hammer us for those bad words I had bought years ago, like *cojible*.

Now I was the one asking myself, *What the hell were you thinking?*

What can I say? Back in my twenties, I thought I was going to be some sort of tech entrepreneur. Sure, I can dismiss it by saying "They're just words" because I had no content and no websites whatsoever. But not only did it reflect poorly on me, it was also coming down on people I cared about—my family. It was then I realized that as a candidate, and possibly as a congressman, whatever I did would affect more people than me. The Internet knows no bounds. The news went viral. After all, it made for a great combination: politics, bad words, and—gasp!— a Republican, of all people! My yearning to be an "entrepreneur," coupled with our digital tactics, made me look bad and embarrassed my family.

It was time to call in the professionals.

You sending the Wolf?

★ Jules, *Pulp Fiction*

Up to this point, our campaign had been a bare-bones, bootstrap operation. While the other institutional candidates had consultants for TV, radio, digital, direct mail, and ground operations telling them how to walk, talk, smile, and shake hands, Matt and I relied on our own skills as well as our handful of indispensable volunteers, who ranged in age from eighteen to eighty.

We had two experienced consultants. The first was a general consultant, Rob Cole out of New York, who was a master of polling and understanding the demographics in our area. When we launched our campaign, his polls showed that we had a significant amount of name ID, making our campaign immediately viable and credible.

The other guy, who was now critical to us, was Todd Harris, our media and communications consultant, who had worked on Marco Rubio's Senate campaign. Todd helped Matt and me better understand some of the unique aspects of imaging and branding. We needed him badly now.

I called Todd in Washington. I was at home pacing in my living room, which was now my permanent office. "Man, I have a serious issue we gotta deal with. *Mother Jones* is hounding me about something I did in my twenties. Years ago, I bought some domain names."

He stopped me with a laugh. "Ha! More domains?!"

I dropped my head. "Yeah, yeah, I know. I know." I tensed up as I told him what they were, saying the word *cojible* out loud along with the questionably naughty *pinche güey*, which is Mexican slang for "effing idiot" but is mostly used as an affectionate term among friends. I also pointed out that some of the names were innocuous, like Visite Chile dot com.

Todd Harris is an assessor. Even casual answers about his favorite wine or the weather take awhile, as if he has thought out each and every response with great depth. Ask a question. Wait. He tilts his head. Wait. Then an answer comes at a slow, deliberate pace.

As I waited for him to speak, wanting to rip the answers out of his throat, I began to think, *Why am I doing this? Why would anyone in their right mind do this? If buying domains in my twenties was going to come back and haunt me, what else? Christ, is Chauncey's dad, the former spook, watching me?* Memories began haunting me. Late nights clubbing in Chicago. "Degenerate!" Spring break smoking pot. "Junkie!" That one night in middle school when we played baseball with mailboxes. "Delinquent!" Or . . . oh, my God, in second grade, I pissed myself! "Disgraceful! No self-control whatsoever!"

This barrage of thoughts was cut off with Todd's drawn-out "Ohhh . . . kay." Then he sped up. "Okay, okay, okay, this is good news. No, this is great news!"

Shaking my head in disbelief and anger, I began pacing around even faster, and yelled, "Good news? Good news! Sure, the domains didn't have any websites, but, Todd, if I am my opponent, I'm gonna call me a goddamn pornographer!"

He started speaking even faster. "No, no, no. Calm down, Trey. This is great news. The fact that *Mother Jones* called is all we need. Here's what we're going to do."

Todd Harris, *the brilliant Todd Harris*, who helped Marco

Rubio decimate the popular, lovable Charlie Crist in the Senate race only two years before, launched into a tirade. "This is an ultraleftist communist rag trying to smear you! This is an attack from the left! No. You know what? This is a badge of honor!"

As he got excited, so did I. I yelled, "Yeah! They're trying to stop us! It's an assault on conservatives all over the country!"

By the time we got off the phone, we had drafted a statement for a press release. Then we did something no one else had really thought of. We took the controversy and began raising money directly from it.

It was clear that one or more of our opponents got this information after some digging. We later learned they had shopped it around to the local press and bloggers, but no one would bite. The only website that would do the story was *Mother* freaking *Jones*. Our opponents thought the revelations would bury us. Instead, we wore the attack from the socialist publication as a badge of honor. We made it a national issue and raised money far beyond Southwest Florida.

Maybe you think that I am a dirtbag for buying those kinds of domain names and raising money off the controversy . . . disgusting!

Well, the moral implications of buying a word followed by dot com are one thing. Sure, I regret it. If you're disgusted by our raising money off the entire situation, though, I get that. The campaign process can look, and at times *is*, undoubtedly, unquestionably sickening.

Here's a dose of reality, though. These situations are what separate successful candidates from the people who don't win.

There is no second place in an election. And you win by dealing with high-pressure, volatile, crappy situations, whether they're your own fault or not, and exploiting them to make the best package you can. In politics there are no good decisions, only the least worst ones.

This kind of problem solving is what separates the best consultants and spin doctors from those who end up advising the local dogcatcher. The best of them go on to run presidential campaigns, like Todd Harris eventually did for Marco Rubio, even if it didn't work out the way they wanted.

This is the tone and style of our American political process. In today's world of campaigns and digital footprints, everything, and I mean everything, is fair game, now more than ever.

Did you get drunk and do something stupid on video one night? That'll be on the Internet and around the world in minutes. Did your better half once e-mail something remotely liberal or conservative? Your spouse will be crucified all over the Internet, TV, and radio. Bare your chest at Mardi Gras? Send a dick pic? The world is about to see your cup size and length and girth—or lack thereof.

In fact, things you haven't necessarily been a part of can and will be held against you in the court of public opinion. An undocumented immigrant once worked for you? If you're a Republican, you're dead. A Democrat? You have a big heart. Were you at the same park where someone held a pro–Second Amendment rally? Republican? Congrats. Democrat? You support terrorists.

Your parents, your spouse, your kids, your ex-mailman, your former dishwasher's owner can and will be tied to you and hung around your neck to bring you down!

The public bemoans it; the media criticizes it. But here's another dose of reality: The public votes on it; the media lives by it.

When the dust settled after our own little Domaingate, I got back to what all candidates live and die by—fund-raising. Through all the turmoil, *ya gotta get that money.* Now was not the time to lose focus. We needed to gather another few hundred thousand so we could get on TV and advertise the hell out of our campaign before the primary, which was closing in quick.

> Money, get back. I'm all right, Jack, keep your hands off of my stack. Money, it's a hit. Don't give me that do goody good bullshit.
>
> ★ Pink Floyd, "Money"

Asking for money is the absolute worst thing a candidate has to do. At least it is for me. I know some men and women love it, and they end up running massive nonprofits that depend on contributions or head up the fund-raising arms of the Democratic and Republican parties. I despised asking for money. Aside from a bank loan and my parents, I never asked anyone for anything. I was getting good at it, though, and I'm not proud of that.

I knew that hitting people up for money was "just part of it," as my consultant Rob Cole would tell me, but at some point you have to step back and ask yourself, *Am I running for the right reasons?* While I am the first to make fun of myself and soak my words in sarcasm, the unabashed truth is this: I love this country.

America has accomplished amazing things. The United States has lifted more people out of poverty than any other society, offered more opportunities to more people than any country on earth, and while we make and have made plenty of mistakes in our short history, we remain a role model for much of the world. The whole damn planet wants to come live here.

In my backpacking days, I saw living conditions no person should ever have to live and breathe in, and not only in Cambodia. I've also lived in and seen the way old Europe functions— many people living in a stagnant economy with little to no upward economic mobility. And if you're an immigrant to Europe, you can forget about assimilation like we have here.

My world travels cemented my love for our country.

Yes, I'm that cheesy guy who gets choked up and emotional John Boehner–style when I talk about our role in the world and our incredibly diverse, amazing society at home. I have no problem using a word like "patriot." I love America.

As a young man, I never set my sights on being a TV news anchor, radio-show host, or any other sort of publicly recognized position. I never gave a damn about titles or being on the air. Throughout my career, I loved what I did and wanted to do more—interact with people, share stories, and, in the case of this opportunity in Congress, I loved the fact I'd be able to try to help the country and our people where I could. *Romantically naïve or honorable?* A little of both.

I knew this, though· If I made it into the United States Congress, I would work my hardest to serve this country and our great people regardless of their political leanings or backgrounds in the best way I could. My love for our country knows no end. And as we approached Election Day, it was time to seal the deal!

I just needed more freakin' money!

It was time to crank up the fund-raising and amass dollars like Jay Z and Jermaine Dupri singing, "Money ain't a thang," and tossing hundreds of dollars into the air!

Like a scene from a Road Runner cartoon, every person had a bull's-eye on their back, and its size was in proportion to the dollar signs floating over their head.

Three types of people donate to your campaign: The first are friends and family, the second are the believers, and the third are people who want something from you.

Friends and family are where you go first, and when you start fund-raising, it is uncomfortable, awkward, and just awful. You call parents, grandparents, aunts, uncles, and the distant cousins you haven't seen since the last funeral or wedding. You hit them up for the maximum contribution allowed by law, known as "maxing out." Maybe this means a few hundred bucks into your campaign account; if your family has some dough, it can mean thousands. If you're born lucky with a really big rich family, it's hundreds of thousands of dollars.

As you begin to expand your campaign, you move on to the believers. They are people who simply do that—believe in you as a person or the policies you stand for. I had a mix of both. Through my community and political connections, I had a wide spectrum of supporters that included grassroots activists and wealthy donors who supported causes, such as conservative think tanks like the Heritage Foundation and the libertarian Cato Institute.

When seeking donors who will max out, you triage, meaning you go for the wealthiest first. It is cold. It is calculating. It just is.

You never ask for large contributions by phone, and you absolutely do not do it over e-mail. You arrange meetings and talk with people face-to-face. When it comes time for the "ask," you ask for their entire family to max out—the husband, the wife, and every one of their kids. If you're really aggressive, you go to the kids who, if they're old enough, may also have children. No one is beyond an "ask."

Just as important as the people who max out are the believers who give you five bucks. These are the "small-dollar donors," and they are critical. If someone who might not have a lot of money is willing to donate even five dollars, it sure as hell means they are going to go out and vote for you.

The third group of donors are the people who want something. It can include political movers and shakers, CEOs, and lobbyists. But contrary to the public stereotype, these donors never explicitly ask for anything. It's never the kind of typical scenario you see in a Hollywood flick, where you're in a back room filled with cigar smoke and evil fat old white men slip you a check saying, "Son, you're going to have to vote this way." There was never anything attached with a donation. They were always pretty straightforward: This is what my client wants or this is what our "ask" is. But there were never any demands or ultimatums.

The money was coming in. And for all the crap the press was giving our "tech-savvy, aggressive, cutting-edge" campaign, we were killing it online. We thought we would raise maybe $10,000 through our digital campaign. We were pushing $100,000.

We'd be able to afford TV advertising every day for at least two weeks leading up to Election Day. Furthermore, we saved hundreds of thousands of dollars by doing our snail-mail and digital campaign ourselves. I came up with general concepts and language. Matt knocked the designs out of the park.

And we were killing it in the candidate debates. Debating came natural for me. After all, I had been doing it on the radio for four hours live every weekday.

I'm not superstitious, but I did do one bit of debate prep consistently. Before getting out of the car at a debate crowded with octogenarian voters and Kenny G music in the background, I listened to two songs: Public Enemy's "Welcome to the Terrordome" and N.W.A's "Straight Outta Compton." They got my blood flowing like nothing else. Maybe it was the young boy in me from years ago when I first heard them; maybe they're just good tunes. I'll go with both.

Debate after debate, we got across our conservative message with libertarian leanings and connected with the audience. With each win, we solidified our lead in our internal polls.

All good! *But*, this being a political campaign, things gotta go south soon.

The phone rang. It was Matt. "Hey, man."

Damn. Another serious "man" from Matt. "What now?" I asked, as if the shitstorms I had caused were somehow his fault.

"Chauncey landed two endorsements, and they're kinda big, man."

"Lemme guess," I said, turning my volume up. "Paul Ryan."

"Yep," he snapped back.

"All right, no problem. We knew that was coming. They're friends. I don't think it's that big of a deal."

Matt paused. "Yeah, but the other one is kind of a big deal."

"Did they reincarnate Reagan's corpse? Can the CIA do that?"

Matt wasn't interested in my dumb jokes. He had two words, "Jeb Bush."

Damn.

Jeb was a beloved and popular governor here in Florida. I knew him, not well, but we had met numerous times when I was a reporter. Shortly after being "that idiot" in the hurricanes (we had five in one year!), I was "that really good reporter" doing the 24/7 coverage on cleanup and recovery. Governor Bush came to talk with local leaders and the press. Knowing he spoke fluent Spanish, I always made it a point to throw down my *español* with him. We were both gringos with an affinity for Latin culture. Years later, through political circles, I also formed a relationship with his son, Jeb Jr., who is a hell of a nice guy.

The Goss endorsement, though, was business, not personal. That's something you have to learn quickly in politics. I understood it, but it still stung.

Would the endorsements be a game changer? *The ad war was on.*

Chauncey and the other candidates were blasting old-school,

'90s TV commercials. They were awful. Chauncey's flashed still pictures like a PowerPoint presentation and featured the stiffest, blandest voice-over I'd ever heard. I was shocked at the meaningless scripts, which used words and phrases like "federal budget" or "was endorsed by" or "debt and deficits." They lacked even the remotest sense of emotion. The other candidates also had consultants from Tallahassee and D.C. who led them into the same old traps and formulas: Voice-over. Still picture. Voice-over. And then the obligatory closer: "This commercial just wasted thirty seconds of your time, cost me $30,000, and I approve this message."

I've always believed that *it's not what you say; it's how they feel.* Todd Harris and I were on the exact same page and developed ads that were personal and direct. I spoke into the camera in front of a clean white background. I would talk to "you," not "Southwest Florida," and certainly not to my "fellow Americans." In some ads, I stood alone talking directly to the audience. In others, my wife held our young son and stood by my side. Those were particularly powerful.

While the ads were running, I was knocking on doors, which is old-fashioned, hand-grabbing, humbling stuff. The big question with retail politicking like door knocking is: *Does it move the dial?* Does it get a large amount of people to vote for you? No. Certainly not like TV or radio, where you can touch the masses all at once. But I believe every bit helps. Plus, I loved to get out and talk with people. If someone was on the fence, I'd do everything I could to talk and even debate with them in a smart, polite way to earn their vote. It was great—until a door was slammed in my face.

Knock, knock. Door opens. Oh, look, it's a really sweet-looking grandmother! She smiles. "Hi! My name is . . ." Then, as I'm saying my name, she cocks her head like a confused puppy because she knows she's seen me somewhere. "My name is Trey. I just wanted to stop by and . . ." *Bang!* Slams door. Then from inside the house, she says, "Get the hell out of here!" It was often the sweetest-looking grandmas and grandpas who were the nastiest.

But as doors were closing, others were opening. The same newspaper, the Fort Myers *News-Press*, that was on our butt from the beginning hired an outside company that specialized in political polling. They published an in-depth, district-wide poll. And as much as the paper loved to hate us, they legitimized us, if unintentionally.

From the beginning of our campaign, many voters had reservations about me. After all, I had never held elected office or even run for one. While I was knocking on doors, I would hear, "Trey, I loved you on the radio! I love where you stand on things and how you say them, but c'mon, you have no chance! You've never been elected to anything." I never brought up my huge win in high school for class president.

Now a week out from the primary, the *News-Press* poll gave us our biggest boost. We were on top! We led by a few percentage points, with Paige and Chauncey tied for second. Anyone who had a reservation about wasting a vote was now certain to cast a ballot for us.

On election night a week later, my campaign team and family headed to a hotel. We had two adjoining rooms. My family in one; the campaign in the other. As the results began to come in, I was pacing like a madman in between the rooms. I had not sat down or slept in weeks. Every second had been devoted to walking, knocking, calling, pacing, screaming, freaking out, and more.

Minutes after the polls closed, big numbers started to roll in for us from absentee ballots. Those votes always pop up first, and they looked really good. But they weren't calming me. By that point, I was even more insane than before. For nine months, with the exception of doing my best to be a new dad and husband, I had been focused exclusively on this day and this day only.

As our numbers shot up, Rob Cole, our New York City consultant, called. "Congrats, man!"

I snapped! "Rob, it hasn't been called yet!"

He laughed. "Come on, Trey."

"No, you come on," I screamed, infuriated. Then I hung up like a jerk.

Then Connie Mack called. "Trey, congrats!"

The same reaction from me again. Frustrated but more restrained because I was responding to my congressman, friend, and current Senate candidate, I said, "Connie, look. man, I—" Then I was cut off. Family, friends, and volunteers all started huddling around the TV. "Here, here, here! Here it is. Shhh!"

We were watching WINK news. My former coanchor, Lois Thome, announced, "We are calling the race for Congress, District 19, for Trey Radel. Trey Radel has won the Republican primary." I tossed the phone and started screaming, running around the room, and hugging everyone. Some people were jumping up and down while my family was crying tears of joy. I ran around more. I couldn't contain myself.

It was a rush and exhilaration like nothing I had ever felt.

It was over.

Now the real work was about to begin.

Enter John Boehner.

★4★
THE SOFT PARADE

'm in the backseat of an armored SUV doing a hundred miles an hour down a main road of Naples looking at John Boehner, Speaker of the United States House of Representatives, third in line to the presidency. I'm behind the driver. The Speaker is to the right of me. The two men up front, undoubtedly armed to the teeth, are driving, talking in their sleeves, and peering out the window as if Naples were Baghdad and mortars might rain down at any moment. John Boehner is taking the longest drags from a cigarette I've ever seen.

Crazy was now being replaced by surreal.

An hour earlier we were having cocktails in the lobby of the Ritz-Carlton Golf Resort. (In Naples, one Ritz isn't enough. There's the famous one on the beach and the one we were at, sometimes referred to as Ritz Golf.) Speaker Boehner was in Naples to headline our fund-raiser. Once a candidate, Democrat or Republican, wins the primary, the party's top-ranking members, called leadership, often show up to lend support and help raise money going into the general election, which was only a few weeks out.

Before this event, I'd asked the Speaker's staff for time alone with him before the event so I could get to know him personally before the circus of donors and supporters overwhelmed us. They granted it. And there I was sitting in a corner of the lobby waiting for the freakin' Speaker of the House. He came down to the lobby alone, although I figured security was lurking nearby. "Hi, Trey!" he said, like we already knew each other.

"Hello, Mr. Speaker." The words rolled out of my mouth as we shook hands. I'm not one to get starstruck, but as I was a passionate follower of politics who was now participating in the process, sitting with Speaker Boehner was like a basketball fanatic having a beer with Michael Jordan.

We headed to the bar and ordered a couple of drinks. As he sipped his merlot, I pulled out a gift. I gave him a blue-and-gold tie—the colors of his alma mater, Moeller High School in Cincinnati. Cheesy? Definitely. But I knew Boehner was a stylish guy, so I bought him a stylish tie. I graduated from Moeller's archrival, Elder High School, so I teased Boehner by saying, "Don't tell me you played football for Moeller!"

He nodded, and said, "Oh, yeah, under Faust. I was a linebacker. Not the biggest, but scrappy." His deep, from-the-gut voice sounded like he had just finished his third pack of cigarettes that day. Coach Gerry Faust was a high school football legend—he went on to coach at Notre Dame—and Moeller dominated Ohio football for years. The Speaker and I proceeded to talk about our beloved Bengals as well as Cincinnati staples like

Skyline Chili, the Montgomery Inn, and Graeter's ice cream. We ordered another round of drinks and stepped outside for a cigarette. I rarely smoke, but you bet I was going to bum a Camel from the Speaker of the House.

On the sweeping balcony of the Ritz that overlooked palm trees and a golf course, the Speaker shared his famous story about "growing up in a bar" where he "swept the floors to help out the family." He took a long drag of his cigarette and exhaled. "I grew up with eleven brothers and sisters. It was tight!" His Catholic parents worked their tails off in that bar to provide for their twelve kids and send them to local Catholic schools. I thought to myself, *Man, could his parents ever have imagined their little Johnny would go on to become Speaker of the House?*

At the pace Boehner speaks, combined with his deep voice, he sometimes sounds like *Fear and Loathing in Las Vegas* author Hunter S. Thompson—just swap Wild Turkey for wine. As he took another deep drag, I kept hoping he'd shout out, "We were somewhere around Barstow on the edge of the desert when the drugs began to take hold."

He asked, "Does your family still live on the Westside?" As a Cincinnatian, he knew that there are really only two locations in the 'Nati—the Eastside and the Westside. Generally speaking, the Eastside is extremely wealthy, cultured, and sometimes, according to Westsiders, a bit snobby. The Westside is blue-collar, highly cultured in Friday-night football, and sometimes, according to Eastsiders, a bit hillbilly. Boehner was right; I'm from the Westside. While I might be slightly cultured, I do love my football.

I shared a bit about my family. "My mom passed away a

couple of years ago, but my dad runs a funeral home on the Westside that's been around for a long time. It still bears our name, Radel Funeral Home."

He nodded. "Oh, sure, I know. Is that still by Elder?"

"Yeah, right near the Pit!" I said, using the nickname of Elder's football stadium, which easily drew ten thousand people every Friday night. "They still use it for parking on game night!"

The Speaker and I hit it off, and we began a new friendship. Even after talking with him for only a few minutes, you feel like you've known him forever. He is warm, friendly, and immediately likable.

After a few more drinks, it was time to head to the fundraiser. "All right, Radel!" Boehner said. "Let's go raise some money." With that, he put his smoke out and we strolled across the lobby. We walked to the valet area, overlooking a long driveway lined with palm trees. I closed my eyes for a second and inhaled the saltwater air of Naples. It was a beautiful fall evening, incredibly peaceful. Then Boehner broke the moment with "All right, let's go!" and his security detail ushered us into an SUV.

As soon as we clicked our seat belts, the driver hit the gas. "Oh, shit!" I blurted out, caught off guard by the sudden acceleration. I quickly looked over at the Speaker and apologized. He already had his lighter poised to fire up a new cigarette. With a big grin, he just nodded, as if to say, *C'mon, man, all good.*

After ripping a bottomless drag, he started asking me about the campaign, although it was clear he knew a lot already. "Now, you ran against Porter Goss's son, right?"

"I did," I said. "Porter is an amazing man . . . served in Congress . . . was CIA."

Boehner chimed in. "Oh, yeah, I served with him."

"It was a difficult race. The Goss name holds a lot of sway here. I hope they don't harbor any bad feelings, though, because it got rough."

"Yeah, primaries often do," he said nonchalantly, while exhaling out of a cracked-open window.

He then asked about our fund-raising. "How much did the race cost?"

"Almost a million," I told him, shocked at how easily the number rolled off my tongue.

He nodded. "Anything left?" he asked.

"Just a few thousand, but as you know, tonight is a big night for us. We hope to raise anywhere between twenty-five and fifty." Thousand that is.

I told him some mutual friends from Cincinnati would be at the event. Smiling in between drags, he said, "That's great. This'll be fun. Trey, you know I spend a lot of time here, right?"

I did know that he had a place in the area and played a lot of golf, so I gave him some flack. "Yeah, I know. I'm just trying to figure out if this is the district you represent or if you're my constituent."

He ate it up. "Ha! Well, I wouldn't go that far. But I do have quite a few friends here. I can introduce you to them. They can be helpful."

"That'd be great. I'd really appreciate it."

As I got to know Washington insiders, I quickly learned that "helpful" is code for "They can raise you a ton of cash."

Our mad dash in the SUV was about to end. It was a ten-minute drive to our destination. We made it in under four.

We pulled up to Mercato, a swanky entertainment complex with everything from high-end condos to restaurants, bars, and shops. Having thought about this night for more than a month, I knew the following: John Boehner is a smoker. John Boehner enjoys a good drink. John Boehner is a social guy who loves to mingle. I knew exactly what we needed: BURN by Rocky Patel, a local cigar lounge. He could smoke, drink, and hang out as long as he wanted.

We rolled up to unload.

Start the slow mo. Cue up some swingin' Frank Sinatra cocktail tune. Zoom in to the SUV.

Boehner stepped out, cigarette in mouth, and buttoned his suit jacket. "Radel," he barked out of the side of his mouth the cigarette wasn't occupying, looking again like Hunter S. Thompson. He removed the cigarette and put it out. While exhaling, he said, "Don't let me forget. We'll cut you a couple of checks for ten grand. Talk to staff."

I nodded, eyes wide open. "Again, thank you, Mr. Speaker."

He walked into the bar without another word.

Ten. Thousand. Dollars.

Might sound like a boatload of cash. Might sound shocking. But it wasn't the first time someone in Washington tossed ten grand my way. Whenever it happens, you question what you're doing. *Am I an exotic dancer? What do I need to do for this kind of cash?* Or worse, *What do I owe? Is this what Washington is all about?*

In some ways, yes.

Again, three types of people donate money to political campaigns: family, the believers, and the people who want something. But it's this member-to-member, behind-the-scenes money that drives more things than you can imagine. Money moves the infrastructure of political parties.

When a member of Congress cuts you a check, they want something. Sometimes it's a vote to get them into leadership because posts like Speaker of the House, majority leader, whip, or conference chair are elected positions. Members currently in the leadership want a vote for them to remain there. Or they want you to vote a particular way when an important piece of legislation hits the House floor.

As soon as I cleared the primary, the calls started coming in from members in leadership positions and from the rank and file who were looking to move into leadership roles.

One weeknight after the primary, I got a call from Eric Cantor, the majority leader, second behind the Speaker. "Hi, Trey," he said in his distinctive southern drawl, which was very different from Matt Pusateri's Cracker-ass accent. While Eric's rhythm is slower, he is fantastic at communicating with people from all walks of life. He's down-to-earth and easy to get along with. But when he talks, you know he has put a lot of thought to his statements, delivering every word with a slight pause, letting it sink in. "Trey." He paused. "I read a bit about your background. Tell me more about your media experience."

Without trying to sound like a bloviating jerk yet wanting to leave a good impression, I described my work in TV, radio, and print.

He took an interest in my media experience and language skills. "Trey, that's great. We could really use someone with your kinds of skills and experience to help us with messaging, especially with your Spanish skills."

"Messaging" is a word I would hear a million times in the next year. That's because—unless it's about bombing some country you can't point out on a map or how "those damn gays are all going to hell"—Republicans have an especially hard time "messaging," meaning how they talk and what they say. For years the Republican Party has lacked a positive, heartfelt message, which has undoubtedly limited its constituency.

Eric was a policy wonk, but he knew how to communicate. He told me that he wanted to avoid social issues and change the overall tone of the party's message. "Trey, we spend too much time talking about the policy when we should be talking about the benefits of the policy. We need to make it real for people."

We tossed around some ideas. One of mine from my days in radio had been reflected in my campaign ads. "I think we need to do a better job speaking to people in the most personal way possible, using the word 'you.' We need to be peppering the word 'you' with talking points about 'your family, your job, and your future.'" I was convinced that we needed to convey in the most personal and positive ways possible that we would no longer be the party of "hell no" and become the party of "opportunity." And if appropriate, we needed to stop the Washington-speak about "prosperity for all" and shift to aggressive and specific language like "getting you a job" and "getting you paid."

"Eric, it's like I've been standing on the sidelines watching the Republicans get whooped not by policy but by talking points. Obama and Bill Clinton, in particular, are masters of understanding how to connect with people emotionally. I've always believed it's not what you say; it's how they feel. Overall, whether we're in the South or the south side of Chicago, I think our language needs to be universal when we go out to talk to people so that we cut across generational, ethnic, and cultural lines."

Before the call wrapped up, the majority leader let me know he would be cutting some checks for $10,000. Ten thousand freaking dollars. After a fifteen-minute conversation!

That first time, I was shocked. I hung up the phone, looked at it, raised my bushy, caterpillar-like eyebrows and just said, "Whoa!"

These examples of Eric Cantor or John Boehner doling out cash have nothing to do with their character, policy, or beliefs. They were simply cementing their positions in Congress and building coalitions. And money can definitely sway and influence coalitions, especially when leadership or other members help fund incumbents who never stop campaigning in tight, tough districts, which means they never stop spending money.

My belief today is that both John and Eric were—and still *are*—in politics for the right reason. The reason is simple. They want to do good for the country. I believe the same is true of Nancy Pelosi and Steny Hoyer, the two top Democratic House leaders when I served. Sure, I may radically disagree with their positions and policies, but they fight hard for their beliefs and their constituents.

I get how superficial this all sounds. I get how jaded we are as a country. Hell, maybe you've already burned this book or vomited on the pages in disgust. But as Americans, we're responsible for it. It's our system. And these examples of how our system works are just the tip of the iceberg. *Just wait till I get to Washington!*

Let's put party back into the Republican Party and fun into fund-raising!
★ a drunk donor at the Speaker Boehner
and Trey Radel event

The music was pumping, the drinks were flowing, and the air was thick with smoke. "Hey, man, the Speaker's time is almost up," Matt shouted in my ear. Boehner was scheduled to be in and out of the event in forty-five minutes, which had passed.

The Speaker had given a nice speech, dropping a few personal tidbits to the crowd about some of the bonds he and I shared from our hometown. During Boehner's speech, Matt leaned over to me and whispered, "Twenty bucks says he cries like a baby."

I tilted my head toward Matt. "C'mon, this ain't *Oprah*. He's talking about tax policy. No way."

Boehner, infamous for crying during even the most mundane interviews, was talking tax policy, which led to "opportunity" which led to "kids in America," which led to a pause.

I looked over at Matt. "That's a burp, man, not a . . ."

Boehner paused again.

"No way," I said, anticipating a breakdown.

When Boehner knows he's about to cry, he does everything in his power to stop it. His face convulses in the most bizarre ways. His mouth tightens, the corners of his lips begin to turn down, and then his forehead wrinkles. It's the dead-on signature Robert De Niro face that everyone makes when quoting his character in *Taxi Driver*. "You talkin' to me?"

Clearly choked up, the Speaker's face started to tighten.

Pusateri leaned over to me. "Go buy me a drink now."

Before I could respond, the Speaker pulled his tears back, worked the frog out of his throat, and continued on about "prosperity for all" and some other Republican talking points. Not one to drag on too long, he wrapped it up without going full De Niro or shedding a tear.

The politics were over. This was now a party. Pusateri and I walked over to one of the Speaker's staffers to see if he would stay longer. He was gazing at Boehner. I asked, "Is his time up? We'd love to have him stay longer."

Without breaking his stare, the staffer said with a smile, "I don't know if the Speaker is going to leave. At all."

I looked over, and Boehner had a cigarette in one hand, a glass of wine in the other, and a huge grin on his face as he swapped stories with people from Cincinnati who were now snowbirds in Naples.

Boehner was supposed to stay forty-five minutes. He stayed for four hours.

★5★
DO YOU REALIZE??

Gazing at the Capitol, I started to tear up. A massive range of emotions began to wash over me.

It was a beautiful September night and my first trip to Washington since winning the primary. Behind me were the Washington Monument and the Lincoln Memorial. The sun was just starting to set, casting everything in an orange glow. Fighting back tears, I took in a deep breath. The smell of the trees and freshly cut grass was different from Florida's salty air. It took me back to home in Cincinnati. I closed my eyes and thought about my mom, who had passed away three years before in a tragic accident. Pushing bad memories out of my head, I thought to myself, *She would have been proud*. I wiped away another tear before it could roll down my face.

We were now two months away from the November general election. The excitement of the primary victory was being replaced by pure, unadulterated joy and a touch of fear. I thought to myself, almost incredulously, *This is real. This is going to happen. I will be making decisions that directly affect our country. I will be making decisions that will directly affect the lives of our soldiers abroad— literally, life-and-death decisions. This is something that only a small portion of the population has ever had the chance to do—to serve our country in one of the most direct ways, as a United States Congressman.* Another tear rolled down my face. I wiped it away and laughed. "Man, pull it together."

I had been selected to be a member of a group called the Young Guns, founded by Eric Cantor, Paul Ryan, and Kevin McCarthy. Tonight, Leader Cantor was hosting a dinner for candidates who had just won their primaries and were, like me, in safe Republican districts. They called us the Young Gun Vanguards. It was yet another way to build networks and, of course, raise more money.

It was time to head to the Young Guns dinner. I was excited to take a brisk walk on this beautiful night. I headed up Pennsylvania Avenue but felt compelled to stop again and take another look back at the Capitol. I let out a loud laugh right there! "I'm going to be a congressman! That's crazy! Ha!" Anyone nearby must've thought I was a drunk or an insane tourist as I laughed and stared at the Capitol.

More thoughts raced through my mind. *How did I even get here? My parents didn't have political connections. No one I know graduated from an Ivy League school.* With the exception of people I've interviewed, I've never even known anyone who went to Harvard or Yale. I thought to myself, *My life has become that Talking Heads song, "Once in a Lifetime."* I started singing, "You may find yourself behind the wheel of a large automobile. And you may find yourself in a beautiful house, with a beautiful wife." And there, with the massive dome of the Capitol hanging over me, I was asking, *How did I get here? How did all the dots connect to put me here smack in front of the Capitol of the United States of America?*

At warp speed, cities and experiences all began to connect in my mind—Cincinnati to Chicago, a stop in Rome, an internship in Atlanta, Mexico, a job in Houston, then Naples, a reporter gig, newspaper publisher, anchor gig, radio, people, politicians, relationships.

Why am I here? What is my purpose? My mind slowed down. *Deep thoughts for another day. Time for dinner and a drink.*

I turned and started back up Pennsylvania Avenue to my destination, Bobby Van's Steakhouse.

Walking in, I was greeted by a twenty-something girl and escorted to a private dining room. Immediately, people were shaking my hand and introducing themselves, including current members, like Steve Stivers from my former home state of Ohio. I also met other freshmen, like Doug Collins from Georgia and two other Floridians, Ron DeSantis and Ted Yoho. And just like the invitation read, there were "members of the D.C. business community."

John Coltrane's "Blue Train" played from speakers as servers zigzagged through the crowd of about fifteen with trays of red and white wine. What I really wanted was a cold beer, like an IPA, but I didn't want to step out of line, so I grabbed a red. As I did, a big portly guy with intense eyes and a big smile stuck out his hand, "Hi! I'm Kent Knutson."

"I'm Trey. Nice to meet you."

Then he said a little more sternly, "Congressman, nice to meet you."

I fired back, "Man, I hear the word 'congressman,' and I still look behind me to spot a congressman." He let out a good laugh.

We chatted about family and work and our love of travel. I shared my love for "throwing on a backpack and just going!" He had just returned from a trip to Paris with his wife. He told me he worked with Home Depot and was "good friends with Leader Cantor." At that moment, *Oh, a lobbyist!* popped into my head. I didn't dare say that out loud, though, knowing full well what a dirty word "lobbyist" had become. Most people prefer something vague like "government relations."

Kent introduced me to other "D.C. businesspeople" as well as other members of Congress. Clearly, he was a player. He knew everyone and everyone knew him. Energetic, engaging, fun—I would learn that these are quintessential characteristics of the best lobbyists.

The wine continued to flow. Kent and I made our way into the dining area. I was taken aback. Trays of food were spread out on half a dozen large circular tables piled high with food skewers. The trays were piled so damn high that the food was falling off, and bits of fat and oil dripped onto the floors and tables. I blurted out, "Skewers!" Kent shot right back, "Skewers." It was all finger food, and each type had its own dipping sauce—soy, peanut, horseradish, sweet, spicy, you name it. I started identifying them out loud in the style of Ben Stein in *Ferris Bueller's Day Off.* "Beef skewers." Pause. "Chicken skewers." Kent nudged me and pointed to our right. "Shrimp skewers."

Kent licked his lips and hit his wine. I took a swig of mine and said, "Man, what a spread!"

Our crowd had gotten larger and the number of servers had doubled. I thought, *Where the hell are these servers coming from? And all this wine? There's no way a bartender could pour that fast, and I've tended bar!* The servers must've been dipping glasses in some sort of garbage-can-size vat of wine. I flashed back to my time in Rome, studying the downfall of the Roman Empire. This must've been just like those Roman parties where everyone gorged on food, drowned themselves in wine, then puked to make room for more. Then I thought, *Nah, man. This isn't Roman. This is Greek, with old men, in this case leadership, taking out young boys, the freshmen, to get us drunk and teach us God knows what. Let's just pray they don't want sex.*

I took another sip of wine and asked Kent, "This is a steakhouse, right? How about a bloody red New York strip?"

"Can't do it." He turned and looked me right in the eyes.

I then held up my glass of wine. "I whack down a few more of these, I'm gonna need a big steak."

He then explained why two grown-ass men, neither of us exactly petite, had to abide by specific rules for however long I held office or he worked as a lobbyist. "It's the toothpick rule. A few years ago, the rules changed on how and what people in government relations and members can eat together. I'm not even certain what applies tonight, but I do know this: Everyone always sticks to the strictest reading of the rules. So, we get"—he paused and put out his hand like a *Price Is Right* model—"skewers."

The rules were first drafted in 2007, yet even today they are so silly and complex that questions are often raised about what's allowed and what's not. Highly paid attorneys try to figure out the rules, then push them, pull them, and bend them as far as possible. There are rules and regulations for anything and everything a lawmaker receives, whether it's a meal at an event or a gift as simple as a coffee mug.

Take, for example, National Hot Dog Day, when lawmakers must take a pause from their duties in Congress to recognize the importance of perfectly formed cylindrical hunks of meat. During this time, two groups who are at odds with each other take to the Hill—the American Meat Institute and People for the Ethical Treatment of Animals.

The rules dictate that if your group uses registered lobbyists you cannot give anything out for free. You have to charge. The AMI uses registered lobbyists. So, on National Hot Dog Day, you will get no free flesh made out of lips and buttholes from them. You gotta pay! However, PETA does not have a formally registered lobbying arm, so it is allowed to sling veggie hot dogs all damn day.

"This is crazy," I said.

Kent agreed. "They don't mess around here." Then he delivered some words of wisdom. "This is Washington. Everything we do is analyzed and scrutinized by the parties and by ethics." He put his hand on his chest. "That's just us, though." He paused and pointed at me. "It goes double for you, Congressman."

I took a long drink of my wine. I didn't want to think about the spotlight and scrutiny I would be under. And, dammit, I was still uncomfortable with the title of congressman. I hadn't even been elected yet!

This kind of silliness pervades Washington. Representatives and their staff, paid with your hard-earned tax dollars, sit around and think up these ridiculous situations and how to regulate them. The goal is to stop corruption. Sure, that's noble. But what the hell is the difference between finger foods and an overpriced steak at Bobby's, Ruth's, or the Palm? Is a fifty-dollar steak going to be just enough protein to push a congressman over the edge to vote a certain way? Silly. Petty. Illogical.

Now think about how much money goes to pay Congress and its staff who sit around jerking one another off with compliments about the great work they're doing while they come up with this asinine stuff. While it might come from the good intention of trying to cut down on influence and corruption, it's within a system where one single wealthy person can help get you elected with billions of dollars run through a super PAC, and one single person with a solid fund-raising network can collect millions of dollars to directly fund your campaign.

You can bitch all you want about how money influences lawmakers, but think about this: At this point in my story, I'm not even an elected congressman. Even with the strict rules and regulations, you see the kind of money being thrown around. For every new rule, for every new ethical boundary, for every new guideline, there's an entire floor in some anonymous, unremarkable building on Washington's infamous K Street filled with high-priced lawyers finding ways to skirt that law, bend that regulation, and push that ethical boundary as far as possible in order to contribute large donations and do whatever is possible to influence your government.

Long before I ran for office, things like subsidies for some businesses, tax breaks for others, government funding for a few, and even gay marriage helped shape my beliefs as a conservative. If there is one thing I am more certain of now than ever, it's this: If you want politicians to quit picking winners and losers in society, get them out of the game. After all, that's the reason the "D.C. business community" warms up to members of Congress. Lobbyists aren't bad people. They're not out to corrupt anyone. They're just doing their job, which is to exert influence over the laws that regulate their clients. That may include demanding changes in tax law or asking for more subsidies to compete with their government-subsidized competitor. The job of a lobbyist exists because government—intentionally or not—created it.

Do you hate tax credits for Big Oil? Don't revamp the tax code, blow it up.

Do you despise watching your money getting thrown at green energy, like the failed Solyndra, a solar company that went bankrupt after getting more than $500 million in loans from the government? Then stop the government from picking and choosing which companies they'll fund, which are more often than not big contributors to campaigns.

I understand the importance of tax dollars being used for research and development. However, I hope the big picture shows you that the more government gets involved, the more susceptible members of Congress are to influence. Those stewards create tax law and dish out tax dollars—your dollars. *That's your money.*

On some social issues, I make the same argument. If you want to quit pitting people against one another, stop the government from picking sides.

Take marriage equality. If two people love each other, let them marry regardless of sexual orientation. There's not enough love in the world; the more the better!

The real question is: Why is government involved in marriage at all?

Marriage should be between people, not a governmental contract. In fact, some far-left liberals and far-right conservatives have argued in favor of marriage privatization for decades. By privatizing it, it becomes an intimate choice between people, not something affirmed by some dude in a suit in Washington. Furthermore, it also removes the issue of religious liberty, and rightfully so. No church should be forced to marry two people against that religion's doctrine. Unfortunately, when the government steps in and deems who is getting tax breaks or incentives based on relationships, it muddies the water.

If government is involved in gay marriage, grandstanding Republicans can leverage it as a wedge issue, often in vile ways, by using religion as an instrument of hate. If the government wasn't involved, it wouldn't be an issue. A married couple doesn't need to be blessed by somebody in Washington. The public despises Washington anyway. I've never understood why they keep inviting it into their private lives, especially on this issue.

Using one of the more polarizing Republicans in recent history, I often ask my gay friends, "Why do you need Dick Cheney to validate your marriage?" A close friend's answer: "The more dick at my wedding, the better!"

Well then, invite Dick Cheney to your wedding. I envision it as a dystopian movie directed by Terry Gilliam. It's totally black, with spotlights beaming down on Dick Cheney, who is hovering behind two men holding hands at an altar. Dick's holding a twelve-gauge shotgun. He cocks it. *Click, click.* Then, in that creepy whisper voice of his, he asks, "Shotgun wedding, boys? I'm a wicked aim."

I'm also talking to you, you government-hating, free-market-promoting, guns-and-gold conservatives.

Why the hell are you inviting Nancy Pelosi, Harry Reid, and Barack Obama to your wedding? Nancy just imported a dozen Cher drag queens from San Francisco to your wedding in the beautiful hills of Arkansas. The church organist is being drowned out by uncomfortably masculine voices all singing, "Do you believe in life after love?"

Too much for ya? Sorry, "conservatives," but it's what you asked for. You may have scorned government officials for intruding into your private life with Obamacare and gun rights, but you demanded the government dictate norms for society's most intimate choice—love.

Many of our public-policy fights boil down to issues of the tax code and funding. Whether it's a tax break, an incentive for corporations, or something tied to your professional or personal life, Congress makes these decisions. And members are real-life, regular people like you. And people are susceptible to influence. When they, *meaning government*, aren't picking, choosing, favoring, or shunning, there's a lot less to fight about.

Surrounded by these people eating tons of skewers, I finished my second serving and last glass of wine. It was time for bed. I had an early coffee meeting with Kent's friend Majority Leader Cantor and more members of the D.C. business community.

When my alarm went off the next morning, I sat up and smacked my lips. The cheap red wine from the vats in the kitchen and greasy skewers had left a nasty taste in my mouth. *Not even a steak! What kind of fat-cat Republican Party is this?* I was sure we'd have massive bloody hunks of cow still attached to the bone, complete with men lighting cigars with hundred-dollar bills while downing a vintage of wine from long before I was born. Nope. Just skewers.

I rolled out of bed, grabbed a shower, brushed my teeth, and scrubbed my tongue for about an hour. I would need the standard hangover remedy—a double espresso and something greasy to eat.

Luckily the event was at a Starbucks, so I got there early, tossed back a doppio and some sort of sandwich with eggs and sausage or bacon. Feeling great, I went upstairs to the private room where the event was being held.

As soon as I got to the top of the stairs, a twenty-something staffer addressed me as "Congressman," took my arm, and shuffled me over to a bunch of guys hovering around coffee and pastries. This was the second time in twelve hours I had been grabbed by the arm and handed off to a random group. "Look what I found! It's a real-life person who was insane enough to run for Congress! Here you go! Now corrupt him!"

Oh, and don't forget, I'm not even a congressman yet; I still have a general election to win!

I've never been to a speed-dating event, but I've seen them in comedies like *The 40-Year-Old Virgin* and sketches on *Saturday Night Live.* This is what they must be like. Shake hands. Fast intro. Grab business card. Repeat.

After meeting with people from Monsanto to Microsoft, I stuffed a bunch of business cards in my pocket just as Cantor pulled everyone together. "Can we have everyone get together in a kind of semicircle here?" He stood in front of the crowd, coffee in hand, and pushed his glasses up the bridge of his nose. "I want to thank y'all for coming. It's very kind of you to take some time out of your morning. Now I know everyone has to get to work, so let's go ahead and introduce everyone." He then looked for us soon-to-be congressmen-elect. "Guys, can I have y'all come up here?"

We awkwardly stood behind him, standing shoulder to shoulder like pieces of meat on display. The majority leader continued. "We wanted to bring this group here today because all of them come from Republican safe districts. We fully expect to see them back here after November. So we want to give y'all a chance to connect. We really don't have a particular order, so let's just go down the line."

I was second to last, so I watched my soon-to-be colleagues introduce themselves. One of them was Ted Yoho. Ted is a big guy, six-foot-four. He took a step forward. "Hi. My name is Ted Yoho," he said, in a big booming voice with a touch of a southern accent. "I am running in Florida's Third District. I'm a small-business owner. Own a veterinarian clinic." Ted turned it up a notch. "I specialize in large animals." He then held up one of his massive hands with thick kielbasa fingers. "So you can imagine where these hands have been!" The crowd busted out laughing, picturing Ted's hand up the ass of a cow or horse.

Smiling, Cantor said, "Now, Ted, you pulled off a major upset against Cliff, right?" He knew the answer. He just wanted to hear more from Ted. "That's right," Ted said. "Cliff Stearns."

Cliff Stearns had served for twenty-four years. That kind of seniority used to mean power and security. It used to be nearly impossible to unseat an incumbent. He had constant media attention, huge name identification, and his campaign coffers were always full. Not anymore. Just two years earlier, in 2010, many incumbents had been defeated by so-called tea party candidates. Frustrated, angry conservatives had yelled on my radio show that incumbents were "part of the establishment" and "part of the problem."

By 2012, most incumbents were on guard and prepared to spend big to fight off challengers flanking them from the right. But Stearns was notoriously cheap, and he had underestimated Yoho. Frustrated establishment Republicans often remarked, "That guy was so tight with money, he still had a million bucks left in his campaign account!"

Ted Yoho was a giant symbol of the antiestablishment mood, and his victory over Cliff exemplified the new political reality: *Once powerful incumbency was now a liability.* Getting elected to Congress had become a lot like when a cool underground punk band lands a radio hit, and as soon as they get airtime, everyone says, "You sold out! You suck!"

Now the leadership had to deal with Ted whether they shook one of his massive hands or not.

Ted turned more serious. "I'm here to stand up for our kids and grandkids who are facing debt that will cripple this nation. Our deficits are out of control. We have forgotten our way when it comes to the Constitution. We need to stand up for what's right."

Ted was a quintessential member of the tea party, which is not a political party at all.

The Associated Press defines "tea party" like this:

Lowercase—the populist movement that opposes the Washington political establishment. Adherents are tea partyers.

Ask fifteen people from across the political spectrum what a "tea partyer" is and you'll get fifteen different answers. Ask fifteen Republicans, you'll also get fifteen different answers. Ask fifteen Democrats, and you'll get, well, some not-so-nice definitions.

First, let's take the word "establishment." If you're in office for even one day, doesn't that make you part of the establishment? Take Louie Gohmert, a Republican congressman from Texas. He has been in office for more than a decade, but ask any member of the D.C. press corps and they'll tell you he is a quintessential hell-raising member of the tea party. Louie would be proud of that, too.

So what is the political establishment? Once again, ask fifteen different people and you'll get fifteen different answers.

The tea party organizers I met early on were good people who could care less about social issues and race. Some were barely Republican; many were libertarian or libertarian leaning. They were concerned with both Bush and Obama shredding the Constitution, bailing out big banks and Big Auto, putting us in nonsensical foreign wars, and destroying the country's future by spending us so far into debt we can never get out.

Overwhelmingly, the original tea party movement focused on two things—the Constitution and spending. They wanted the power in Washington to have checks and balances; they wanted the same when it came to spending. Contrary to the way Democrats and some in the media have portrayed the movement, it was never about race, religion, or anything social. Those are cheap and easy ways to dismiss and discredit a movement.

A few years later, another group came along that I felt mirrored the tea party in many ways—the Occupy Wall Street movement. Both groups felt cheated and abandoned. Both saw the heavy hand of government always choosing the side of the wealthiest and most powerful.

Those were some of the issues Ted addressed in his quick speech. But when leadership knew you were aligned with the tea party and talked about silly things like a balanced budget, it signaled two words: "hell" and "no."

Hell, no, Ted wouldn't go along with the system. Hell, no, Ted wasn't going to vote the way you wanted. Hell, no, Ted wasn't going to partake in any Washington games.

In my campaign I was proud to have support from across the spectrum. Moderate and establishment types came to our side, and even though the local tea party was divided up, we had a ton of grassroots supporters. With my Spanish-speaking skills and the fact that I openly supported a Republican version of the DREAM Act, we also captured Hispanics.

Sure, I shared some of the tea party sentiment. I was and am especially passionate about our massive spending problem in Washington. But I wasn't going to D.C. to be a hell-raiser *just to be a hell-raiser.* I made it a point to get to know Democrats and find ways to work with them. In fact, in my campaign I never identified myself as a tea party candidate.

A few weeks into my term in Congress, though, I discovered that the media labeled almost every Republican congressperson who was sworn in after 2010 as a member of the tea party. Even with my eventual outreach to Democrats as well as my libertarian leanings that could be construed as liberal, I was still labeled as a tea party wacko and part of the problem.

It is what it is. People might label you and put you in a corner, but you've gotta define yourself. I would have to work hard to do so.

To draw parallels between business and Congress, a member chooses who he wants to be like a business brand does. As Rob Cole told me during the campaign, "Trey, you need to figure out your role in the play." Once I figured out that I was heading to Congress, I knew what I did *not* want to be. I didn't want to be the angry guy going *South Park*, and yelling, "They're taking our jobs! Durk a der." I also wasn't the guy who would go along to get along. I knew I would stay true to my libertarian values, vote conservative, yet always make an effort to bridge gaps and work with people from all walks of life.

I saw my role, and ultimately my vote, as a constant balancing act between what the voters wanted and what I wanted, *meaning voting my conscience.*

Occasionally, it's a push-pull scenario. You may have groups in the district who are passionate about issues that don't move you. For me, those were social issues. Other constituents might be lax about things that infuriate you; for me, those concerned foreign policy and civil liberties.

Ted finished his speech, and others followed. Then it was my turn. I looked out at the lobbyists, uh, I mean government-relations staff. They were bored stiff and getting antsy. I gave a quick spiel, telling them that I was from a part of Florida where "at least a few of your parents or grandparents have retired to." The group laughed and, sure enough, at least two people raised their hands. I touched on my history in business and as a journalist. I also said I had never served in office and was eager to meet people and learn from them.

In my experience, lobbyists, either on the campaign trail or in arranged meetings, often don't give a damn about your stump speech, your values, or your policy. They just want to know you'll listen, hear out their case, and not be a jerk. Pretty simple. They're just doing their job for the businesses they represent.

My meetings were over. My trip lasted forty-eight hours. It was time to get back to Florida.

My plane descended into Southwest Florida International Airport. As soon as I hit the ground, I was smacked in the face with the brutal September heat and humidity. I wanted to take a break, go home, sit in the air-conditioning, play with my son, and strum the guitar, anything to zone out. But my phone kept blowing up.

More calls came in from people at the Republican National Committee, known as the RNC, as well as other members of Congress from Florida. Those I expected.

Others I didn't.

One weekday I got a call from a guy named Armando Gutierrez. "Hi, Trey, my name is Armando. Jeb Jr. gave me your number," he said, referring to the governor's son. Armando explained that he was politically active with the Maverick PAC, known as MavPac. He asked me some questions about my history and résumé, but not much about where I stood on any issues. He then said, "MavPac supports young conservatives in office or running for office. We'd like to support you." "Support" is a Washington code word like "helpful." Money was about to be thrown at me. Dance.

I thought deeply for a second. *Hmmm. Someone's tossing money at me. Why? What's the motivation? Maybe I should hold off on accepting contributions.* That second passed. "Great! Thanks! I'd really appreciate it."

Armando then suggested I speak to a congressman from Georgia. "His name is Tom Graves. He is a rock-solid conservative and also a young professional."

"Sure, set the call up. I'd love to get to know as many colleagues as I can."

Armando wasted no time. A day later I was on the phone with both of them.

Our conversation started with the basics about work and family. Tom also had some young kids, so we talked a little bit about trying to juggle the demands in Washington with family. "It's tough," he said in a smooth Georgia accent that I hadn't heard since I'd lived in Atlanta. "One piece of advice I'll give you is when you go and hire staff, make sure you and your wife both meet the person doing your scheduling."

Naïvely, I asked, "Wait. You have someone in the office just devoted to scheduling? Can't your chief of staff do that?"

He chuckled. "Trey, you'll see soon enough. When you get to Washington, you'll be pulled in more directions than you even know." Tom, with classic southern charm, offered up his chief of staff to help answer logistical questions and more.

Armando broke in. "Trey, not sure if you really know about the election process in D.C., but people run for all sorts of positions like Speaker and leader, but there's also an important committee, the RSC."

"Oh, yeah," I said, having heard of it. "The Republican Study Committee, right?"

"That's right," Tom said. And knowing I was still green, he added, "It's not an actual House committee like Ways and Means or Transportation and Infrastructure. It drives conservative policy for the Republican Party."

Tom then got more specific. "So, Trey, I'm running to be the chairman of the RSC, and I'd really like to have your support. We'll eventually vote on this as a party. Can I count on your vote?"

Silence.

From a sales perspective, when the seller asks a question and the buyer goes silent, he wins.

Green as hell, *naïve as hell*, I said, "Yeah. Uh-huh. Sure." I didn't have the slightest clue who he was running against. I didn't even know the position existed before this phone call. I mumbled on. "Yeah, yeah, happy to."

This is one of those situations that some freshman members go through yet never share with other newbies coming in. Maybe lifetime politicians who had served in their state house or senate knew about these things, but I sure didn't. Like a boy desperate for a prom date, googly eyes wide open, I committed to the first person who asked.

I may have been naïve and clueless about these internal elections, but I knew there was a bigger picture. These positions are just the start for many members who use them to climb the ladder. Tom Graves would go on to lose the RSC chair spot to Steve Scalise, who had his eyes set on bigger positions, too.

Steve reached out to me just before the election, but I was so embarrassed about being so green and already committed to someone else that I didn't get back to him until after the vote. Steve is from Louisiana. We got along really well, sharing our affinity for New Orleans, its culture, restaurants like Tujague's, and local entertainment, including the semifamous 610 Stompers. A year later, when Eric Cantor lost his primary and his spot as majority leader, Steve went from RSC chair to majority whip.

While the RSC chairmanship might have led to higher positions for Tom Graves, why would Armando Gutierrez be connecting the dots like this? Why did this fellow Floridian have a vested interest in a random member from Georgia, the RSC, or, for that matter, me?

MavPac had built a solid reputation and powerful network of both elected officials and supporters. Armando's family was politically active, and he'd run for Congress, too. His first phone call ran through my mind again. "Jeb Jr. gave me your number." I later found out that Governor Bush's older son, George P. Bush, was also a major figure in the PAC.

People like Graves were building networks to gain support for higher positions in Congress. But why do groups like MavPac build their networks so far and wide? There was never any "ask." I certainly couldn't categorize them as a group of donors who "wanted something." Their organization didn't have a common thread in an industry or a business. They did what they said—supported up-and-coming young politicians who leaned right.

On June 15, 2015, John Ellis "Jeb" Bush, the former governor of Florida, announced he was running for president.

Was this PAC built and sustained to create a network of support for Jeb? Or how about future Bush political players, like George P., who is considered a rock star in Texas? Is that how far and wide other seasoned political players think? My guess is yes. And if I, a political novice, started connecting these dots, I am certain that longtime players like the Bush family and their entourage of consultants thoroughly understand this.

After all, even as a rookie, I understood the power of a network, both for fund-raising and grassroots support, as well as the power of relationships, and the *power of powerful people*; members tend to wield influence over their constituents and sometimes their colleagues.

I now had to figure out the bigger picture for myself: *What committees did I want to get on? What kind of a political player did I want to be?* To answer these questions, I would need to start building my own networks.

And, oh, yeah, I'm not even friggin' elected yet!

★6★
MO MONEY
MO PROBLEMS

The general election was drawing near. It was of no concern.

It was time to get the band back together. The campaign team had taken a break from one another for a few weeks while I traveled. It was a nice respite; Pusateri had certainly had enough of my crazy ass. But now it was time to start thinking about what we would do when we got to Washington.

That's right. The general election to officially become a United States congressman was two months out, but we were looking way past that.

Think about what's happening. I haven't even won the spot. I'm being wined and dined in D.C. with the supercool title of Young Gun, and now I'm figuring out what I'll do as a congressman, but I'm *not yet a congressman*. Don't get disgusted. Just thank your local state legislators for the safe districts they carved out for me and Democrats alike.

Now it was time to pin down some of the people who would come to Washington with me. I never made any promises to anyone during the race, but in my head I knew a few people on my campaign team who would be a huge asset if we won. Officially, I could not tell them what I wanted for them. That's a big no-no: You cannot promise anyone positions in return for their campaign services or volunteer work. But anyone who has half a brain knows that if they have skills, a decent résumé, and work hard on the campaign they'll more than likely find a spot in the federal office.

I began to settle on the main parts of the team.

Matt Pusateri would be my district director, heading up the team at home. Matt would oversee Southwest Florida staff and have a wide range of responsibilities, including coordinating all local outreach—attending regional meetings of political clubs, civic groups, and industry organizations.

Matt would also have to take a lot of crap from a lot of people. Properly said, he had to relay what's called "constituent sentiment" to the office in Washington. So, if we were doing something in Washington that the people didn't like, it was his ear they'd chew off. Then he'd do the same to me.

It was a perfect fit for him. He had a knack for people and politics, and now he knew the district and all of its political, business, and industry players better than anyone. It also worked well because he wanted to remain in Southwest Florida with his family.

I wanted two others from the campaign to join the team in Washington—Jason Moon and Abby Dosoretz.

Jason and I had known each other for years through political circles but soon became friends, sharing a love of sports and food. Jason worked as an attorney but, like me, was ready to do whatever he could to serve the country. He is smart, driven, and has a sense of humor. The latter was very important to me as I looked at new hires. I wanted to work with people who not only had as much drive as I did but could also have fun. I would hire him as chief of staff.

I wanted Abby to work as our legislative director. Abby is Jason's sister-in-law, and because they knew each other's work style, they clicked professionally and got things done quickly. I knew they could do the same in Washington. Plus, it just so happened that Abby's fiancé had a job lined up in D.C. Jason would travel back and forth with me to D.C. and Abby would live there.

Abby was detail oriented and could manage and coordinate. This was a big asset, especially when Matt and I would blow things off or not take certain events or responsibilities seriously enough. Abby knew not only when *but how* to crack the whip. If Matt asked, like a smart-ass, "Aw, come on, what's walkin' door-to-door gonna do?" Abby would look up over her thick-rimmed glasses, and reply, "We have to do it. This is a campaign. We need to be out campaigning."

She'd stay up all night making maps for us to campaign door-to-door. We even dragged her fiancé, Steve, into the campaign. He had just finished law school and had moved to Southwest Florida to be with Abby while he studied for the bar exam. He'd stay up all night hitting the books, then she'd send him to Starbucks in the morning to whack down a strong coffee and chauffeur me around to various neighborhoods. He'd drop me off at one end of the street; I'd knock on each door, circle back, get in the car, and repeat on the next block. Abby kept us in check, and she kept our feet on the ground demanding we *put in and appreciate* the hard, detailed work it took to win a campaign.

While I kept my eyes open for other potential hires, it was time to focus on things I had no business focusing on while still a candidate and *not yet a congressman*. I was looking at what committees I wanted to get on.

Jason and I would huddle every day, typically over a churrasco and empanadas at a restaurant called El Gaucho Inca, owned by a local Argentinean and Peruvian couple.

One day he cut into his steak, stopped, and looked up at me. His face was a little flush, but then again he's fair skinned and has red hair. He might poke fun at himself and say he's a ginger, but not quite. Growing up in Florida gave him a little color. Plus, he has a thick build. With his massive chest and usually serious demeanor, no one would dare call him a ginger! At least not to his face.

So the ginger went on. "We're going to have to raise a lot more cash," he said, in an intense whisper.

"Yeah, I know," I said, dismayed. I didn't want to think about the campaign. I wanted to enjoy my steak, but we had just won a grueling primary and there was a lot more work to be done.

We had already raised and spent nearly a million dollars, but now we needed more. Frustration began to consume me. "Man, the last thing in the world I want to do is go ask people for more cash, especially the people who just gave to us. I mean, do you know how that looks?"

He nodded as he chewed. I set down my knife and fork, and put my hand up to my head with my thumb and pinky finger extended like I was on a phone call. I laid on a deep announcer voice, mocking myself. "Hello. I know you, your wife, your children, and your children's children just donated thousands of dollars to our campaign . . . but wait! There's more!" I picked up the pace, speaking like Billy Mays hawking products on TV. "Now you have the one-time opportunity to donate in this general election! And if you donate now, you can donate in the next primary that starts in just a few months! And the next cycle and the next cycle after that!"

I picked up my fork and took a bite of bloody red meat. In between bites, I said, "Screw that." Jason, not playing along, continued in his hushed voice. "We have to. We need somewhere north of $25,000 in the next few weeks."

"I know. I know."

But why? After all, I've got this election wrapped up! *Seriously, why the hell would I need tens of thousands of dollars more for a campaign that is all but assured victory?*

The money is not for me. It's for the party. And this brings us to a dirty little secret in Washington: The more money you give, the more powerful you become as a player within your party.

I needed to *donate to* or *raise money for* the Republican Party's political arm, the National Republican Congressional Committee—the NRCC—which is devoted to electing representatives.

Don't think for a second this is just a Republican thing. The Democrats' arm is the Democratic Congressional Campaign Committee, or the DCCC, pronounced *D-triple-C.*

These committees get involved in campaigns all over the country. They fight to get or maintain control of the House. In some cases they recruit candidates. And in districts where the race is close, they spend millions of dollars in advertising to tell you that their candidate is Jesus reincarnated or that the competitor is Satan.

They also raise money in all sorts of ways. They have events with prominent speakers where the attendees donate big bucks for a mediocre meal and the chance to hobnob with political celebrities and leadership. Sometimes the event has a theme, like Bright Lights and Broadway, which is held in New York City, and you get a ticket if you contribute $15,000 to the NRCC. On top of that, you have to pay for your hotel and expenses, which in Manhattan are totally reasonable.

The NRCC and DCCC are headed up by members who perform these duties outside of their responsibilities as federal lawmakers. During my campaign, Representative Greg Walden from Oregon was the head of the NRCC. He had deputies with titles like finance chair or recruitment chair. Regardless of their titles, the most important thing the members who serve on these committees do is raise money, and they are consumed with it. They're responsible for their own fund-raising benchmarks and making sure other members are contributing. They set goals and call them "dues." Bigwigs in the leadership raise millions of dollars. Important committee heads raise hundreds of thousands to millions. Rank-and-file members raise thousands to hundreds of thousands—or more than a million if, of course, they want to ascend to a better committee or leadership position.

Every year members are expected to raise and pay dues to the committee. And you're reminded of it often.

Phone rings. "Hi, Trey, it's Congressman So-and-So. I work with the NRCC. Just wanted to catch up on your dues. Think you'll be able to make it this cycle?" Not even a "Hey, how ya doing?"

Or the worst: Every time you walk into an NRCC meeting, a giant goddamn tally sheet is on prominent display that lists your name and how much you've given—or haven't. It's a huge wall of shame. The big players, people in leadership positions and chairs of powerful committees, always dominate the board, raising millions for the NRCC. Furthermore, if you are in leadership or the head of a big committee, your dues are higher, *much higher.*

Just as a member of Congress's federal business cannot overlap or mix with their campaign in any way, these political campaign arms must be separate entities.

What a joke. It is abundantly clear that the more you help the party, the more leadership will help you in your role as a federal lawmaker, whether it's giving your legislation a chance or getting you on a good committee or, as years pass, a better committee. It's not directly pay to play. It's not overt. It certainly isn't on paper. But when you donate big to the congressional committee, you land on a better committee.

And that, my friend, is exactly what we planned to do!

"So you think the magic number is twenty-five?" I asked Jason.

"I do. I think it's attainable and it's a good number going to the NRCC even before we get elected."

"And you think we can pull that off?"

"Yes. I'm working some angles now to bring in some of the people we didn't have in the primary. I'll need you to make calls or maybe we have lunch with some of them."

"Man, do you know how incestuous this is?" I asked. "All that money we got from Boehner and Cantor just goes right back to the party, back into some imaginary NRCC pot."

Finishing his steak, he said, "I know. It's ridiculous. It's just back and forth."

"Right? It's not even sneaky like a shell game or anything like that. It's just one pocket to another. It's a giant, not really that intricate, incestuous, cyclical bucket of money."

Jason raised his voice, "Well, we need to put money into that bucket."

"Yes, we do."

"La cuenta, por favor." I asked our waiter for our check, making the signing gesture with an invisible pen.

Jason went over other details of our plan. "We also have to approach House Steering Committee members."

The House Steering Committee assigns you to a committee or committees. It is made up of leadership, committee chairs, and individual steering chairs who oversee regions.

An example of this would be Region 1, represented by Doc Hastings, made up of his home state of Washington plus Oregon, Idaho, Montana, Utah, Colorado, Nevada, and Alaska. Quite a big territory, right? Well, Doc gets that much because there are so few Republicans in the northwest, plus those states are sparsely populated. Other regions include the Midwest, parts of the South, and so on.

Then there's Texas, which is its own region because of its size and because it has so many Republicans.

When it comes time to put people on committees, each person has one vote, with the exception of the Speaker, who has five, and the majority leader, who gets two.

I tell Jason, "Cantor's office helped me with some names. Some people from his team had some great suggestions on how to approach this."

"Really?" he asked.

"Yeah, let's go get a *cafecito* and talk more. I couldn't sleep last night. I was consumed with trying to think up new ways to ask for money. I need a strong coffee."

We paid the check and got into Jason's beautiful BMW— he'd made some decent coin in his years as an attorney—and headed to the nearby Cuban Cafe for a colada, a tasty Cuban coffee that is basically five shots of espresso with sugar. He started the car and both the air-conditioning and Jay Z's voice singing "Ball so hard" kicked on full-blast. Jason turned down the volume, and we continued talking.

I started. "So, man, I got a list of names. The steering committee members are our targets."

"Oh, yeah, you an assassin with those targets?" he asked.

I played along. "Damn straight! There is an art to this, ya know. Like a sniper, you gotta identify your target, zone in, and bang! You fire away. You unload your weapons—charm, friendship, relationships, you name it."

Suddenly Kanye's voice singing, "That shit cray," danced over the beats. I turned the music up. "That shit cray, J!"

Jason rolled his eyes at my stupid antics, turned the stereo back down, and asked, "So, these are all steering committee members?"

"Yeah, they're broken down by region."

"What do they want from you?"

I laughed really loudly. "What do you think?"

He fired back with "Money."

"Yeah, man. Money. But it's not for them." I let that sink it.

Jason asked, "Who is it for, then?"

"So here's the deal. The steering committee members appoint everyone to committees. They have these regions they oversee. Our guy in Florida is Congressman Jeff Miller from up north. He'll suggest where we go, and then the steering committee votes on it. But check this out. These steering committee people also pay close attention to races in their regions. And when someone's in a tight race, they can always suggest you help out." I held up air quotes on "help out."

"Okay," he said, nodding.

"And so I'll *help out* any candidates that might be in a tough race."

Jason pulled into the Cuban Cafe's parking lot, shut the car off, and laid it all out. "Okay, so we'll do $25,000 to the NRCC, hopefully more. You make the calls to other members, see who needs help, and we'll cut checks to them, too."

"Yeah, that's pretty much it," I said.

"We'll hit those other candidates with anything from a thousand to a max out of twenty-five hundred." He paused in thought. I looked out the window and nodded toward the restaurant. *"Vamos."*

It was time to get to work again.

Several weeks passed. I knocked down hundreds of coladas and made as many phone calls reaching out to steering committee members.

One of my first calls was to Congressman Lynn Westmoreland from Georgia. Connie Mack had once told me he was a great guy who would be helpful as I navigated my way through Congress. And I mean "helpful" in the genuine way, not the Washington way.

Lynn was the representative for Region 8: Georgia, Alabama, and South Carolina.

"Hello, Congressman Westmoreland. My name is Trey Radel, calling from our friend Connie's district."

In his thick, friendly Georgia accent, he said, "Hi, Trey! Connie speaks highly of you! Please, call me Lynn."

I love people who drop formalities right away. "All right, Lynn, thanks for taking my call. Connie also speaks highly of you."

We chitchatted about my time in Georgia and how much he loved Naples. "What are you interested in when you get to Congress?"

What am I interested in?

I was prepared for this question. Before I made the call, I'd done a lot of research.

There are good committees and great committees, bad committees and terrible committees. As you may have guessed, I wanted to go big. I wasn't going to settle for some half-assed committee that I was neither passionate about nor had any significance to my district.

Committees even come with labels, A and B. Those labels aren't official; they're just a way for members to categorize them. An A committee is powerful, like Ways and Means. Something like the Committee on Education and the Workforce is a B committee. Of course, there's another reason A committees are held in such high regard—money. The more a committee is directly involved in a private business, such as setting its tax policy or creating new regulations, the more likely its lobbyists and people from that industry will donate to your campaign.

Some B committees do hold serious sway, even if they don't pack fund-raising power. Transportation and Infrastructure, known as T & I, and Agriculture are powerful because they set policy that directly affects the entire country. Likewise, Foreign Affairs and the Committee on Oversight and Government Reform are important committees.

Foreign Affairs has the spotlight during any sort of overseas conflict. Oversight drags people to the Hill to beat the crap out of them, from IRS personnel targeting people to Secret Service members deciding to pay for a BJ after a heavy night of drinking.

Then there are the long-winded committees like Science, Space, and Technology, and the committee that thought it might be more compelling if they used the word "House" twice—The House Committee on House Administration. While I bet Neil deGrasse Tyson is pissed that no one is clawing to get on Science and Space, most members are trying to get on the better B committees. Usually, they try to make their way up to either be a chair of one of the better B committees or plot a move a few years down the road to get on an A committee. Don't get me wrong, all of these committees are important. In fact, B committees like Space and Science are critical to the constituents and communities they serve.

But who signs up for the House Committee on House Administration? Sure, they help with important things like getting you an office, but come on. Who says, "When I get to Congress, I want to be in charge of issuing phones!"? Or worse, there are the people who sign up to be on the Ethics Committee to bust other members of Congress. What kind of Napoleon complex do you have to have? It's like the annoying person in elementary school who was always tattling on everyone. *Ethics! Hope I never have to deal with those people!*

The reality is those committees handle mundane duties most people would prefer not to. And neither one raises you money.

Over the years, some committees have lost their luster and even some of their power. One in particular is a sad example of how screwed up Washington has become. Not long ago, Appropriations was one of the most powerful committees in Congress. Everyone wanted to be on it! Why? You doled out the money! It's like asking someone why they rob banks. That's where the money is!

Lawmakers used to pass financial legislation through an appropriations bill. Bills that go through the regular appropriations cycle are more specific, targeted, and responsible. They're broken down line by line with direct oversight. But now, massive pieces of legislation, known as omnibus bills, have replaced the way money is allocated. With an omnibus, which comes from the Latin word meaning "for everything," thousands of pages of individual measures dealing with everything from spending issues to national security measures are thrown together for a one-time yes or no vote and so are rarely debated within committees or on the floor.

Another way to fund the government is through a continuing resolution, known as a CR. A CR keeps things as is. Nothing new can be funded or created. The status quo stays the same, if not better protected. These CRs are such giant blobs of ambiguity that they leave no one responsible, and so, ultimately, they protect lawmakers, who can easily point their fingers at someone else.

Not so surprising, lawmakers rarely read these thousand-plus-page bills. Some are open about that; others are full of it.

Many members do not read every bill. That may sound shocking or disheartening, but it's the reality. It's why you have staff. Like a CEO of a company, you have employees to help you read and carefully vet these bills. After all, if you were an accountant, would you want your boss hovering over your shoulder breathing heavily in your ear as she reads every line of your spreadsheet? If you do public relations, would you want your CEO writing your press releases for you? Sure, I know some do, but those are the kind of micromanaging CEOs who lose their focus and eventually their minds.

Bills can sometimes hit the floor with only a few hours to read and then vote on them. The only people who have read what's in the legislation are the people who wrote it—a random mix of staff from various committees, who are all under the thumb of the leadership of whichever party is in charge.

Occasionally, if it's politically expedient, members will openly admit that no one is reading the bills.

In 2009, when Democrats had control of the House, John Boehner, then minority leader, took to the floor to complain about one of these instances. Democrats gave the House twelve hours to read and vote on a 1,100-page bill. On the floor, Minority Leader Boehner said not once but twice, "Not one member has read this."

Once again, both parties are guilty of this.

In December of 2015, with Republicans in control of the House, an omnibus bill was released. A headline on *Politico* read: "2,200 Pages, $1.8 Trillion, Dead of Night."

Voting has become like the movie *Gladiator*, with Joaquin Phoenix giving a bill a thumbs-up or thumbs-down. Except nothing in Congress is like a profound Ridley Scott film; it's more like *History of the World: Part 1* by Mel Brooks.

Back to the committee search!

The crème de la crème is the Committee on Ways and Means. It's like Manhattan's hottest restaurant. You call and ask, "Could I get a reservation for this Saturday?" The snooty young girl on the other end lets out a sigh, and replies, "No, but I can get you in next month on a Tuesday at 11:45 at night." No freshman gets on Ways.

Ways is the tax-writing committee. It determines the tax code, including tariffs and tax incentives, which are better known as "breaks." Whether it's 501(c)(3) status or something as specific as a tax incentive for pharmaceutical companies operating in Puerto Rico, Ways and Means members have their hands in everything.

Lobbyists are so desperate to get to its members that if you have even the smallest connection to or semblance of a relationship with the chairman, they will beg you to mention their issue in passing.

Dave Camp, the chair when I was in Congress, was one of the few committee heads to really make an effort to reach out to the rank and file, even us lowly freshmen. He was always attentive and listened to concerns, but if the committee is like Manhattan's hottest restaurant, Camp is the celebrity billionaire owner. Everyone wants to hang with him, get to know him, and, more than likely, ask him for something.

So one way for a freshman to get on an A committee is by donating a ton of money to the NRCC. We were working on that, but there is another way. Candidates from a swing district, one that doesn't heavily favor Republicans or Democrats, have a better chance of getting on an A committee.

Why's that? C'mon. Haven't you figured out the answer? Money!

When you're on a better committee, you can raise more money. And for candidates from swing districts, that means more money to spend on their campaigns, which means victory, which means the party in charge stays in charge by maintaining their majority in the House.

But there is a big catch to being on a great A committee. You are responsible for even higher dues to the NRCC or DCCC. In other words, because you have the opportunity to raise more money, you've got to shell out more money. It's like a protection racket in 1929 Chicago. You pay to remain on the committee and not be demoted or harmed. If you don't raise that money, Al Capone's hitman, Frank Nitti, will demote you. Off to the Education and Workforce Committee you go!

One committee had recently moved up in stature and was on its way to becoming an A committee. It's the House Committee on Financial Services, and freshmen had a chance to get on it! I wanted on. It would be a great fit for me. Banking is a huge industry in Florida and loads of constituents worked in the financial sector.

Financial Services oversees the entire financial industry, and I mean everything—from Fannie Mae and Freddie Mac to securities to regular commercial retail banking. After the housing bubble's burst ushered in the Great Recession, the committee, under the Democrats, began playing a more powerful role, especially after the Dodd-Frank Wall Street Reform and Consumer Protection Act was passed. Appropriations may have been losing some steam and power, but Financial Services was getting more powerful by the year. *And when a committee becomes more powerful, so do lobbyists.*

Don't take my word for it. In a 2007 *Washington Post* article headlined "Democrats Offer Up Chairmen for Donors," Chairman Barney Frank said, "Financial services companies are inclined to give to me because I'm chairman of the committee important to their interests." Frank was asked "whether banking interests feel obligated to give to Democrats when he asks them for contributions." He answered, "Obligated? No. Incentivized? Yes."

Frank said, however, that those donating "understand, and others do, too, that there are no guarantees of my doing what they want, or even my being pleasant." Barney Frank has never had a reputation for being the most pleasant guy, but the man knows politics and he knows policy.

The same article notes: "Frank traveled to Charlotte, home to two of America's largest bank companies, for a similar fund-raising breakfast, for a fellow Financial Services Committee member. Donors got to hear firsthand about Frank's plans for upcoming banking legislation. He assured attendees that more federal regulation of banking is on the way and that it will help banks to prosper."

Prosper they would, especially as competition thinned out over the next few years. During and after the economic collapse, many banks, including Southwest Florida banks, went under or were bought up by larger competitors.

Whether you are a constituent or someone aspiring to serve in Congress someday, you can throw away any idea that you or your representative will be a powerful player in Congress based on a "knack for good legislation" or a "strong will to fight for the people." Sure, those things are great to have, but "strong will" is nothing unless it comes with a big fat check.

And for candidates like me, elected in a safe district, I was asked to "consider giving" pretty quickly. Whether I was net-working with staffers, lobbyists, or members, the same question was always asked: How much have you donated to the NRCC?

After raising nearly $30,000 for the NRCC, I circled back and checked in with Congressman Westmoreland and others.

We cut checks to Lee Anderson out of Georgia, who lost; Dan Benishek from Michigan, who won; and Frank Guinta from New Hampshire, who lost but was reelected in 2015.

Our next move was to lobby Speaker Boehner and Leader Cantor and their staffs to express my strong desire to get onto Financial Services.

The day for votes came!

Get ready to play the Price Is Right *loser horn.*

We didn't land on Financial Services.

And blow horn.

Other freshmen from tough swing districts landed a few spots on the committee, such as Andy Barr from Kentucky. Tom Cotton, who was not in a swing district but was a prolific fund-raiser, also ended up on the committee. I was told he raised $100,000 for the NRCC. That guy was in a different league than we were. By the way, he's now in the United States Senate.

It was time to move on. We may have lost out on an A committee, but I would land two of the greatest B committees—Transportation and Infrastructure and Foreign Affairs. I was learning the ways of Washington and would soon officially be part of it. The general election was only days out—not that we were paying attention.

Ever since winning the primary, I asked myself over and over, *Why is everyone giving me this money? Am I doling out table dances?*

Now things had changed. We didn't get the committee we wanted, but I was no longer dancing for dollars. *I was tossing them out.*

RING OF FIRE

We breezed through the general election, winning handily by almost thirty percentage points. Amy and I traveled in and out of D.C. frequently, usually getting a hotel and bringing our parents with us to watch Jude. One cold and gray November day, we both attended freshman orientation for members of Congress and spouses.

Like the last time you heard the words "freshman orientation," it's a lot like the first few days of college. I was dealing with mundane stuff like securing a new office, getting a government-issued phone and computer, and attending a briefing on House ethics rules.

Amy's orientation was quite different. She had attended a Congressional Club orientation, a social group for members' spouses, that went over the difficulties of being a spouse to an elected member. In the first packet she received, one of the pamphlets they handed her was about suicide prevention.

"Suicide?" I asked, my voice high-pitched in disbelief.

"Yeah," she said with a glazed look, as if asking, *What have we gotten into?*

I was furious. Why would this group bring up suicide? Talk about being set up to fail. The club set the bar on spouses' expectations to: You're gonna love it here! Try not to slice your wrists or put a gun to your head. Thanks for playing! Buh-bye.

I'll never understand why the group handed out suicide prevention pamphlets. Maybe it was to raise awareness on the issue. Maybe it was because the life of a spouse is very difficult. Either way, Amy and I quickly learned that the upcoming year would be grueling.

Once you're elected, you essentially hold two jobs. The first is to fulfill your duties as a United States representative; the other is to continue your campaign.

In the House, you serve two-year terms, which means as soon as you are elected, you begin campaigning for the next cycle. However, the two roles, congressman and candidate, must be kept completely separate. Within federal offices, in Washington or district offices at home, lawmakers and staff are strictly forbidden from conducting any business related to the campaign—no calls, no organizing, and absolutely no talk about fund-raising. While many rules in Washington are bent, poked, and prodded, this one is not. At least not among anyone I knew.

With those roles running simultaneously, the demands on members and their families double. I had an idea of the stress because of my long relationship with Connie Mack, who had filled me in over the years. But now it was *my* schedule. Outside the office, I knew I could keep up a strong campaign and, of course, continue fund-raising, but privately, I worried. *I need to be a husband to my wife and a father to my young son. How will family fit into this schedule?*

The Republicans controlled the House, so they set the yearly calendar. They were known for keeping a tight, disciplined schedule. It's as if they played into a stereotype: Republicans are like your stern, somewhat out-of-touch grandfather, and Democrats are like your free-spirited, somewhat out-of-touch hippie uncle. Now there might be upsides and downsides with both, but before Republicans took control of the House, the schedule was insane, with no order or thought put into it at all. It was complete chaos. You'd be in session one week, out the next, and on the random weekdays that you thought you would spend at home with family and constituents, you'd get called back to Washington. House Democrats often remarked that they were thankful for the new tight schedule and order. Everyone knew when and where they had to be for the full year unless a government shutdown was looming. *But c'mon, how often does that happen?*

Congress was set to be in session roughly three weeks every month, Monday through Thursday or Tuesday through Friday. Coming from Florida, I would leave early Monday or Tuesday morning and be back home in my district late Thursday or Friday night. More often than not, to members and staff, the word "district" refers to home, not the District of Columbia.

Amy and I had to find an apartment in D.C. and work out how often we would be traveling to and from Florida, all with a soon-to-be two-year-old. She was visibly and justifiably concerned. "How are we going to work this schedule?" Amy asked.

"We'll work it out," I tried to assure her, but in my head I wasn't so certain. "I'll talk with other members, and you know I can always reach out to Connie."

"Connie is divorced," she sternly reminded me, and walked away.

Quite a few Republican members live in their offices and sleep on cots or on their couches. They practice what they preach, fiscal conservatism, but those members do not have their families in Washington with them. As a steward of other people's money, I vowed to be responsible with tax dollars. But I was living on my paycheck. While I understand this paycheck is taxpayer dollars, there are no stipends or per diems for an apartment or any other living expenses, for that matter. If you go to breakfast, lunch, or dinner, or if you rent an apartment or shack up at a hotel, that money comes out of your $174,000 salary.

And while orientation may have felt like college, this was not college. I had already been through my twenties and slept in plenty of dorms and hostels and shared enough bathrooms. I was a grown man and would live like one. Besides, this was Washington, D.C.! I wasn't going to absorb this great city by barricading myself in my office. I wanted to get out and get to know the city and share the experience with my family.

"Where should we live?" Amy asked.

Doing that thing spouses do, I answered her question with a question. "Where do you think?"

My wife and I went apartment hunting, staying mostly in

D.C. proper. Washington, for as much as its safety has improved over the years, still has some really rough neighborhoods. We fell in love with Dupont Circle, which was full of young families and young professionals. We found a great apartment in the basement level of a row house, with shops and restaurants all within walking distance. We could afford it, but it was more than we wanted to pay, and we wouldn't be saving much money. Amy and I talked it over.

"The most important thing to me is that you two feel safe," I said.

"I know," she said reassuringly. She loved the place. So did I.

"Let's do it," I said, getting enthusiastic. "There's a Metro stop nearby, so I can take the train to work. You and Jude can hop on, head to the museums, and meet me for lunch! Plus, we know I have a two-year term at a minimum." *At a minimum, right?*

Do you solemnly swear or affirm that you will support and defend the Constitution of the United States against all enemies, foreign and domestic?
★ Speaker John Boehner, January 3, 2013

With that, I was sworn in, given a funny-looking pin to attach to my lapel, and officially became Representative Radel.

After the swearing in, my family was paraded through the Capitol to have a picture taken with Speaker Boehner. He must've shaken a few thousand hands that day. We had our picture framed and sent copies to extended family and to the local press.

It was time to get to work. Again.

And I'll be takin' care of business every day. Takin' care of business every way.

★ Bachman-Turner Overdrive,
"Takin' Care of Business"

The mornings in Dupont started with feeding Jude, making my beloved Café Bustelo Cuban coffee, kissing Amy good-bye, and hopping on the Metro. I'd walk out at my stop, Capitol South, with my headphones still on, jamming anything from Jay to Janis. And every trip was more electrifying than the last. I always took the slightly longer route to my office, heading a block north to Independence Avenue, just so I could gaze at the Capitol while heading into work.

As I arrived at my office at 1123 Longworth on one of my first mornings, my new communications director, Amanda Nunez, was waiting outside to greet me. "You have to be the only member who takes the Metro," she said.

"I'm also the only member who makes hip-hop beats and plays guitar," I said, referring to my hobby of making terrible to semitolerable music. "Neither of which is very special."

"For a Republican it is!"

I smiled. "Good point."

She opened the door. New faces were buzzing around,

people who would soon become like family. Both Jason, my chief of staff, and Abby, my legislative director, had spent long weeks poring over hundreds of résumés to fill slots including communications director, legislative correspondent, legislative aide, and a scheduler, just like Tom Graves had told me. Jason and Abby had done a great job of hiring young men and women who worked hard and had fun, outgoing personalities.

Going from the campaign to Congress is an extreme change of pace and style. The campaign is like a start-up business. You create your brand, identity, logo, and even raise capital. Although, in a start-up, you have months or years to dream about, create, and formulate your company, and in a campaign, you only get a few weeks. A federal office is more corporate. Pusateri, now officially my district director, and I were no longer running and gunning on the fly. As he set up district offices in Southwest Florida, I was in Washington placing my life and reputation in the hands of my new and still unknown employees.

Along with a physical office, a member of Congress also gets a little more than a million bucks a year. It's the office budget, usually referred to as the MRA, which stands for Member's Representational Allowance. There are some stipulations on how you use the money, which is for "official use only." A big chunk goes to staff salaries. It also covers expenses ranging from travel to constituent services.

Oh, you can also use the money to communicate how wickedly awesome those constituent services are! That last part, the wickedly awesome part, is one of the ways members could maybe, possibly, potentially abuse taxpayer dollars, or at least the public might view it that way. Allow me to explain.

Any official mail paid for with the MRA must be marked with a label stating, "This mailing was prepared, published, and mailed at taxpayer expense." The mail cannot single out certain voters or even Republicans or Democrats. But you bet the pieces are still strategic. Let's say, for example, a member was in a district whose constituents were rabidly against abortion. That member, *theoretically*, could send out mail saying they just signed off on legislation to defund Planned Parenthood. On the flip side of the spectrum, a member could mail constituents announcing they just voted to make sure Planned Parenthood is funded. Sure, it shows constituents how a member is voting, but it also shores up the base that the member might need for re-election.

Back to hiring our squad.

Shortly after receiving our million bucks, Jason and I made our final decisions. Given my background in media, the job of communications director was an exceptionally important position to me. Tasked with writing and crafting press releases, creating an overall media strategy, and sometimes becoming a designated speaker, the comms director essentially becomes the face of the office, hence the face of the congressperson.

Amanda Nunez was a perfect fit. She had more than media contacts; she *understood* media, traditional and digital. Amanda, who was currently living in D.C. and had been in another congressional office, also grew up in Fort Myers. In fact, most of our staff had local ties to Southwest Florida.

Another hire was Greg Dolan, who worked in Senator Rubio's office. A lot of Greg's family had left Pittsburgh and ended up in Naples. I put aside my hatred for the Steelers from my

Cincinnati days, and we hired him to work directly with Abby. Both were policy nerds, and Greg, a hard-core fiscal conservative, fit in really well. He was as fun and passionate as he was wonky.

As we were settling in, it was important for me to talk to everyone at one time. Jason gathered the entire staff into my office for a pep talk. Looking out at the faces, either near my age or younger, I couldn't help but smile. This was my crew. I was glowing. "I hope this is as exciting for you as it is for me even if you've been working here in D.C. for a few years. And I want every day to be as new and exciting as your first."

I then took a more serious tone. "A few things I want to make clear right off the bat. From here on out, you will no longer address me as Congressman." I paused dramatically. Then I continued, my game face on. "You will be beaten and flogged if you do not address me as Your Holiness, the Shiz, Homie, TreyDawg . . ." It took them all the way to "TreyDawg" to start laughing.

Trying to break the ice, I said, "Seriously, though, I hope this experience can be fun for us all. Work is never work if you enjoy what you do. And while all of us have put in an insane amount of time and energy and emotion to get here, I sometimes feel like I've never worked a day because it's been such a fun ride. I love this. I love people. I love politics, and now, with us working as a team in Congress, I want to come to love legislating." I paused. "But I have a lot to learn. A lot. I've never held elected office. That means I can only be as good as you are. I will rely on many of you to navigate me through Washington, whether it's how to sponsor a bill or find an espresso that I'm told might be near the elusive cafeteria that I've heard is somewhere downstairs."

Next, I stole a line Pusateri once shared with me. "The last thing I'll leave you with is this. I'm not your boss until you make me be your boss. As far as I'm concerned, we are equals. We are a team and in this together. I will never"—I paused to let the next part sink in—"I will never ask you to do anything I haven't done myself. I'm not one to ask anyone for crap like fetching me coffee although I've fetched plenty. But there will be days and nights you will be asked to put in long, intense hours. And while I love to joke and have fun, I take this very seriously. We carry a responsibility that goes far beyond a job or work. If you are ever bothered by something or think I've asked too much, the best thing you can do is communicate that to me. I will always, always be here to listen, help, and, again, learn from you."

Throughout my life, whether it was as a TV news anchor, a radio-show host, or now as a congressman, I lived by and loved the words my father taught me at a young age: "Trey, take what you do seriously; never take yourself too seriously."

Before getting to Congress, I would often watch Fox and MSNBC and ask myself, *Do Democrats or Republicans shank one another in the hallways of the Capitol?* By late January 2013, just before the president's inauguration, all the staff was hired. I felt somewhat settled in, and now I had a plan. I hadn't been shanked or even spit at. After getting to know my fellow freshmen, Democrats and Republicans alike, I decided I wanted to set a positive tone and reach out to senior Democrats.

Many of the freshman Dems were really good people. One in particular, Patrick Murphy, was a helluva nice guy. Therein lies the difficulty of Washington. I'm supposed to hate this guy. After all, Murphy is the "kid" who beat Allen West on Florida's east coast. West was highly respected among House Republicans and loved by the grassroots. He was also occasionally bombastic. After redistricting, West's district had changed. So did the constituency and its leanings. Murphy beat him in one of the nastiest, toughest congressional races in the country. At twenty-nine, he was now the youngest member of Congress.

Other Florida Democrats in my freshman class included Lois Frankel. She was like the Jewish grandmother I never had. She was frank and blunt but somehow maternal and caring. We served on the Foreign Affairs Committee together. There was also Alan Grayson, who was even more bombastic than Republican Allen West. He came in with our class but had also served from 2009 to 2011. Then he lost to Dan Webster, but with redistricting, he had found a new district and won. Grayson is an eccentric bomb thrower who occasionally takes contrarian positions especially on civil liberties and fiscal matters. He even voted against raising the debt ceiling, a big no-no when your own party is in the White House.

During these first few weeks, I had Jason set up face-to-face meetings with every Democrat in our Florida delegation. The only way I ever had any success in business was by building relationships. I looked at Washington the same way.

The initial reactions to my requests were funny. Scratch that. They were pretty sad. Democratic staff asked my staff, "Whuh? Why?" Essentially: "Why the hell would a Republican want to meet with a Democrat?" It was as if a get-to-know-you meeting was like having ISIS put in a request for a face-to-face with the pope. *Do you mind if we wear large jackets and loose-fitting clothing to the meeting?* A little curious, they obliged.

One of my first meetings was with Alcee Hastings, a long-time Democratic congressman who represents an area directly across the state from Fort Myers/Naples in South Florida. I felt like I was connecting with an old friend. Alcee is immediately approachable, friendly, and outgoing. I told him the same thing I'd say to other Dems: "I just wanted to meet and get to know you. I'm not here to call you names or shout you down, like I unfortunately sometimes see on TV." We talked about music, sports, and his nearby district. In my meeting with Kathy Castor, we talked about Tampa, her district, where I have relatives. She, too, was gracious and appreciative.

I didn't talk about policy at all. Instead, I focused on what we had in common, whether it was family, friends, or a love of Florida.

Then it was time to meet the most vile, terrible, god-awful Democrat ever. It was time to meet the devil incarnate, Debbie Wasserman Schultz. Boo! Hiss!

At this time Debbie was head of the DNC and had spent years communicating the Democrats' message, which had occasionally resulted in some provocative and nasty comments about Republicans. Boo! Hiss! I'd never met her before, but you bet I talked tons of smack about her when I hosted my radio show. After Obamacare was ramrodded through Congress, I ran sound bites from Wasserman Schultz and called her a "mouthpiece for Democrats."

Now, as I was about to meet her, I wondered, *Oh, no! Is she going to shank me?*

Far from it. Debbie turned out to be one of the kindest members of Congress. We met on the House floor, shook hands, and sat down next to each other. After talking about lighter things, she struck a serious tone. "Trey, one of the important things for us is to remember what happens here"—she paused and looked around the chamber, even nodding up to the gallery—"is different from what happens outside."

I got it right away: We have work to do for every American, but on the "outside," campaign rhetoric will always exist and—gasp!—may even occasionally rub people the wrong way.

This reinforced why I made the effort to reach out to Democrats. As members of political parties, we often need to get over ourselves, stop focusing on the occasional provocative rhetoric and campaign speeches, and find commonality.

My tiny effort to meet Democrats soon brought about one of my best memories in Congress—an invitation to a unique bipartisan dinner.

Debbie and Florida Republican Dan Webster hold a dinner once a month to bring together lawmakers from both parties. *Sounds like a bad sitcom, right?* It's like the segment "Cleopatra Schwartz" from *The Kentucky Fried Movie*: "She was a red-hot liberal! He was a fire-breathing conservative! She fought to have people pee where they wanted! He fought to stop the gays from marrying! Together, they were the 'Ideological Ideologues'! And together, they wined, dined, and won over Washington!"

The dinner was by invitation only. The only requirement was that I invite a guest from the opposite party. I picked Patrick Murphy.

Dinner was fun and friendly, with about a dozen people. We talked about our districts and shared warm stories about our families. Some of the more senior members dished out advice to us newbies about constituent services and the importance of working with the other party to pass legislation. Unfortunately, events like this are rare. More often than not, lawmakers skip an event like this to fund-raise. Shocking, right? Raising money instead of trying to form relationships and legislate!

I'd been in Congress for a few weeks when I realized that the anger and resentment on both sides was a huge problem. But why? Well, some people were judged based on an offhand comment on the House floor during a debate or, worse, an appearance on a partisan, opinionated cable news show. And ya know what? That's like basing someone's entire personality on the moment after they get in a car accident. "Hi! I see you just wrecked. How are things?"

"Terrible! Get outta my face!"

"Wow! That guy's a real dick."

If there was even just a small effort focused on personal relationships, I believe Congress could get more done. Am I talking about landslide solutions for immigration, the tax code, or foreign policy? Of course not. At least not right away. However, it becomes a lot harder to ignore people or throw shade when you know them personally. Furthermore, it gets lawmakers out of their political echo chambers.

As I was trying to reach out to Democrats, I was also doing a lot of interviews with the local and national press. One of the local stations followed us around for a "day in the life" story. The national stories gave a brief overview of my life followed by some questions on policy. Overall, the interviews were mundane. While I wanted to have some fun, I kept myself in check and maintained a serious disposition, which is not always easy for me.

I kept that demeanor even when I got a call from a Florida political blogger who I knew fairly well. Javier Manjarres and I had hung out before, even had drinks together. He runs a conservative political blog called *Shark Tank*, which covers mostly Florida politics and some national issues. He first made his mark as one of Marco Rubio's early supporters in 2009, when Marco was challenging Governor Crist for the Senate seat. He had done an impressive interview with Marco and began drawing contrasts between the two candidates. With Rubio's rise, the blog started to catch fire, and I did a few interviews with him during both the primary and general elections.

Javier seemed like my kind of Republican—fiscally conservative and socially libertarian. Coming from a family of immigrants, he also knew that we needed a practical solution to our immigration issues.

When Javier came up to Washington, we scheduled an interview for his website, and Amanda and I sat down with him in my Longworth office.

The interview was lengthy, around thirty minutes. He started with relatively mundane stuff, like taxes and fiscal policy, and then brought up President Obama's potential executive orders on guns. He segued into the topic by bringing up the name of a colleague. "Trey, Congressman Steve Stockman . . ."

Record scratch! Gasp!

Steve Stockman had served in Congress from 1995 to 1997 and had just returned for another term. We were sworn in together. Aside from a brief conversation or two over a drink at earlier functions, I didn't know him and certainly didn't know anything about his policy. But if you think Allen West or Alan Grayson is bombastic, Steve Stockman is a loose cannon packing unlimited rounds of insults and tirades. He was the guy who raised money for his campaign by selling Obama barf bags online and invited Ted Nugent to the State of the Union. Barf bags and the Nuge! He said some reprehensible things, but he also had his moments of hilarity, including a few tweets like *"Antiques Roadshow* is coming to town. I'm bringing the last budget passed by Senate Democrats" and "Gas is getting so expensive Obama now has to carpool to drive the economy into the ground." Kinda funny? Sure. Till he wrote something terrible: "Obama has no sympathy for unarmed women raped by criminals. #SOTU Gun control creates more crime." Despicable.

And Javier just linked me to this guy! "Congressman Steve Stockman made an interesting comment the other day about Obama's forthcoming executive orders that will further restrict gun rights." He then asked, "Is President Obama making the case for possible impeachment?"

Like an idiot, I mean *like an absolute moron*, I said, "All options should be on the table," then fumbled to get back on message. Mumbling, I tried to put what I was attempting to say into context, but I was speaking in broken half sentences.

"To be bipartisan for a second, the thing I would stress to Democrats and Republicans is, let's say you're a big fan of President Obama and you support everything he's doing and you want an executive order to ban guns, to take guns away, to raise the debt ceiling with unlimited amounts of spending, or to ignore law. What I would say is ask yourself: What are you going to do when a Republican gets in that you may not agree with or like very much and begins doing the same thing? We have lost our checks and balances in this country. The Congress needs to hold the president accountable for the decisions that he's making right now, and that's why again, I would say that all options should be on the table."

Whatever *that* was, I rambled on for about one minute. And out of the entire thirty-minute interview, that was the only part he used on his blog.

I was attempting to speak to the larger point of keeping power in check, not call for the impeachment of President Obama. I never said I wanted Obama impeached. But following my fumbling and moronic bumbling, Javier posted a headline on his blog: "Radel on Obama Impeachment: On the Table."

Javier sure as hell knew I would have never pursued an impeachment of the president. But hey, as a blogger, he has a business to run based on clicks and impeachment stories get clicks and clicks get dat money.

I'm not one to dwell on "what I should *not* have done" scenarios, but this was a lesson. I should not have expected context or perspective within the piece. I should not have rambled on about my thoughts on "checks and balances." I should have answered with one word and one word only, which I did at a town hall weeks later: "No!"

Even with my years in media, my infinite hours on radio, I screwed up and would pay a price. Javier's article ran, and the blogosphere lit up. *ThinkProgress* ran a headline: "Republican Congressman Considers Impeaching Obama."

Blogs are one thing; mainstream media is another. And these days, with the push for constant new content on websites, those lines got blurred long ago. After all, clicks mean money for even the most prestigious news websites, too!

This story spread like wildfire in the thirty minutes it took me to ride the Metro from the Capitol South stop to Dupont. Thirty minutes on the Internet is an eternity in which lives can be changed, even destroyed.

On the train I got a text from Amanda: "Call now." But my service kept getting cut off. I couldn't respond. Coming up the escalators at Dupont Circle, I reached her, and right away I could tell she was panicking.

"Trey, this was making the rounds on many of the blogs. But now *HuffPo* has picked it up." Then she paused. "Oh, no." I could hear her clicking at her computer.

"What?" I asked in my high-pitched, freaking-out voice.

"*Politico* has it."

"No," I said, and let out a deep breath. I now got to see my new comms director's tenacious side kick in. She said, "You never called for Obama's impeachment, and that's what the headline makes it look like! Call Javier. I think you should at least see if he'll change the headline to maybe stop the bleeding on this."

I got to the top of the escalator and called him. "Hey, Javi, we gotta talk. I need to ask you something." Like a madman, I began pacing around Dupont Circle.

"Sure, what's up?" he asked, without the slightest clue about how angry I was.

"The headline you ran is giving people the impression I am going to ask for Obama's head. You know me, man! You know that's not my style. I never said I wanted to impeach him."

Javi pushed back. "C'mon, Trey, your supporters will love this! The base will eat this up!"

I interrupted him. "Javi, man, I don't need campaign advice. I am in Congress now. You know as well as I do, this isn't me. I never called for his impeachment or suggested it. I was talking big picture. And now . . . now I'm gonna be grouped with the crazies!"

"Crazies" is a term often used for members or candidates on the far left or the far right who say, do, or make exceptionally insane moves, kind of like a Steve Stockman.

Javier reluctantly agreed to change the headline to: "Congressman Radel on Possible Presidential Overreach—'All Options Should Be on the Table.'" He removed the word "impeachment." When I called Amanda back, she said the story seemed to have stopped at *Politico* and she hoped the headline change would continue to halt the wildfire.

Yes, I should have been more careful about my answer and phrasing, but I was shocked that no reporter—*not one* in the so-called mainstream press—picked up the phone to contact me or my office before doing a story about me. When I worked as a journalist, calling someone I was about to do a story on was Journalism 101.

It's a different world now. And when issues—in this case, ones that were partly distorted by my own ramblings and failings—get out there, I learned just how fast we would need to work to push back to correct or influence the record. *I would have to pick up the phone.* No one was going to call me.

With headlines circulating that I wanted to impeach the president, a nonprofit legal advocacy group targeted me. They, too, failed to give me a jingle, shoot me an e-mail, send smoke signals, or make any attempt to talk. The Southern Poverty Law Center ran an article titled "The Year in Hate and Extremism." With the indication I wanted to impeach President Obama, they put me—a well-traveled, trilingual, lover-of-all-cultures type of guy—in league with a neo-Nazi gunman "who stormed into a Sikh temple in Wisconsin, murdering six people before killing himself." Nice! My "setting a new tone" with Democrats was clearly working really well!

On January 20, just a few days after my interview with Javier, it was time to head to the second inauguration of Barack Obama—you know, the guy I wanted to impeach.

★ 8 ★

SERVE THE SERVANTS

A few months into my term, the team was firing on all cylinders. And so was I, but not in the healthiest of ways.

Once I was elected, I never returned to any kind of exercise routine at all. The last time I saw my boxing trainer, Marcus, was at a campaign event. If I thought I had been gaining weight on the campaign trail, I now found myself getting fat at catered lunches and long dinners. At our lunchtime Republican powwows, they served up Chick-fil-A every chance they could. Yes, Republicans served Chick-fil-A. Sometimes stereotypes aren't that stereotypical.

The evenings offered more choices. Embassies hosted small get-togethers and elaborate parties. Some weeks the Brazilian Embassy offered up caipirinhas and music one night, and days later I was overindulging on some killer hummus and drinking arak, a fire-breathing, anise-flavored drink, at the Lebanese Embassy. With my Lebanese heritage, I felt like I was with long-lost cousins. But the steak dinners were going to be the end of me. In Florida, with the exception of an occasional visit to Gaucho Inca, I didn't eat a lot of red meat. Now I was consuming big fat steaks at least twice a week. Some evenings you could have a regular steak dinner with members at Ruth's Chris and then head to a catered event with steak on a stick. More skewers!

I was also regularly invited out by senior members and those in the leadership. These dinners were never paid for with tax dollars. They were paid for with campaign dollars. In keeping with the old saying, "You've got to spend money to make money," it was spending money to win over and influence people.

Some dinners featured laid-back conversations with topics ranging from family and hobbies to politics. Others involved intense conversation about politics and policy. At the smaller dinners, I was usually the youngest member. It was exciting to meet some of the men and women who had been around awhile, learn from them, and take in their experiences.

But as with everything in politics, there's always the question of motivation. I was happy to eat a killer meal and have a few cocktails, but I wondered what was expected in return. The senior members' motivations were sometimes as simple as wanting to hear new ideas and have a good political conversation. Potential players jockeying for a leadership role wanted to wine and dine you, and get your vote. I again saw the power of networking.

I was never out getting drunk at these things. For better or worse, I've always held my liquor well, and rarely could someone tell whether or not I had just knocked back a beer or quite a few.

But maintaining any regimen of healthy eating and having "just a drink" was getting more difficult. Professionally, I was doing really, really well. Personally, I was fine, just getting a little flabby. The only workout I got the year before on the campaign trail was walking door-to-door. Now my workout consisted of standing on a long escalator ride at my Metro stop while I watched other people take the stairs. Although I did talk to Paul Ryan about his famous P90X workout sessions. He told me they started at something like six in the morning. I laughed and never went.

My schedule was also getting extremely difficult for my wife and my chief of staff. Even when Amy and Jude were in Washington, I was out most nights till late evening. I could have cut down on dinners and nighttime events. But I kept telling Amy, and myself, "This is the first year. Let me get through this intense year of meeting people, networking, and learning. Soon all of this will calm down." I was struggling with something I have struggled with most of my life—balance.

Jason had missed some days traveling back from Florida with me, and I knew the schedule was wearing him down as well as being hard on his wife and kids, whom he was away from for three weeks every month. One day in between votes and meetings, we talked over the situation.

"Trey," he said. "I can't do this anymore. I knew it was going to be difficult for me and my wife and kids. Without them living here, there's just no way I can continue." He took a long pause and looked away. I glanced at the picture of my son on my desk as he continued. "Every time I leave my kids, it gets harder and harder." As he started to get emotional, I stopped him because I was about to well up with tears, too, as I reflected on how tough things had gotten for my own family.

"Jason, it's okay. I totally understand. Before any of this happened, we were friends. It will stay that way."

With that, Jason resigned. In a very kind gesture, though, he agreed to devote several weeks to our office while we searched for a new chief of staff. A month later, we would find someone from Washington.

While Jason was stepping down, I was stepping up my workload and nights out. Outside of work, business relationships soon became friendships. Arizona's Kyrsten Sinema and Tulsi Gabbard from Hawaii often organized bipartisan dinners for our freshman class. Patrick Murphy, who I had also grown close to, ended up moving into a place near my neighborhood. We would occasionally grab a beer together in the evening.

Among the Republicans, I loved to talk policy with Tom Massie from Kentucky and Justin Amash out of Michigan. Both, like me, are libertarian-leaning conservatives, if not full-on libertarians who happen to have an R next to their names. The three of us worked on some legislation together. At one point we even worked with the ACLU, which, contrary to the stereotype of their being a bunch of pinko communists, had taken up some issues close to conservatives' hearts.

I found myself especially connecting to a lot of the members who were sworn into Congress in 2011. Adam Kinzinger from Illinois and Kevin Yoder out of Kansas were friends, and I occasionally hung out with their group. You might not hear it out of them as sitting congressmen, but those two have a wicked good sense of humor, plus something I was never very good at while in the public eye—restraint.

I found many of my colleagues to be engaging, even entertaining, with a genuine concern for our country. Sure, we could all shoot the breeze about sports, music, and movies, but if you get any one of these people focused on a subject they care about, you will find them inspiring and insightful.

I loved being with people who were as passionate—*and as nerdy*—as I was about politics. But the best part was that at night, unlike being in our offices or on the House floor, we could knock back drinks and use much more colorful language.

Most people in Congress want the same results: opportunity and a bright future for their constituents and, in turn, the country. Where it gets difficult is deciding how we get there. *How much government do we need to take us there? How little? How much will it cost? What programs do we cut from in order to save others? Where do we go in debt in order to prevent cuts?*

My nights were getting a little later, and occasionally, my were mornings, too.

> Elections are about fucking your enemies. Winning is about fucking your friends.
> ★ James Carville, political strategist and media commentator, as quoted by Hunter S. Thompson in *Better Than Sex: Confessions of a Political Junkie*

One morning I had to be in early for an NRCC meeting at the Capitol Hill Club, which is a private social club used day and night for meetings and meals. And it has a bar. The Democrats also have their own private club where, I'm sure, they meet and secretly plan how to destroy the country, too.

As I walked into the meeting, the first thing I saw was that big portable whiteboard that lists every House Republican's name and how much they've donated to the NRCC.

As you know, Jason and I raised nearly $30,000 for the NRCC before we got to D.C. I was excited to see where I stood on the board! But I looked through the names—"Radel . . . Radel . . . hmmm." It wasn't up there with the others who had raised tens of thousands; it wasn't even up there with people who had raised only a few thousand bucks. *What the heck?*

Steve Stivers, who worked in the NRCC's finance department and was always happy to answer my rookie questions, happened to be standing nearby. "Excuse me, Steve? I'm wondering why I can't find my name on the board. We gave about thirty grand to the NRCC as far back as November."

In less than a second, he pointed to my name. "There you are."

Next to my name was "$0." Yes, a big fat doughnut. "Zero?" I asked.

Steve explained, "Trey, you donated before this new cycle. So everything you gave got wiped out on the tally sheet. It's a new year, a new cycle." I gave him one of those clenched-jaw smiles that says, *Really? Is Trey Radel gonna have to choke somebody?*

Thirty. Thousand. Dollars. You can buy a nice car with that kind of money.

It meant nothing.

The money we raised did not count *at all* toward my dues for this current cycle. The general election was another lifetime ago as far as they were concerned. After sending thirty grand to the NRCC and trying to get on Financial Services and failing, I was at zero. So I had that going for me.

I found a spot in the back and leaned against the wall to listen and learn. As I sipped crappy coffee, the meeting started with hard-core, bare-knuckle politics.

Using a PowerPoint clicker as if it were a loaded handgun, NRCC chair Greg Walden was standing in front of a couple hundred rowdy Republican members of the House and laying out the "top Democrat targets" in this cycle. Both the NRCC and DCCC find swing districts that are about equally split between the parties, and they do everything they can to keep the seat by defiling and defeating the candidate from the other party. The meeting had a sinister feel to it. I thought to myself, *Nice! This isn't a regular boring policy meeting about debt and deficits! This is interesting!*

My mind wandered dangerously.

I asked myself, *Will Mr. Burns from* The Simpsons *show up?* I could see him rubbing his hands together and giving a pep talk. "Men, there's a little crippled boy sitting in a hospital who wants you to win this game. I know because I crippled him myself to inspire you."

At that moment Walden cocked his gun and loaded up the next PowerPoint slide. *Click, click.* They were about to come on the screen: the top-two dirty, filthy Democrat—stress the "rat" part—targets. The room began to get warmer. The men and women around me were licking their lips. Sweat began dripping off their foreheads. The lighting got dimmer. "Give it to us, Greg!" someone yelled from the back. Suddenly, a spotlight circled around the room, a drumroll kicked in, smoke shot out of the walls, and Metallica's "Enter Sandman" was playing right there in the Capitol Hill Club. "Exit light!" screamed James Hetfield. Speaker Boehner lined up shots of whiskey and tossed unfiltered Camels out to the crowd as if they were beads at Mardi Gras. Leader Cantor threw his coffee to the ground and started headbanging. Whip McCarthy was playing air guitar with his tongue out. Then the music cut off. Lights up! Walden pulled the trigger. *Bang!* The shot rang out.

Then silence.

On the screen were the top-two dirty, filthy Democrat targets, wide-eyed and tilting their heads like confused puppies with bull's-eyes smack in the middle of their foreheads. A headshot would do these dirty dogs in for good!

But wait, wait, wait!

I rubbed my eyes. I did a double take. *No!* I was in shock, then I felt tremendous sadness. My lip quivered as I held back tears. "Oh, no," I whispered under my breath. The targets on the screen were my friends Kyrsten Sinema and Patrick Murphy.

Like a pouting child, I looked around in confusion, and said, "Bu-bu-but wait, those are my friends." No sympathy for my camaraderie! Everyone erupted in applause and began screaming. "Yeah! Top Democrat targets! Let's go get those rats!" With that, everyone lit torches, put on hoods, and ran out the door.

I stood there alone in the room still filled with smoke, staring at Kyrsten and Patrick, who I had just had a beer with the night before.

This, my friend, is the kind of predicament you find yourself in when you are in Congress. As Rob Cole, my campaign general consultant and a hardened New Yorker, had warned me, this is all "just part of it." He knew the deal. D.C. is a world where your closest friends can be labeled your biggest enemy. I never took that sentiment too seriously, but there are definitely people in both parties who do, and they refuse to form friendships or even converse with people in the other party. It's petty, and it's part of what makes Congress so dysfunctional.

The smoke cleared; the meeting continued.

Walden's PowerPoint presentation identified which members needed "help," *and you know what that means.* He ended with the latest info on upcoming dinners and events. And then everyone else who got up talked about how we needed to raise more money. The meeting, not nearly as interesting as it was in my imagination that morning, began to bore me. I slipped out early to grab my second espresso of the day and get to the office.

Two espressos and a half cup of crappy coffee later I got back to 1123 Longworth. Abby was at the reception desk talking to a visitor. She turned to me and said, "Greg and I need to talk to you. Can we meet in your office?"

"Sure."

Walking in, I glanced at a picture of my son and wife, whom I hadn't seen in a few days. I took off my jacket, got rid of my tie, and rolled up my sleeves. Greg and Abby followed me in. Greg, who stands six-foot-three, was at the doorway. Abby sat on the couch, and I took a seat in front of my desk.

Abby and Greg had taken it upon themselves to find and create legislation that would be a good fit for us. As a freshman office, we knew we weren't going to change the world or single-handedly pass tax or immigration reform. So we figured the best way to make a difference was to start small but do something significant.

Abby was smiling, and Greg was clearly excited. He started with "Two words, Congressman." Greg always called me Congressman even when I insisted that no one call me that. "Two words. Sheep shearing." Abby's grin got bigger.

"Sheep shearing?" I asked.

Abby chimed in. "Yeah, sheep shearing."

Greg said, "Fifty million dollars."

"Fifty million for what?" I asked. Greg sat down next to Abby, and they began pulling out papers and notes to show me what they'd "discovered."

Poring over all sorts of legislation, they had found a fifty-million-dollar appropriation in the upcoming farm bill for the sheep industry. Every five years, Congress votes on a farm bill that establishes agricultural and food policy. It is a huge bill, which means there is a ton of opportunity for handouts and deals for special interests, including sheep, apparently.

Greg read from his notes. "Okay, so here are just some of the things taxpayers fund. A government trip to Australia to learn about best practices for sheep, all expenses paid. They fund a social media campaign to market lamb. They provide grants for beginner shearers to buy razors, scissors, and brushes. They also pay for a video on best goat-handling practices."

"Sheep shearing?" I again asked, incredulously.

Abby fired back. "Yeah, fifty million for this. They've already spent a million."

"Sheep shearing," I said definitively. Greg and Abby nodded, still amused.

I then got skeptical. "Okay, but this has nothing to do with our district. Why is this *our* fight?"

"Exactly, sir!" said Greg. The people who have this district won't go against this!"

It hit me right then. I raised my big bushy eyebrows and leaned back in my chair. "You're right. You. Are. Right. This is the type of stuff that flies under the radar, and the only people who know about it are the people who want it or, worse, create it."

I sat back and crossed my legs. Still seated, I hopped up on my soapbox. "You know, I have always believed that when it comes to spending in Washington the only way to fix our deficits and debt is with huge structural changes to Social Security, Medicare, and Medicaid. I get that." I leaned forward. *I was making a dramatic point, dammit!* "But ya know what? When it comes to spending, the individual raindrop does not blame itself for the flood." I paused. Deep stuff. "The appropriation of fifty million . . . that's a lot of money. A lot. While the million or so they spent isn't that big of a deal, that's not the point. This is taxpayer money going to something that's ridiculous. *Why?* No. Not why. *When* or *how* did government decide to pick this group and toss them millions? This is crazy!"

Greg firmly and loudly said, "No, Congressman. It's abuse." Abby nodded her head in agreement.

"Sheep shearing," I said again quietly, and paused.

I stood up and began to pace. "Let's do it. Let's go all out. We'll need to bring in Amanda for the messaging. We don't want to look silly or petty. I don't think we will. We just need to have a solid message." I stopped pacing, turned, and looked at both of them. "Abby, Greg, great find here. This represents the worst of government." I started pacing again. "And, yeah, Greg, I agree, it should be us. No one will touch this. It's doable even for us lowly freshmen, and I think it'll play well. And, dammit, it's the right thing to do! Love it!" I stopped pacing for the final time, and we broke.

When they briefed Amanda, she laughed at the ridiculousness of it all and began crafting a press release and digital strategy. Soon after, we were all hard at work on our first big amendment. The title was simple: The Radel Amendment. The legislation would be equally simple.

A day later I was in between votes with a rare moment to watch some news. As I sat and incessantly flipped between Fox, CNN, and MSNBC, and checked my e-mail, Greg came in with the text of the bill. "Congressman," he said.

"Greg," I replied, in a tone that conveyed, *Call me Trey.*

"I think you'll like this. It's a few words. Nothing more." He sat down next to me and handed me one page. It read:

AMENDMENT TO THE RULES COMMITTEE PRINT OF H.R. 1947 OFFERED BY MR. RADEL OF FLORIDA

Page 590, beginning on line 18, strike section 12101 and insert the following new section:

SEC. 12101. REPEAL OF THE NATIONAL SHEEP INDUSTRY IMPROVEMENT CENTER. Effective October 1, 2013, section 375 of the Consolidated Farm and Rural Development Act (7 U.S.C. 2008j) is repealed.

That was it. With just a few words, my amendment took the handouts for the sheep industry and killed them. The handouts, not the sheep.

Greg said, "So next we'll have to go before the Rules Committee." Not having been through this process, I hung on to every word Greg said. "We'll have a time scheduled, and you will present your case to them. You'll sit down at a table in front of their committee. You'll intro the bill and give your argument. After that, they'll have some questions for you. Then they'll decide whether or not the House will debate and eventually vote on our amendment."

Still looking down at the bill, I yelled, "Sheep shearing!"

Greg calmly replied, "Sheep shearing."

I couldn't resist. "Sounds like a baaaad time."

But the puns and ridiculousness were just getting started.

The Rules Committee room was tightly packed. With the thirteen members on an elevated dais, it's slightly intimidating. The chair was Pete Sessions. Pete has a serious and quiet intensity about him, and his steel blue-gray eyes pierce through you. He does have a sense of humor, but he's so intense that whether he's telling a fun joke or giving his serious take on legislation, he'll grab you by the upper arm to finish his point. Sometimes it's a warm Texan embrace. Other times he'll tighten his grip to show you he means business.

After hearing a million and one possible amendments to the farm bill, Pete welcomed me. "Mr. Radel," he said, mispronouncing it *ruh—DELL*. My name is pronounced *RAY-duhl*, like "dreidel," for my Jewish friends: "Radel, Radel, Radel, they made you out of Trey." But I wasn't about to sing Hanukkah songs or correct the Rules chair. Pete continued. "Welcome to the Rules Committee. I don't know if you've been up here before. We'd normally host you with an ice cream party." I had no idea what his inside joke meant, but people laughed. So did I, with my curious, raised bushy eyebrows.

We were asked to speak briefly. Side note: Politicians always start their remarks with "I'll speak only a few minutes," then they carry on for a half hour or more.

"Thank you, Mr. Chair. You've been here a long time today, huh?

"I only act like it," said Sessions. Once again, he got a big laugh.

I got right to it. "A program deep in this bill, literally filed under miscellaneous, is something called the National Sheep Industry Improvement Center—NSIIC. We're talking about sheep shearing." I noticed a few people giggling. I laughed a little, too; looked at the group; and, still smiling, said, "It would be laughable if it wasn't so sad."

I laid out how our amendment would stop fifty million from being appropriated for sheep shearing. "This is an industry that was perfected in biblical times, in the Old Testament." Diving into the grants, I highlighted a few. "This one grant we have here provides two amateur shearers with their combs, brushes, scissors, and razors to begin"—I paused for effect—"shearing."

A little nervous, I started to highlight my frustration with the irresponsible spending. "Should the government be providing no-questions-asked grants to people? There are people all across this country trying to start businesses today. We can't pick and choose the ones we're going to fund."

Listing more examples, such as taxpayer-funded trips and money for marketing, I wrapped up with the final absurdities. "The list goes on and on of where our taxpayer dollars are being spent." I finished with "we can shear spending now" and promised "that'll be my last bad pun."

Pete shot right back with humor as dumb as mine. "We appreciate your feedback and not pulling the wool over our eyes." The room busted out in laughter at our stupid puns.

We were done. Greg and I walked out.

"Great job, sir."

"Yeah, I thought it went well, especially if Pete Sessions is joking around like that."

Days later, the Rules Committee cleared our amendment for debate and a vote on the House floor. It's voted on before the full bill. Sometimes there are no amendments to a bill; other times, especially with a large bill, there are many.

One afternoon Abby and Greg let me know I would have my first debate on the House floor that very evening. It was on!

Republicans and Democrats put their top people on the floor to debate amendments. The tone and length of these debates can vary, but they're all conducted under a strict format. Sometimes it's as simple as people getting up, giving a spiel, and ending in agreement quickly. Other times there are lengthy, drawn-out arguments.

In these debates you always speak directly to the man or woman who is presiding over the debate and stands at the Speaker's rostrum, the raised area on the House floor. Depend-

ing on what the House is in session for, that member is addressed as Mister Speaker or Madame Speaker or Mister Chair
or Madame Chair.

Debating goes through the presiding chair in order to maintain decorum on the House floor. Arguments are not directed
at the opponent or proponent of an amendment. So, instead of
Hey, Congressman, you and your amendments suck!, you get *Mr.
Chair, this guy and his amendments suck*! It's much more cordial.

As Greg and I made our way from Longworth to the Capitol, I got in the zone with some music. Greg shuffled papers as
we walked. His tall frame hovered over me from behind. As we
crossed the street heading to the Capitol, I had my headphones
on blaring Public Enemy. "Welcome to the Terrordome" rang
out with Chuck D's deep voice. "Refuse to lose!" I turned it
down as Greg began to brief me. He started with "Congressman." Of course he did. "The Republican this evening with
the Ag Committee is Mike Conaway. He's a chair of one of the
subcommittees. The Dem is Collin Peterson. He's the ranking
member on the full committee." The ranking member is the
highest member on a committee from the party not in the
majority.

As we walked up the east steps of the Capitol, Greg reminded
me of some of the technicalities of the debating process. "You'll
have an opening statement, and at the end of each statement you
make, be sure to say you 'reserve the balance of your time.'" In
addition to how you address the chair, there are other rules and
debate guidelines to follow. Reserving your time simply means
you keep the time that has been allotted to you. When the
opposition or even a member in agreement is finished, you still

have your time to speak, a set time determined from the beginning. Some of these rules are archaic, even strange, but it keeps order on the floor. And order among rowdy House members is good, especially because I was unknowingly about to piss a few off.

As we walked onto the House floor, I shut off my music just as the lyrics "In a game, a fool without the rules got a hell of a nerve to just criticize" were starting to play. There were only about ten people in attendance. This is typical. Unless the House is in session for votes, no one ever heads to the Capitol to hear some schleppers debate their schleppy amendments. In fact, the House also gives time for members to speak about whatever they want, typically at the end of the day when no one is there. So the next time you tune into C-SPAN and see someone giving a politically charged speech as if they're addressing an NFL stadium full of fans, just know that there is no one watching, not even a tourist in the gallery.

We arrived at the floor microphone. You have the choice to use one directly on the floor, which looks out toward all of the seats and the gallery just above. Or you can speak from the seating area, facing the Speaker's rostrum. Staff can sit right behind you there. I chose the latter. Greg sat directly behind me and would help with any questions I had during the debate.

Presiding over the House floor that evening was a familiar face, Congressman Jason Chaffetz from Utah. I had hung out with him at a few events and had known of him before I got to Congress. Chaffetz is extremely media savvy. He presents himself really well on TV and works social media like few others do. I also knew he was a fellow fiscal conservative, but because he was presiding over the floor, he would not be able to express his opinion during this debate. But somewhere up in my head was a *wink, wink* that signaled, *Yeah . . . you know what I'm saying!*

My headphones were long off. But do me a favor, cue some circus music.

A little nervous, I looked up at Chaffetz and began. "Mr. Chair, I've been here only a few months. In my short time I've witnessed firsthand just how we spend your money here in Washington—your money, the hardworking, tax-paying American. I was shocked, though, to learn about something that is hidden very, very deep in this year's farm bill. It's actually filed under miscellaneous. It is for sheep shearing." I paused. "Sheep shearing." Pause. "Sheep." Longer pause. "Shearing."

"We have already spent $50 million, $50 million, on sheep shearing, an industry that basically goes back to the Old Testament. Moses was sheep shearing."

I held up my one-page amendment as if I were doing a standup in a TV news report to show and tell.

"So my amendment right here—one page, one sentence— will stop another $50 million from being wasted. But let's take a look at what $50 million of your money has purchased you as a hardworking, tax-paying American. This program funded a trip to Australia for the group called the Tri-Lambs. It's kind of a play on *Revenge of the Nerds*, if anyone saw that movie in the '80s. Look, as much as I love that flick, the purpose of this trip was to get people to eat lamb. And, Mr. Chair, I'm sorry, but I think that we can find a better way to use our money here in the United States."

Continuing to point out the insanity, I said, "In another

grant, two beginner sheep shearers were given—here we go—free combs, brushes, razors, and scissors with our $50 million." I paused to make the next point. "What we're talking about here are start-up costs. Think about that. If you are a business owner and you had $50 million, what could you do with that kind of money? It's start-up money! It's not fair."

On my radio show and during the campaign and debates, I'd often give a nod to bipartisanship to strengthen my arguments. In this case, I felt doing that was especially important to highlight how silly this debate was. So I said, "We have Democrats and Republicans right now who are debating about how hungry children are, and we're talking about $50 million to shave sheep!"

Finally, to make it personal for anyone who maybe, just maybe, happened to be watching C-Span this evening or might click on YouTube later, I said, "This could be your money that you could be saving up for your rent, for your mortgage, for your next vacation. This is as bipartisan as you can get. We are looking for places to save and show how we here in Congress can be more efficient with your money, accountable and transparent with your money—you, working forty, fifty, sixty hours a week. With that, Mr. Chair, I reserve the balance of my time."

I felt great! The butterflies in my stomach were replaced with adrenaline. It was then my fellow Republican's turn, you know, the party that prides itself on fiscal conservatism. You know, the party that was elected to stop the growing deficits and debt crushing our country! Yeah! Let's go fellow Republican! Let's kill this debate, call it a night, pop a champagne bottle, and celebrate!

Mike Conaway is from Texas. His website says, "His background as a CPA gives him a unique perspective on fiscal responsibility and ensuring every taxpayer dollar is being spent wisely." I was ready to hear his persuasive argument in support of my amendment to get rid of this unnecessary spending, clearly a favor for a special-interest group!

He was at the dais just across the aisle from me. *Okay, teammate, whatchya got?* I looked over and smiled as he was about to start. Conaway said, "Mr. Chairman, I started to go down one path, but the disdain with which my good colleague from Florida insulted the folks in this industry is unacceptable. I rise in opposition."

I looked behind me as if I were Robert De Niro in *Taxi Driver.* "You talkin' to me?" Wait, what?

Conaway rolled on. "I wish he would get his facts correct. The total appropriation, the actual money spent, is $1 million. He has confused authorizations with appropriations. So, if he will go and check his records, the $50 million he blasted out over and over and over was just simply incorrect. That is not the money that was spent."

He had a point. I had screwed up, giving him an opening. Sure, it was incorrect to say "spent $50 million" when the money had merely been appropriated that way. But then again, *this entire debate is absurd.*

As a raw debate tactic, though, $50 million sure sounds sexier than $1 million. It also brings us to another dirty little secret about how Washington politicians can deceive the public when it comes to spending. Members authorize huge amounts, like this $50 million, that make a bill insanely expensive. But the money doesn't get spent until a completely separate law is passed, called an "appropriation." So members get two chances to be dishonest—first, by telling their lobbyist friends they authorized large amounts for their industry and then by telling taxpayers it's only a small amount being spent. What's the result? A lot of misleading campaign ads with politicians saying they're cutting spending when they're really only cutting from an over-inflated number that would never have been spent anyway.

Conaway was offering his deep thoughts on the industry. "Sheep shearing is an important issue with respect to growing the wool industry in this country. It is about jobs."

I began to have full back-and-forth retorts in my head. *About jobs?! Ah, so now you're in the business of singlehandedly picking and giving jobs to people. I see.*

Conaway then said something he would return to later. "Sheep shearing is hard work. Throughout the farm bill, we have attempted over and over again to promote production agriculture and the jobs associated with it. While sheep shearing may not be particularly exotic and folks from Florida might think it is beneath them, the folks from west Texas take a whole different view of that."

Whoa! Beneath the people of Florida? Should the kids in poor, rural Immokalee, Florida, who don't have enough money for school supplies, pens, or pencils, give a damn about a sheep shearer outta west Texas? I'm gonna say no.

Conaway went on. "The author of the amendment has disparaged these grants saying that they are for razors and combs for beginning shearers. That's how you do it, Mr. Chairman."

"Check out the big brain on Brett!" I thought in my best Samuel L. Jackson, aka Jules in Pulp Fiction, *voice.*

He rolled on. "A major barrier for beginning sheep-shearing professionals is an initial cost of purchasing the equipment. These small grants assist to create these jobs in an industry that needs our help."

Small grants? I know about a million other people who would love a million bucks for a start-up, too!

Conaway finished. "With that, I reserve the balance of my time."

"Oh, well, allow me to retort!"

I launched right back into it, clarifying the appropriation and spending comment. "Mr. Chairman, we are defending sheep shearing, $50 million in appropriations, $1 million under government accounting." Then I went off, maybe a little too aggressively. But then again, can you be too aggressive when you're attacking $50 million being handed out for such a ludicrous purpose?

"When we look at the industry best practices, Mr. Chair, they could have been written by Moses with how old this industry is. The proposal funds an informational video describing recommended goat-handling practices. They're also using this money on social media." In a nod to Chaffetz's digital skills, I said, "Mr. Chair, you know as well as I do what we're talking about is free—social media, the Internet. This doesn't cost money to 'create a buzz' among consumers."

Wrapping up, I added, "This is why the American people are so frustrated with both Democrats and Republicans picking and choosing industries. Congress has wasted $50 million, yes, *in appropriations*, since 1996 on this program. This House needs to save taxpayer dollars at a time where we have record deficits and runaway spending. I urge my colleagues to vote for this amendment, and I reserve the balance of my time."

I waited. It was now time for the Democrat to pop off. *Come at me, brah!*

Congressman Collin Peterson began by noting that in the 1990s, they "killed off the sheep and goat industry in this country."

Aaaand . . . some quick background.

Collin Peterson has been in elected office since January 1977, when he won a seat in the Minnesota senate. He was sworn in as a U.S. congressman in January 1991. I was fourteen years old. The United States had invaded Iraq, uh, for the first time. Apartheid still existed in South Africa. Guns N' Roses was one of the most popular bands in the world. And get this! The movie that dominated the Oscars that year—*The Silence of the Lambs*! Pun not intended, but that's pretty damn hilarious!

Droning on, Peterson said, of the sheep industry, "We basically gave it away to New Zealand and Australia. Let's be clear about what this is. It is $1 million. One million dollars. This is a modest effort."

I can usually blast out some serious sarcasm, but with that, I just bowed my head in disappointment. "Mr. Chair, only in Washington, D.C."—I paused, shocked by what he'd said— "Only in Washington, D.C., can someone call $1 million a modest amount."

I paused for a longer moment and said, "The individual raindrop does not blame itself for the flood. Mr. Chair, we are in a time of record deficits and a debt that hangs over us to the point that it is a national security problem for our country. I encourage my colleagues to vote for this amendment and slow the wasteful spending. With that, I yield back the balance of my time."

I should have ripped the mic from the podium, dropped it, held up both hands with peace signs, and yelled, "Radel, out!" But the debate was over. It was time to relax. *This was policy, not personal.* And, in fact, I was about to go over to Mr. Conaway and tell him just that. When I turned to walk to him, though, I saw him already in a full sprint toward me. As I extended my hand, and said, "Congressman, of course, this is about policy, not personal," he looked me right in the eyes and asked me the most laughable question I've ever been asked in my life. In a loud whisper, he demanded to know, "Have you ever tried to shear a sheep?"

"Ha!" I laughed out loud from my gut with a big smile on my face.

Then I realized, *Oh, my God, this guy's serious!* I awkwardly wiped the grin off my face. He asked me again, this time even more pissed and enunciating each word, "Have you ever tried to shear a sheep?"

At this point my amusement turned sour. I snapped back, "No, but I started a business, and no one from the government ever handed me a million bucks."

He stormed off the floor without another word.

Standing there in amused disbelief, I looked at Greg, who is an ultraconservative. He had a huge grin on his face and a slightly psychotic look in his eyes. I asked, "The hell was that guy's problem?"

With the slightest hint of smoke shooting out of his ears, Greg's eyes, with tiny little flames in them, followed Conaway off the House floor. Then he looked down at me and said, "We're shaking up the system, Congressman."

I shrugged. "Okay, all done. Let's go grab a drink. We need to celebrate." I figured if I had just pissed off both parties that were desperate to placate silly special interests, I must be doing something right!

Yeah, I felt pretty good. But things were not good. *At all.* And Mike Conaway would be back.

=★9★=
WITH A LITTLE HELP FROM MY FRIENDS

*W*ashington is the nerdiest sexy city in the world.

Aside from the mostly older, sometimes stodgy, politicians in Congress, D.C. is dominated by youth. If you want something done in Congress, you do not go to one of the members; go to their thirty-something chief of staff or their twenty-something aides. Those people are high-energy, type-A personalities, and almost every night after work, they're out enjoying the lively bar scene from the U Street Corridor to my neighborhood, Dupont, and everywhere in between. Having lived in Chicago, Rome, Houston, and Atlanta, I found being back in an urban environment as exciting and exhilarating as I had remembered. Sure, I love my home—the people, the weather, the palm trees, and the beaches. But I feel the blood rush through my veins every time I set foot in a city. Once I'd done the rounds of steak dinners at Del Frisco's and Ruth's Chris, I started venturing off the Hill and away from downtown for ethnic restaurants like Dukem for Ethiopian cuisine and any and all José Andrés restaurants. The Palm, a few blocks from my apartment, became another warm, friendly port off the Hill, and I got to know the owner, Wally Ganzi, who also lived in Naples.

I was getting to know the city; the city was getting to know me.

I'd love to be able to use a smooth cliché and say, "I was working hard and playing harder," but the truth is, I was doing both at insane levels. I hit maximum speed every day, every night. Braking wasn't an option until I crashed in bed well after midnight.

Tuesdays and Wednesdays were full-session days in Congress, and those evenings became my Friday and Saturday nights. I loved and lived for my professional responsibilities. Even if I stayed out late the night before, I'd hop up out of bed the next morning ready to get to work. Work never, ever took a backseat to my social life. And when I was back in the district, I rarely went out socially or even drank.

Congress gets all sorts of shit for being in session only three days out of the week. But those days of legislating barely scratch the surface of what's really being done. You work from early morning until late at night, and the time you put in at home in the district is equally intense.

I'd fly to Florida on a Thursday night, and Friday morning at six I'd start a "day in the district," going to events with Matt Pusateri. At the crack of dawn, he'd be waiting in his pickup truck (of course he rolled in a pickup) in my driveway, sporting aviator sunglasses to block the Florida morning sun. With his shortly cropped hair, shades, and serious look, he could pass for a cop. And Matt did, indeed, have a gun or two or more in the truck or on his person.

One morning I hopped in his truck, and he greeted me with a long, drawn-out, "Dude," and launched into a quick tirade on the district's anger with Washington, immigration, the economy, and life itself. Pausing between each word, he said, "These people are pissed!" Then he said, "But wait till you hear this, man!"

As we ripped down I-75, he told me he had recently gone to a large regional Republican Party meeting, where people who had backed our opponents usually showed up. They were the older, institutional Republicans. "No one's been giving you attitude or anything, right?" I asked.

He smiled. "No, not at all. In fact, I think they've seen the light. *Maybe.* They have some guy in from Tallahassee teaching the group digital strategies. This guy's going on and on about Facebook and Twitter, and, man, I don't even know if anyone in that room ever even used Twitter. But then he gets to the good part." Matt gave me an evil smile. "Domains."

"Domains!" I cut him off almost before he could even finish the word. I was still suffering with PTSD from our campaign.

"Yeah, man, domains! This guy was showing them how the party bought a bunch of domains with Charlie Crist's name."

By this time, Charlie Crist, having lost his Senate bid against Marco, officially switched to the Democratic Party and was running against Rick Scott for governor, the job he'd held two years ago as a Republican.

Matt continued. "They put a bunch of content on the sites saying all sorts of nasty things about him. Get this, though. They also have Florida Dems dot com, where they mock the hell out of Florida Democrats. The Dems' actual site is Florida Dems *dot org*. They got the *dot com* and put up all their own content there!"

Smiling, but a little agitated, I asked, "And did these people, *who all gave us holy hell*, tell this guy what an unethical bastard he is?"

Matt was laughing hard. "Hell no, man! They were amazed! They thought he was the smartest, most tech-savvy guy ever!"

"Yeah, right. Tech savvy, like us."

In our first few months in office, Matt led the way, organizing an intense rollout and presence that our district had never seen before, and we did it to make a point—Southwest Florida was home, not Washington. I went to D.C. to do the work of the people, but I came home at the end of every week and still lived in the same house my wife and I bought years ago, still underwater on our mortgage thanks to the housing collapse. It was an extraordinarily busy period, where the days lasted from six a.m. until as late as eleven p.m. Felt like five minutes.

Ready. Set. Go!

We held multiple town halls, all of which drew capacity-to-overflow crowds, and several roundtable discussions with community leaders and state and local elected officials. We also had a district office open house, and I did in-depth interviews with every local media group, including the Spanish-language networks Univision and Telemundo. By the way, learning Spanish in the streets of Latin America didn't exactly prepare me to talk about the intricacies of immigration reform or tax code.

In the mornings there'd be some sort of breakfast hosted by

either a political group or the Rotary Club. I'd usually give a fairly generic Washington update as people choked down warm, mushy fruit and rubbery eggs that had been sitting in a buffet vat for a few hours. I'd keep my remarks to less than ten minutes and then open the meetings up for questions.

Immediately after that, a couple hours were set aside to have coffee with a small group of big-money donors, who are typically engaged, educated, and interested in the nitty-gritty of legislating. They also tend to be more moderate, not necessarily on policy, but in the way they want their representative to communicate. So I took the time to reassure them I was not working on anything stupid, like impeaching the president.

When you're dealing with multiple groups as an elected official, you have to master how you speak to all of them individually. This isn't to dismiss the validity of what you're saying. It's about communicating effectively. While I might not be the greatest speaker, I've always learned from the best, who taught me that *you have to know your audience.* At every event I'd speak about the same values and principles, but would use different words and tones, focusing on the most appropriate issues for each group.

When lunch rolled around, it was time to speak to yet another group, a political, nonprofit, or business organization, like Realtors or people in the hospitality industry, both big in Southwest Florida. I'd give a speech or a Washington update tailored to what most affected that particular group while they dove into wilted salads drowning in ranch dressing or a soggy sandwich with square pieces of neon-orange cheese. After those delicious meals, I would meet with staff at the district office, take more meetings there, or grab another coffee with a grass-roots group.

Then we were off to the "rubber-chicken circuit." At night all the groups I just mentioned—nonprofit, industry, and political—offered an evening of speakers complimenting one another for hours on end. "You're the best." "No, you're the best!" "Shut up!" "No, you shut up!" This would go on and on while I ate a piece of recently thawed chicken drowning in gravy that maybe had enough flavor so that when the organizer asked, "Congressman, how is everything?" you could look up, show you'd eaten a few bites, and say, "Delicious. Thank you." Insert smile, whack down a few more glasses of wine, give a speech, and then head back home, where your wife and kid have been sound asleep for several hours. Damn. Missed 'em again.

That's it for Florida!

Back to D.C.!

The schedule wasn't intense in Washington; it was absolutely insane. Some days I had back-to-back fifteen-minute meetings from nine a.m. until six p.m. The days were long, but I loved it! I enjoyed interacting with people, talking policy, learning about what was important, what was a problem, and where I could help. And in the bigger picture, though this might sound naïve, I was doing good things for the country even if it was for one person at a time or one small issue at a time.

During these meetings, I'd often get called to vote on the House floor. If a meeting in my office had started, I'd have to say, "I'm so sorry, I need to let you know I might get called for votes any at second." Then, just as someone was about to get into the issue, *ding, ding*! Time to go vote!

It became like the kids' game red light/green light. The bell would ring, signaling, *Go! Run! Get your ass to the Capitol as fast as you can! You gotta name that post office in McCracken County's beautiful town of Paducah!* Or Amanda might rush in, saying, "Trey, MSNBC wants you!"

"Remind them I'm a conservative Republican, and they'll drop the request," was my usual response.

The reality is I did MSNBC and CNN more than Fox. Producers and bookers would call Amanda with requests for interviews, but sometimes they would call the House Republican Conference, which handles messaging and media relations, with a generic request for *any* Republican to come on and talk about *any* relevant issue. The Republican Conference would often request me because they liked my way of communicating. The bar was pretty low, though. They just wanted me to *not* say dumb things on camera. "Okay, I'll try." I loved to spar—and occasionally say dumb things—with anchors like Craig Melvin, a ball of fire, and Chris Jansing. Both were fair, but they sure grilled us Republicans.

As the craziness of the schedule and infinite number of press requests began intensifying, there was an undercurrent of darkness in Congress I had not experienced yet. The country of Syria had just begun a downward spiral into hell. As a member of Foreign Affairs, and as someone who has traveled and followed international politics intensely, the issue of Syria weighed heavily on me.

When you become a member of Congress, you realize that one of the heaviest responsibilities you carry is to declare war. It sure is different, though, when you have to decide it. Your decision, *your one vote*, potentially means life or death for other human beings. While some in that group might include people who pose a direct threat to our national security, it also unfortunately includes innocent *moms, dads, brothers, sisters, and babies.*

That I knew.

What I did not know was how heavy the decision would be.

In my twenties, right after the attacks of September 11, 2001, I had considered joining the military. With my knack for languages and love of travel, I also considered the Central Intelligence Agency. I never acted on either. I was neck deep in being a journalist and always looking ahead at other entrepreneurial opportunities.

Even in that dark time, post 9/11, I could not shake my libertarian leanings. When President Bush ordered the invasion of Iraq, I was heartbroken and, in some ways, relieved I'd never joined the military or CIA. I would often argue with my neocon friends, saying, "We are invading a country that hasn't done anything to us! And what the hell happens when it falls? Are we going to prop up another dictator? That didn't work well in Iran or half a dozen other places in Latin America! This is bad for everyone!" Ever since I was young, international issues and politics has fascinated me.

Now keep in mind, when a serious issue like Syria is discussed and members are asked to authorize the death of thousands of people, including innocent women and children, some of their foreign policy experience is, in fact, very international.

International in the sense that they once went to Mexico for spring break, where they bought a killer T-shirt reading "One tequila. Two tequila. Three tequila. Floor! Cancun '88." Other members have never left the country. Some would even have a tough time pointing out specific countries where we are bombing or arming rebels.

At this time in 2013, members were potentially going to be asked for life-and-death decisions on Syria. Over the past few weeks, Amanda had been crashing into the office with media requests to share my noninterventionist views. As Syria was beginning its downward spiral, I was not about to hop on the bandwagon of Republicans or Democrats advocating for the overthrow of *yet another dictator* where we would more than likely lose control of *yet another country*. After the disaster that was Iraq, it was time for the United States to stop supporting regime change even in the case of Syria's Bashar al-Assad.

The rhetoric was stepping up at this time from both parties, but it was especially sad to hear this type of neocon interventionist policy from President Obama. While I might disagree with some of President Obama's policies, one thing I really hoped for—like many other libertarians in the Republican Party—was that he would *not* adopt a Bush-type doctrine and send our troops into foreign countries for more empire building or dictator toppling.

When Amanda would grab me for an interview, she would answer my question before I asked. "Yes, we have a minute to grab an espresso!" And we were off. Espressos in hand, we marched to the Cannon Rotunda to get harassed, in a good way, by MSNBC. There I'd pop in my own earpiece I kept from my days of anchoring the news and do what's called a talk-back, where a show host from New York was in my ear asking questions while I looked at the camera and answered.

Week after week, the schedule and even the issues them-selves seemed to get more intense—immigration, the economy, Syria. While it was exciting, it was stressful.

Finding ways to blow off steam was not a problem.

In the evening I met more people and formed new bonds. I was also discovering that the "circuit" in D.C. was no low-rent rubber-chicken circuit. This was a refined cocktail circuit. This was Fellini's *La Dolce Vita*, but without Marcello Mastroianni having an existential struggle between intellect and celebrity. In D.C., politicians, lobbyists, and even the semifamous interns on social media pull off both.

Cue up some '60s Rat Pack music.

When I wasn't participating in policy meetings, there were always loads of swanky fund-raisers where I could put in an appearance. That means showing up so the lobbyists who are donating the big bucks know their recipient is "connected" and "engaged" with other members of Congress. And making an appearance at one of these things often means you just eat free food, talk shop, and have a martini or two—or more. Some-times you hit multiple parties before the night even begins.

Of course, I held my own fund-raising gigs. Personally, I hated the country club atmosphere on the Hill, so I chose other options, like entertaining groups at a local comedy club. One week, Second City, the famous improv group in Chicago, was in town playing at the Woolly Mammoth Theatre. We held a fund-raiser there. Both the show and our event were big hits. This was certainly different from whacking down cocktails at the Capitol Hill Club while pretending to be interested in a member's monologue on super-compelling issues like the Export-Import Bank or a tax incentive for Big Pharma.

I was finding my groove and having fun, but I was alone. My work responsibilities were consuming me, and any extra time I had outside of the office was now dedicated to my social life. Amy was coming up to D.C. less and less with every passing week.

> 'Cause I've got friends in low places, where the whiskey drowns and the beer chases my blues away.
> ★ Garth Brooks, "Friends in Low Places"

One evening after work, I was standing on the Metro platform waiting to switch to the Red Line and noticed a guy staring at me. In his early to midtwenties, with light hair, blue eyes, and wearing a suit, I figured he was a congressional staffer. He approached me. I pulled off my headphones, which were blaring Daft Punk. "Congressman?" he asked.

"Hi, I'm Trey," I said, and stuck out my hand.

"I knew it! I follow you on Twitter."

I let out a quick laugh. "Ha! Okay. Cool. That's a sign of the times."

"My name's Mike." (Of course his name's not Mike. It's been changed.)

As fate would have it, our train was delayed for a good forty-five minutes, and we ended up talking about everything from his recent marriage to where he grew up.

"Mike, you work on the Hill?"

"No, I finished an internship a few weeks ago and am looking now."

With an ear for accents, I pegged him to be from either Chicago or Buffalo. "Where are you from?"

"Chicago," he said.

"Great place! I lived there for years."

"Yeah, I grew up there. And now, here, I'm kind of a late bloomer. I went to culinary school and just now started to get involved in politics."

"Culinary school, huh? What do you think about the food scene here?"

His eyes lit up. "I love it!"

"Yeah, me, too. I live in Dupont. I'm always on the hunt for good food and drinks. You got any suggestions?"

As if he had a list in his head, he started naming the best places by cuisine and cocktails, with a particular focus on the old-fashioned at Hank's Oyster Bar. He asked, "Hey, wanna grab a drink there? I'm meeting my wife for dinner later in the area."

"Sure," I said. "Why not?"

With that, after the almost hour delay on the train platform and a drink, a random friendship was struck up. In the following weeks, Mike and I occasionally hung out. He also introduced me to his friends, including a guy named John. (And, of course, his name isn't John.)

John, who was about my age, immigrated to the United States at an early age and ran a business (that's all I got for ya). He, too, was married and had some kids. He was outgoing, interesting, and we shared a passion for travel and foreign cultures.

The three of us were soon hanging out often. Since I didn't go out on the weekends at home, our nights out together were like my Friday and Saturday nights. But, of course, they were actually my Tuesday and Wednesday nights. It was great having friends who didn't work on the Hill; I didn't have to be constantly on point or talk policy or politics.

One night Mike, John, and I were having a beer. "Cheers," Mike said.

I replied, "Cheers. *Carpe diem!*"

John cocked his head. "What's that mean?"

Like a smartass, I replied, "Well, I'd give you crap for your limited English, but it's actually Latin. It translates to seize the day."

For me, "seizing the day" was occasionally an issue, and not a good one.

> The future's uncertain, and the end is always near.
> Let it roll, baby, roll.
> ★ The Doors, "Roadhouse Blues"

I have always had an insatiable hunger for life, a voracious appetite for everything—learning, seeing, doing, tasting, touching, experiencing. It's been the same with work. Professionally, nothing has ever been enough. And even with the success I've had, rarely have I felt a sense of accomplishment. *I've always been happy, but never content.*

Why?

Dead people. I see dead people.

Long before my brush with death in Mexico, one of my earliest memories is of a dead body lying on an embalming table. This was normal for me. Almost one hundred and fifty years ago my great-grandfather started the Radel Funeral Home when a baby girl died in his neighborhood and there was no one to help with a proper burial. He was the owner of a furniture store, so he stepped in to build a casket. My dad still provides care for the community today. Our family never lived in the funeral home itself, but it was a small business with only a handful of employees. Both my mom and dad worked there full-time, and when I was sixteen, I was helping run funerals and driving the hearse in the processions. During weeknights, if I didn't have sports after school, my dad had me run my own visitations, sometimes called wakes. Some were heartbreaking, like the time I buried a close friend's older brother who had committed suicide. That weighed heavily on me. Memories from long before did, too.

When I was a very young boy, I remember walking to the back of the funeral home. It had been built in the late 1800s and was full of old antiques and, of course, caskets. I walked into the embalming room and saw the body of an older woman partially covered by a white blanket. It had become normal to see dead bodies. It wasn't freaky or scary. I was a kid and had nothing to judge it against, no Hollywood movies or even neighborhood stories from other kids about zombies. The body was just there. Dead.

I know today that seeing dead bodies at such an early age profoundly affected me. Carpe diem wasn't just a saying; it became my way of life. And sometimes it was a problem. From my earliest years, I knew that *any day, at any hour, at any minute, at any fleeting second*, life could disappear in a heartbeat. Knowing this, I have tried to live every day to its fullest—consciously, subconsciously, maybe even unconsciously.

And in Washington I was seizing the day, and the nights, too, which were about to get longer.

One night John and I met up with his friend Ryan, who worked as a club promoter. Club promoters are like Las Vegas. They'll do anything for you as long as you stay and keep spending. We headed to his lounge, and after more than a few drinks, I started making choices not only as if I were *not a Congressman* but also as if I were invisible.

★10★
WE ARE THE CHAMPIONS

Today's the day," an excited Abby proclaimed as I rolled into Longworth a little later than usual.

"Farm bill!" I fired back, my headphones playing the Doors. As I pulled my headphones off, my new chief of staff stood up and followed me into my office.

There he was, Dave Natonski, in all of his six-foot-four glory. Before leaving, Jason was true to his word and helped us find Dave. It took me about three seconds to hire him. Although Jason and I had troubles keeping up with the insanity and schedule of Washington as outsiders, Dave had no problem whatsoever. He was the consummate Washington insider and had been grinding it out for years. Dave was just a few years younger than I was and had worked about every position you can in a congressional office—deputy chief of staff, communications director, legislative assistant, and more.

Rarely am I the shortest guy in the room, but with Dave

being even taller than Greg, I loved to ask them to walk by my side when we went in and out of the Capitol, wear sunglasses, and talk into their sleeves. Never happened.

"Morning, Dave!" I said loudly, with a smile. He made his way from behind his desk and followed me into my office.

While Dave's height is imposing and he often carries an intense look on his face, he's kind and caring. He has this great head of thick dark hair, which he prides himself on and constantly pushes back with one hand. He is also proudly quirky. There were two things he absolutely could not tolerate—socks and hot drinks. He didn't wear socks, ever, and he was not knocking down multiple espressos a day with me, not even a cup of coffee. "Hot drinks, don't like 'em," he'd say in half sentences. Weird. And, since this was mandatory with any hire in our office, he also had a great sense of humor.

Abby, Greg, and Amanda joined us. "We're getting the band back together," I said, with a smile. Not only did we have the farm bill coming up, we also had the most important, critical, paramount amendment known to mankind, born right here in this office—the Radel Amendment to cut sheep shearing.

"So," Dave said. He often started his sentences with a word like "so" or "look," then he would pause before launching into the issue. Dave's "so" was Pusateri's "man." After his pause, Dave said, "It's not looking good."

"What's not looking good?"

"Leadership is whipping against our amendment."

Before a vote, leadership puts together a list of their suggestions on votes. The "whip" is the person who rounds up, suggests, or violently enforces votes for his or her party. And now leadership was "whipping" against me. Sexy, right? Picture old white Republican men in black assless chaps cracking whips and telling you which way to vote. You better do what they say! "Good news though," Dave added. "The outside groups are for you."

I exhaled, and like a villain from a Batman movie, I said, "Ahhh, yes, the feared and revered outside groups."

Some of the more prominent and influential outside groups that advocate for or against political issues include the Club for Growth, the Heritage Foundation, and FreedomWorks, which grade lawmakers' conservative credentials. For example, they'll issue an alert that an upcoming vote will be "graded" or "scored." Vote *with* them, get a higher score and, in effect, a higher ranking. Vote *against* them, get a lower ranking and possibly, quite possibly, a challenger in your next primary. These groups can dump a few thousand to hundreds of thousands of dollars into a race against you. That kind of money moves the dial. For the candidate they support, it's an instant game changer. In Senate or presidential races, they can easily contribute more than a million. This scares people; incumbent Republicans pay attention.

Even if an outside group isn't financially supporting a challenger, if you want to run against an incumbent Republican, one of the first things you do is look at the groups' scorecards. The incumbent with the least conservative score will be the one labeled "not conservative enough." After all, a rookie candidate who has never taken a vote in Washington doesn't have a report card.

That's where it gets complicated. If a candidate wins based on defecating all over his opponent with these Holy Grail score-cards, the question then becomes: How will that new member vote—for their constituents or for the outside group?

Now these votes, policies, and issues might simply be a part of a lawmaker's principles and beliefs. In fact, I agreed with many of the groups most of the time. After all, the 501(c)(4)s are based in conservative or libertarian philosophies. But another dirty little secret in Washington is that when leadership asks lawmakers to consider a vote, some won't answer until they hear how these outside groups are grading that vote.

I was ecstatic that our amendment had the support of outside groups. Being the eternal optimist, I said, "This is great!"

But Dave was shaking his head, almost physically caution-ing, *Yeah . . . but.*

"You don't think we can pull together enough votes, do you?"

"Leadership is against this." As Dave delivered the bad news, he somehow did it with a smile. This was something I came to appreciate about Dave. Even after several years of working in D.C., he wasn't jaded at all. Instead, when things didn't look good or got rough, he shrugged his shoulders as if to say, *This is Washington. Yeah, it's a circus. With or without our doing what we're doing, the merry-go-round will keep spinning. Let's get to work.* And in this case, even though no one in leadership would justify their opposition to our amendment, we all knew it was more freebie handouts for yet another industry.

If I tried to be the eternal optimist and Dave wasn't so sure, Greg was beyond confident. Ever since the debate, he'd had a fierce look of determination. Even if we had only one win in Congress, for him, this would be it.

But then more bad news. Abby said, "Democratic leadership is also whipping against our amendment."

Greg angrily shouted, "Of course they are!" The only thing he left out was "those damn communists!"

In a calm voice, I said, "It's all good. All good. If it happens, great. If not, so be it. We worked hard and did our best," adding, "Sorry if I just sounded like a bad '80s inspirational poster."

This was going to be tough, if not impossible. We were so concerned that Amanda took the extra step of drafting two press releases, one with an exuberant "we are awesome and saving the world one sheep shear at a time" tone. The second said, "Our country is doomed if we can't even shave off this appropriation."

With the final puns in this argument coming to a close, it was now time to vote on the critically important Radel Amendment, several others, and, eventually, the final farm bill.

Abby and Greg walked over to the Capitol with me. As we hustled across Independence Avenue, Abby handed me the day's long list of amendments with vote suggestions. I was familiar with most of them. (Staff members suggest votes for the members just like leadership does.)

One amendment was a provision added to the bill by what's called a "voice vote." This means it was debated but *unanimously* agreed upon by both Democrats and Republicans without objection. The provision gave individual states more power over how their food stamp programs were administered, including the possibility of drug testing food stamp recipients. While I didn't like it, it was a states' rights issue for me. I also thought it couldn't be that controversial if both conservatives and liberals were agreeing on it. The way I looked at it, I'd vote yes any day to give our states more freedom to decide what they want for themselves, whether it's legalizing marijuana or addressing how they treat drug laws.

I didn't think much about it, but that provision would come back to bite me in the ass harder than I've ever been bitten before.

We got to the Capitol, and as if I were a teenage boy being dropped off at the movie theater by Mom and Dad, Abby and Greg hugged me and said good-bye. They also gave me some extra money to buy popcorn. One hell of a movie was about to come on.

When I headed onto the House floor, I liked to walk in on the Democrats' side, say hello to some colleagues, and then make my way over to the Republican side. This time I took Dave's advice. His instructions: "Work the floor. Democrats and Republicans. Tell them your amendment. What it does. Whip them right there on the floor." He finished with the two words we had said out loud to each other over the past few weeks— "Sheep shearing"—as if to say, *Look, if these idiots are really focused on keeping sheep shearing, just move on, man.*

First, I approached the people I knew well, including Patrick Murphy, who had a large bull's-eye still stuck to his head that read, "Top Democrat target." I peeled it off. *There you go, now you're safe, buddy.* I said, "Hey, Patrick, if you get a chance, check out my amendment. It's cleverly labeled the Radel Amendment. I'd love your vote on it. It's simple. It knocks off $50 million in appropriations for, get this, sheep shearing."

He said, "Okay, got it," and marked his paper. I thought to myself, *Hope I get at least one Democrat's vote!*

I worked some other Dems and then did the same on the Republican side—let people know about my amendment, what it did, and how easy it was to remember. "It's my last name!" As I said that, I thought, *Damn. If it fails, it's also easy to remember that it's my last name.*

During a long series of votes, I wandered around talking with people or I headed to the cloakroom. *Sounds cool and clandestine, right?* Each party has a cloakroom just off the House floor. You don't dare go in unless you're with that party. As secretive as it sounds, the Republican cloakroom is more like a dive bar in Hell's Kitchen, like Rudy's Bar & Grill if you're familiar with that establishment. While both places serve food, the main difference between the two is that you have to pay for your hot dogs in Congress; at Rudy's they're free. And like in the good old carcinogen-filled days of Rudy's and other bars in New York, you can also smoke. *Damn you, Bloomberg.* The Republican cloakroom reeks like an ashtray. It probably smells a lot like the bar Speaker Boehner grew up in. And guess who was puffing away right in front of me?

Seeing John Boehner brought a flood of great memories from the campaign, and he still made things seem new and exciting. Whenever we'd talk about Cincinnati, it was like catching up on childhood memories. "Mr. Speaker," I nodded, and half-jokingly said, "Mr. Speaker, you should vote for my amendment."

I was teasing him. More than likely he would vote the way his leadership team suggested. But hey, if all hell broke loose, maybe he would be the swing vote.

Getting the farm bill to the floor for a vote had been problematic for leadership. The Speaker had explicitly asked for and intensely lobbied conservative House Republicans for their support. He noted that he had voted no on previous farm bills, but he said that he was going to vote for this one because it was responsible, conservative legislation. However, the outside groups that supported our amendment did not support the bill. They thought it was not conservative enough. This was a problem for the Speaker and the Ag Committee, but in the end, the farm bill was a rare case where many conservatives broke with the outside groups to vote yes because they considered the bill sensible and conservative, and saw that it genuinely reined in some of the big spending programs it had been laden with in previous years.

It was soooo conservative . . .

How conservative was it?

It was so conservative that even tea party wacko Ted Yoho was all over it! Working with the Ag Committee, he even whipped for it—sans chaps.

The vote happened just as a wave of animosity and anger against the leadership began to build among House Republicans, some of it fueled by the outside groups. Months before, I had received calls about a plan to oust Boehner. Even though I had a personal relationship with the Speaker, I would always listen. I never gave the calls much credence, but I listened. Congressman Tom Massie called one night. "Trey, we are lining up votes to do this. We are going to overthrow the Speaker!" But in the course of the conversation, I learned that the insurrection had no designated person lined up to replace him—no option, no conservative, not even a sacrificial lamb (pun fully intended as we approach the vote on our sheep amendment!). There was no plan. Just chaos.

A few years later the anger, resentment, and chaos would climax in Boehner's resignation, but even then no one had a viable replacement until a revered young icon stepped up. And as the Radel Amendment was about to open up for votes, I was standing smack in the middle of the House floor next to him.

Paul Ryan and I had first met during the primary. I shot up to D.C. to network, and Paul was crossing the street near the Capitol Hill Club. I instinctively called out, "Paul!" Not exactly respectful considering I didn't even know the guy. But, hey, he is a midwesterner like I am. He's down-to-earth and really passionate about policy, with a work ethic to match. He reminded me of the people I grew up with. In fact, he left Wisconsin to go to college just north of Cincinnati, at Miami University of Ohio, and knew some of the older brothers of guys I went to high school with.

When I yelled his name, he looked up, smiled, said, "Hey," and stuck out his hand.

"Uh, Congressman, Congressman Ryan. Sorry. Nice to meet you. My name is Trey, Trey Radel. He, of course, had no idea who I was until I said, "I'm running for Congress against your buddy Chauncey, unfortunately."

As if a lightbulb had turned on above his head, he said, "Oh, yeah, you're the radio guy."

I laughed. "Yeah, that's kinda how Chauncey's referred to me in debates. Sure. I just wanted to meet you."

He shrugged his shoulders, and said, "Hey, Chauncey is a friend, I've known him a long time from our working together."

"I totally understand. I just wanted to say hi, meet you, and thank you for the work you're doing." And I did understand. Like so much else, it was politics, not personal.

Shortly after getting elected, I sought out Paul for his advice and to get to know him. Before I knew it, we were talking about our mutual love of music, including the Beastie Boys and Rage Against the Machine. Actually, it was only a year before that Rage's guitarist, Tom Morello, penned an op-ed in *Rolling Stone* on how much of an asshole Paul Ryan was for proposing a budget that—*get this*—tried to address some of our country's spending concerns. *What a dick Paul Ryan must be, right?* Who the hell wants to be responsible with taxpayer dollars?

Ryan let it roll right off. The eventual Speaker wasn't going to take shit from Tom Morello, who wrote: "You see, the super rich must rationalize having more than they could ever spend while millions of children in the U.S. go to bed hungry every night." Tom Morello is worth *$30 million.* If he gave just half that away, he could feed those millions of hungry kids in the United States and still live a really comfortable life with $15 million. While celebrities like Morello fly on private planes and bitch about global warming, Paul Ryan slept on a fucking couch in his office and flew coach to return home to the kids he barely saw while he was serving the country.

Many celebrities are given soapboxes and megaphones in the media because they have a talent for playing guitar or singing or acting. Those are great talents, which I respect and admire. And many, like Tom Morello, who is probably a good, honorable man, do tons of charity work. But can *any of them* who ignorantly damn Republicans to hell while talking about peace, love, and open minds propose some solutions to our country's serious issues, like mandatory spending, instead of just taking shots, typically using words like "racist"? In that *Rolling Stone* piece, Morello proposed no such solutions, but he did call the highly educated and wonky policy wonk of all wonks "clueless."

And now, as I'm standing on the House floor next to this clueless, couch-sleeping, coach-flying, unabashed Rage fan, the Radel Amendment was about to open up for votes.

Ryan smiled and said, "Radel, you're up!" Like Boehner, Paul also always addressed me by my last name for some reason. He stood there with his arms crossed, which he often does, as if he's deep in thought.

For a while, Paul Ryan was the poster child for the ultraconservative, crazy far right. While people like Morello and other liberals slammed him, conservatives adored him for it. It was when he was chair of the Budget Committee that Ryan proposed a budget that—*gasp!*—tried to shore up and actually save Medicare and Social Security. *Again, what a dick, right?*

At that time there was a beautifully constructed video with a Paul Ryan look-alike. It is truly touching. In it, you see the handsome, young, gentle Paul Ryan pushing around a sweet-looking older woman in her wheelchair, undoubtedly his grandmother. Soft music plays in the background while graphics come up to educate you on issues important to seniors. In this serene and beautiful setting, Paul continues pushing around his beloved grandmother. Soothing music continues in the background while birds chirp. Paul and his grandma gently ascend up a hill in a wooded area that looks a lot like Wisconsin. Then, so smoothly and beautifully, they arrive at the top of the hill. It's a scenic wide shot of a stunning cliff overlooking a gorgeous body of water.

Then Paul Ryan pushes that bitch off the cliff!

In trying to do good for the country and actually recognize there is maybe, just maybe, a slight spending problem—*those words dripping in sarcasm*—and that maybe, just maybe, someone needs to address our mandatory spending issues, a political group made a video showing the sweet baby-faced Paul Ryan murdering his grandmother. Nice!

What's even crazier is that Ryan, who was once the darling of the conservative movement in some circles, *is no more*. He isn't far right enough. So, in short, for some, he's so far right, he'd throw his own grandma off a cliff; for others, he just hasn't done enough. He should have killed his grandpa, too. Weak.

As soon as these concerns crossed my mind, I wondered, *Uh-oh! How will this communist vote on the Radel Amendment? After all, he killed his grandma but skipped grandpa!*

Before I could ask, he said, "I'm voting for your amendment, by the way."

"Thanks, man. Me, too, so that's at least two of us."

Just as I was feeling a bit optimistic, he brought me down a notch. "But it's not looking good, Radel."

I laughed. "Yeah, yeah, I know. I got both sides whipping against me today. All good, man. Rage against the machine."

He let that sink in and laughed. "Just gotta watch the board,

Radel, because the board will get ya," he said, looking up at the electronic board hanging just above the Speaker's rostrum. It's a lot like a scoreboard that shows each and every member's name and how they voted. The votes pop up live in real time.

You vote by taking your assigned card, putting it in one of the inserts that are scattered all over the floor, and pressing YEA, NAY, or PRES. The last means "present," which is less a vote and more like "I know my most basic responsibility in Congress is to vote. I know I'm being paid nearly $200,000 a year to vote. But ya know what, I'm gonna go Swiss on this one."

The vote was allotted fifteen minutes. *Bang!* The Y's and N's started popping up next to members' names. The tally went from single digits to 10 to 10, then quickly hit 27 to 25 in favor of nay. Seeing that I wasn't getting destroyed out of the gate, I nodded slowly. "Okay. Not bad."

His hands still crossed, Paul looked over and smiled. "Nah, the board's gonna get ya, Radel."

I fired back with a smile. "C'mon, man! Have some faith!"

The numbers continued to climb. Like a close March Madness basketball game, one second my amendment was on top, 49 to 42, then seconds later, I was falling behind, 51 to 49. "Damn," I said out loud.

Adam Kinzinger, my colleague from Illinois, walked past us and barked, "Sheep shearing!" Then Patrick Murphy yelled, "Sheep shearing!" In this party atmosphere, as everyone walked around popping their cards in slots and having loud conversations while these two guys yelled, "Sheep shearing," the numbers moved into the hundreds. We were getting close, and Paul said out loud what I was thinking. "We're getting close now."

Then he smiled, looked at me, and repeated, "Board's gonna get ya, Radel."

The spread remained in single digits, then the nays started to pull away. Then the yeas made a comeback! Yes, no, yes, no, winning, losing. *Ahhh!* Then, winning, winning!

By a handful of votes, the Radel Amendment started to pull away with only seconds left on the clock. "Man, we might do this," I said to Paul, as calmly as I could. But in my head, I was screaming, *We're gonna nail this!* I had visions of shooting the AK-47 from Cambodia at the scoreboard as soon as we won.

Arms still folded, he slowly nodded. "Maybe." Then he cut himself off. "Uh-oh."

Seconds away from closing the vote, with the Radel Amendment nearly victorious, leadership walked over to the people who manage the floor and the clock, which was also in the Speaker's rostrum. They ordered them to stop the clock. "They're holding it," Paul said.

Aw, c'mon! I almost yelled.

Near the center aisle, a group of hard-core conservatives were sitting together. The group included Justin Amash, Tom Massie, and others, and they are some of the guys who would form the Freedom Caucus and push Boehner out. They started yelling, "C'mon! Let's go! It's over!" As fellow fiscal conservatives, they were of course supporting my measure.

Leadership continued to huddle. Then some Democrats started getting riled up, too, yelling, "C'mon! Let's go!" I looked back up at the board. I had won quite a few Democratic votes but had lost a lot of the Republicans—you know, the people who pride themselves on cutting wasteful spending.

The leadership and committee chairs kept the clock locked up. Then I saw them pull into the huddle some members who had voted for my amendment. *Oh, no. They're flipping them.* I was in disbelief. Before Paul could say "the board," I said, "Dude, don't say it!" He laughed out loud.

Suddenly, I spotted Jason Chaffetz rushing up the aisle looking intense. He locked eyes with me. "What the," I mumbled. He pointed directly at me. *Am I in trouble?* I asked myself.

Chaffetz said, "Trey, you've got to get people to flip. You need the CBC." Since I was a rookie, it took me a second to process what he'd said: That I needed to start working people like leadership was and concentrate on a group that, oddly enough, this Mormon from Utah had a great relationship with, the Congressional Black Caucus. Jason freakin' Chaffetz, who was presiding over the House floor the night I debated with Democrats and Republicans over sheep shearing, was here to help me!

He put his arm on my back and steered me over to where many of the CBC members were sitting. He started working the crowd. I went right to Greg Meeks, who represents a Queens, New York, district. We served on Foreign Affairs together. I adored the guy. He has a huge personality, and from the moment I met him, he helpfully answered many of my questions. I didn't know if he had even voted yet. I didn't care! After a few words, he went back to his colleagues. Jason spoke to the prominent longtime congresswoman Maxine Waters, and a minute later she was walking down to the well in front of the Speaker's rostrum, where you go to—*get this!*—change your vote. Maxine flipped. A huge line of fellow vote flippers formed behind her. At this point, it wasn't just the CBC, it was Democrats and Republicans who knew the amendment was going to win, and they wanted to be on the winning side!

The vote closed. Done. With 235 yeas and 192 nays, the Radel Amendment passed. "We did it!" I shook Chaffetz's hand. "Thanks, man! Thank you so much!" A few people gave me high fives as if this were a sporting event and I had just destroyed an opponent. It was hilariously weird. I wanted to run up the aisle flipping the bird at the board. Instead, I calmly walked off the floor.

All that for—insert long, dramatic pause here—sheep shearing.

Soon after, the farm bill narrowly passed.

This example is a microcosm of so much in Washington. Our country is pushing $20 trillion in debt while similar nonsense is debated day after day. As a freshman office, we knew we weren't going to lead the charge on structural changes to mandatory spending, reset corporate tax rates, or reform immigration. We picked something small that we thought we could accomplish. And even with the evil forces of Lord Vader presiding over the Ag Committee and henchmen in assless chaps "whipping" against us, we got our amendment passed. How I went about this once again highlighted the importance of relationships. Without the Congressional Black Caucus, the Radel Amendment would never have passed.

Maybe you think all of this is petty and not worth discussing. But ask yourself: What's important to you? What's *your* issue? More money for education? More money for our military? While our teachers and veterans occasionally get crapped on by the government, the fact that we had to debate sheep shearing highlights the insanity in Washington.

My philosophy has generally been: If the private market can pay for it, let the private market have it. But there are some things the market won't touch. For example, one of my constituents, Rob Whan, came by my office to share his heartbreaking story. His three-year-old son had died after being diagnosed with a rare form of leukemia called hypodiploid. Rob and I talked about funding for research into rare diseases and how I could help raise awareness for childhood cancer.

Typically, pharmaceutical companies don't fund research and development into rare diseases. Why? Because they're rare! There's no money to be made treating such a small segment of the population. On the flip side, why is Viagra so popular? Because millions of older men are willing to pay billions of dollars for it. While it is inappropriate and absolutely horrendous of me to use this terrible story of losing a child, I do so to make a grim, cruel, jarring, and savage point about the harsh reality of capitalism.

However, where capitalism will not go is potentially an area government can, by providing money for research and development, and just maybe helping save the next young child's life.

Sigh.

But instead, we fight over who can piss in which bathroom, hand and dick sizes in presidential debates, and how much money to allocate to sheep.

With the sheep dead and gone, I took away another lesson.

As fired up as I was, I should have toned down my speech on the House floor. After that debate, I never spoke again with Peterson or Conaway.

In retrospect, I should have taken Debbie Wasserman Schultz's advice that there is "in here" and "out there." My debate rhetoric was more suited for a campaign or my days on radio. My intention was to highlight the absurdity of sending money to a special interest. While I might not have been as bombastic as Alan Grayson or Allen West, I still went over the top. I would later tone down my speeches on the floor.

That was about the only thing in my life that was getting toned down, though.

★11★
FEEL THE PAIN

My nights got later; my days got darker. And there was death. Lots of death.

By September, the Syrian civil war had gotten so bloody that it was hard for experts to decipher who was fighting whom. As Bashar al-Assad's government fought multiple rebel groups, and rebels fought both the government and other rebels, some of whom had outside support and influence, the civil war morphed into complete chaos. On one side, Syria had teamed up with Russia and Iran, with Hezbollah fighters from Lebanon lending a hand. At first, they were fighting against a rebellion made up of Syrians that some in the West called "moderate." Then, as Syria quickly descended into Dante's violent seventh circle of hell, it was impossible to tell the difference between moderate opposition groups and radical terrorist groups. Add to the mix the clashes between the Syrian government and the Kurds, and you can see what a nightmare the country had become.

During this time, some of our allies in the region supported the rebels—well, at least some of the rebels, just not the bad ones. But then again, "bad" is an ambiguous term when an organization like Hezbollah, a terrorist organization by United States declaration, is fighting ISIS. Which side do you cheer for in the cage match when it's Hitler versus Pol Pot?

This is just the CliffsNotes version. The intricacies were enough for me to question our own government's involvement.

Behind closed doors, some bomb-happy, missile-toting Republican neocons talked about "getting in there" and "providing resources to the right groups." After all (insert southern accent here), this was "fer freedom!" Yeah, right. What both Republicans and Democrats wanted was regime change. And plenty of Democrats were as open to an all-out war as the neocons.

In order to push back, our office added a simple amendment to a defense appropriations bill, which read:

AMENDMENT TO H.R. 2397, AS OFFERED BY
MR. RADEL OF FLORIDA

None of the funds made available by this act may be
used for United States military involvement in Syria
without express authorization of Congress.

When our office pushed for it, leadership asked us to compromise and make the language simple enough to have broad application. But my concern was that it was so broad, it was ineffective. After all, is "funding" a "rebel group" *really* military involvement? Meh.

As Syria continued to spiral out of control, Bashar al-Assad gave the West a reason to bomb the hell out of his country. He used chemical weapons on his own people. Here's the catch, though: At the same time al-Assad gave the West a reason to attack militarily, President Obama had already given people a reason to attack him politically. Back in 2012, Obama had explicitly declared that if chemical weapons were used it would be a "red line for us."

President Obama had made that now-infamous comment at a press conference, and I'm certain it was unscripted. My guess is that, in private, the president would admit that it was a mistake to answer a question with such an ultimatum because I felt that, like many of us in Congress, he didn't want to get involved in the mess either. In some ways, it was crappy to see him bashed over and over for this, but as we see time and time again, there's politics in politics.

Any sympathy I had for the president evaporated when, in response to Assad's use of chemical weapons, he and his advisors overreacted with a strategy that they'd put as much thought into as they had his "red line" comments. The administration began a concerted effort to get Congress to authorize a strike against Syria. The rhetoric they were pushing in the media and to Congress was that it wouldn't be full involvement; they only wanted to bomb "specific, strategic, high-value military targets." Once again, I found myself longing for the Obama whose position in his campaign was that he was not going to resort to bombing countries and asking questions later. My position on Syria was and is: Stay out. Maybe by the time this book is printed things will have changed to alter my opinion, but proxy wars have cost us billions if not trillions of dollars over the decades of our involvement in Southeast Asia, the Middle East, and Latin America. Have our proxy wars really made us "safer"? Given us more "freedom"? No.

We are in the business of protecting our people at home, our interests abroad, and our allies. As formal and informal discussions continued among members, and pundits opined on the news, I never heard a persuasive argument that Bashar al-Assad posed a direct threat to the United States or our neighboring allies, including Turkey or Israel. I couldn't agree to any measure that called for invading Syria or funding "rebel groups" we were barely familiar with. Over and over, I would plead, "Who will replace Assad? Potentially someone or something that's even worse or less stable. What you're asking me to do is replace Ebola with cancer."

The Foreign Affairs Committee received classified briefings from top military brass on the situation in Syria. In these briefings, everything is expected to be off the record. While that sounds super secretive, the reality is that 99 percent of what I heard at these briefings I had already learned from the news or other members.

The top brass were struggling to clearly lay out all of the intricate difficulties and differences among the various rebel groups as they recommended strategic bombing. The goal seemed to be the eventual overthrow of Assad, with the rebels serving as our proxy. I asked, "Do we know which rebels will prevail and control the country when or if Assad is taken out?"

206 ★ TREY RADEL

"No, and we're not really trying to take him out, per se."

That was a typical answer. "Per se."

I'm not a military man. I don't pretend to know war strategy. But some pretty simple questions lacked specific answers. Part of me wondered, *Are they hiding something? Did they really have some sort of master plan they were keeping to themselves?* The unfortunate part is that I don't believe they were hiding anything. It's complicated militarily and politically, which, for better or worse, must coexist in our democracy.

We often think we can drop a few bombs and change things overnight, but these regions have been waging wars on each other for thousands of years. The United States has existed for fewer than 250 years; we cannot fathom the deep complexities and hatred among the religious factions and warring tribes that were established thousands of years before the British marked up maps and carved out countries.

Furthermore, long before I was a member of Congress, when I heard some of President Bush's top-level advisors on Iraq argue publicly that we would be warmly received, I didn't think they had a clue what they were talking about. Violence rages on today, and the Iraqi government is hardly a reliable, transparent ally to the United States. And in Afghanistan, where we were also—using an oft-repeated cliché here—going to "win hearts and minds," the government is corrupt, and remnants of the Taliban, coupled with al-Qaeda in Pakistan, are still major problems. Once again, violence pervades a country that is hanging on by a thread.

Let's take a look at how well bombs, boots on the ground, and even rebel support have worked out for the United States in the last few decades. We supported the Afghan mujahideen in their fight against the Soviet Union. You might remember someone else who helped in that fight—Osama bin Laden. When he founded al-Qaeda, he was joined by many of these fighters; others formed the Taliban. Later, in Iraq, we not only overthrew Saddam Hussein, we also hanged the guy. The country has been a bloody mess ever since. The instability in the region has led to an emboldened al-Qaeda and its evil, psychotic twin brother, ISIS. How absolutely effed up is it when al-Qaeda says, "ISIS? Those dudes are crazy!" Meanwhile, we turned a blind eye—or maybe, allegedly, possibly got directly involved—when Gaddafi was toppled in Libya. It, too, is now a breeding ground for ISIS, whose propaganda videos are more horrifying than any Wes Craven film.

When I left these classified briefings, I was firm in my stance. I would not be an old man in a suit sending our young kids in uniform to die. I was also convinced that if we started with a "strategic" bombing of Syria, as the White House continued to call it, we would most certainly end up sending troops. I had seen enough kids die, and in my own district I had befriended a soldier not much younger than I was who had lost both legs and a hand in Afghanistan. No way.

Many other committee members came out of those sessions unwilling to authorize strikes. At times, I felt like the military men and women who were tasked by the White House to sell this strategy to Congress were embarrassed. They were merely doing political pickup in a complicated world—complicated for President Obama, complicated for Congress, complicated for the military, and, sadly, complicated for the innocent men, women, and children who were being slaughtered for no other reason than they happened to be living in Syria at the wrong time.

While I could not be sold on war, the most persuasive selling points in the briefings for doing something were the pictures of dead women and children killed by chemical weapons or cross-fire. Those images still haunt me.

The weight of death, the news, and the stress of work, coupled with barely seeing my wife, child, or talking with my dad by phone, was bearing down on me. Around this time, I'd find myself leaving the Hill a little earlier to go hang out with John and even the club promoter, Ryan.

> Some people like the way it feels. Some people wanna kill their sorrows.
> ★ Kendrick Lamar, "Swimming Pools (Drank)"

Like my days, my nights got dark, too. The nightlife I came to love so much in D.C. was no longer contained by dinners here and there. I was out. Often.

John introduced me to a few new friends, and our group got larger. Like me, everyone was in their thirties. Most of the guys were successful, and some of them were a little obnoxious—think new money and bad cologne. They threw a lot of cash around and made sure people knew about it. Maybe it's just the midwesterner in me, but that kind of pretentious, flamboyant display always made me roll my eyes and wonder, *You need a tricked-out, jacked-up Hummer to compensate?*

We'd grab a bite to eat near my place in Dupont and then stop at the apartment for even more cocktails. By this point, Amy and Jude were staying in Florida almost every week. The apartment became more like a bachelor pad, with seven-day-old pizza, empty condiment bottles in the fridge, and a pile of laundry on the floor.

John, a new friend, and I went out one night and the scene had me saying to myself, *This is getting out of hand.* Leaving my place, we caught an Uber to head out for the evening.

Hopping in the car, I asked John, "Where we heading?"

"We're going to meet some more friends at a nearby lounge. You'll love it. It's just downtown."

The word "lounge" conjured up the kind of place I like— low lighting, couches, chill music, cocktails, and good craft beer. I said, "All good, man, just as long as it's not a club with hundreds of people, light shows, and DJs."

When we pulled up in front of the place, I noticed a line out the door. "Uhhh," I said. With that, John and his pal walked on either side of me, and we were ushered through the doors immediately.

Cue up DJ Snake and Lil Jon and ask yourself, *Turn down for what?*

"Over there," his friend yelled over the blaring music. "There" was a table behind a red-velvet rope. A table with bottles of Grey Goose. A table with mixers. A table protected by a bouncer with a shaved head, tight fitting black jeans, and a tighter fitting black T-shirt riding up his massive arms to expose tribal tats from the early 2000s. A table where a beautiful six-foot-tall blonde, blue-eyed model zoomed around serving cocktails. A table where I would be surrounded by guys wearing Drakkar, Cool Water, and gold Rolex watches.

The bouncer pulled back the red-velvet rope without even looking at us or saying a thing. We walked over. Around us, people were dancing. White people did whatever that thing is that they do with their hands when dancing to electronic music; black people got their groove on. One girl twerked.

Suddenly, it was just like my days as a reporter in sleepy Naples and leaving late on Friday to head to ritzy, Euro-trash-infested, house-music-blaring South Beach. But this time I was in Washington, D.C., and at a club, *not a lounge like John had said*. And, oh yeah, as a sitting United States congressman.

As we strolled over to the table, I grabbed John, put my hands on his shoulders, and looked him in the eyes. "John, I am not itching to tear up the dance floor to Drake or Daft Punk. I'm in my thirties, and dammit, I'm a congressman! What the hell am I going to do if someone snaps pictures of me? This isn't like having a steak at the Palm. This is bottle service at a club with a freakin' table, a red-velvet rope, even a bouncer with terrible tribal tats! How's that gonna look?"

He laughed hard. "Trey, relax man! No one knows who you are!"

"Ha! Good point!" I said.

Who *am* I?

It was a legitimate question.

Recurring descriptions and phrases from other parts of my life began to circle around in my head again—*cavalier, total disregard, what the hell are you thinking?*—even though things were going great for me professionally. I was killing it. I was raising money for the party, exceeding all expectations in my committees, and serving Southwest Florida with a constant presence. I was appearing on all of the networks, including Telemundo, Univision, and CNN en Español. And I was sharing a conservative message on social media with people who had never even met a Republican. Amanda and I were planning a speech about social media at next year's hugely popular South by Southwest Festival in Austin, Texas.

When it came to policy, I was all over environmental issues, which garnered the respect of Democrats at home and throughout the state. And I was building solid relationships with leadership, but I stayed true to the principles I ran on. I managed to stick to my guns and not toe the line or take votes to go along and get along. In fact, the outside groups scored me as one of the most conservative members. In the entire House! Conservatives in my district and other parts of the country had started taking notice.

At this point, I was a machine, a robot focused on work and my social life. The weeks were flying by.

"Good-bye, Amy and Jude." Hop on plane. D.C. Drinks. Bed. Wake up. Espresso. "Hello, Congressman." Committee. Work. Espresso. Event. *IPA*. Morning. "Sir." Go on camera. Exude confidence. "Thank you, Congressman." Committee. Death. Espresso. Budget. War. Event. Ketel One, rocks. "Congressman!" Speak to crowd. Smile. Get on camera. Work. *Did I leave the iron on?* Espresso. Committee. "The Honorable." *Honorable?* Syria. *Stress.* Go out. Drinks. Bed. *Sleep?* Wake up. Hop on plane. "Hi, Amy and Jude." A day. A night. "Good-bye, Amy and Jude."

Several months into my term, with my family a thousand miles away, I was doing *everything* too much—working, socializing, and drinking.

But I always found ways to justify my behavior. I justified late nights with early mornings. Partying didn't start till long after work, and work was *always* the priority. I flew out of bed every day ready to take on the day. Finally, I justified my bad habits with my good habits: When I was at home in Florida, I didn't drink or go out.

I could justify all I wanted. I was flirting with being out of control.

And as the son of a mother who struggled with alcohol, pills, and addiction all of her life, I, of all freaking people, should know how out of control things can get.

★ 12 ★
AT LAST, LAST DANCE

My mom was dying.

On the dance floor at our wedding reception.

I was standing in my tuxedo next to Amy, my beautiful new wife of about an hour, watching as my mom appeared to slowly pass away in front of our eyes. She was choking on a piece of steak.

Dying.

On our wedding reception floor.

How could this possibly be happening? It was like some twisted scene from a Quentin Tarantino flick.

Dying.

On our fucking wedding reception floor.

Someone in our wedding party happened to be an EMT. He tried his best Heimlich maneuver. Nothing. Finally, the paramedics arrived.

About a hundred of our closest friends and family were at

the reception. Roughly half of us formed a large circle around my mom as the paramedics worked on her. I stayed close to my mom as Amy paced frantically. She was torn between watching, not watching, and crying. I felt weak and stunned.

After an eternity of a few minutes, Amy whisper-screamed at me, "Tell them! Tell them what is going on, Trey!" Shocked out of my barely conscious state, I walked over to the paramedics and very quietly told them, "My mom has recovery issues. She may be medicated." I paused. "Pills," I discreetly whispered.

After all, I had been whispering and covering for my mom all my life. Why speak up now? Why speak up now while my mom was dying on the floor of this beautiful ballroom surrounded by a year of my wife's work—the designs, decorations, specific colors, specific flowers, specific candles, specific linens, and things called sashes that I still have no idea what they are. *Why the hell should I speak up now?*

They carried Mom away on a stretcher. Ten of us in our immediate family tailed the ambulance in our cars. I was convinced she was dead. I didn't say anything out loud, and in my heart, I hoped she was still alive. After all, my mom had survived years of abuse to her body. She was not in recovery or clean and sober at this time. She wasn't drinking alcohol, but she was definitely abusing painkillers. Incredibly, though, she remained in good health.

My mom drank heavily before I was born and then stopped for well over a decade during my entire childhood and well into my teen years. When I left for college, she started drinking at night. She was neither mean nor exceptionally happy, just intoxicated and quiet.

Years later she substituted prescription pills for the alcohol. Xanax and painkillers were her choices, and they were readily available from doctors who tossed them out like candy at a parade. The pills made her completely out of it. When she sobered up or got the pills out of her system, she was one of the happiest, most outgoing, and most caring people I've ever known. She had a huge heart, with an especially soft spot for people going through a rough time. I needed her now in my own rough time. Unfortunately, we were losing her in the ambulance we were following.

I could see that the ambulance wasn't "running hot," a term I learned as a journalist. If someone was in critical condition and just starting to knock on heaven's door, they raced to the ER with the lights and sirens blazing. But they weren't going to endanger anyone else's life on the road when their passenger was already dead.

At the hospital we stood in the waiting room decked out in our tuxedos, gowns, suits, and dresses. You'd think we'd just come from a wedding.

During the year of our wedding, Amy and I were living and working in the Fort Myers/Naples area. I was finishing up my stint as a TV news anchor—although I was occasionally confused with the much-better-looking meteorologist, a blond, blue-eyed, California-surfer "weather dude." Amy was the beloved news anchor for the local Fox affiliate. There we were: two local quasi celebrities whose wedding celebrations in ritzy Naples were ending in the emergency room.

We were shown into a tiny room, and a doctor came in with a clipboard. Just over his shoulder, I could see a few empty beds as well as curtains drawn around others. *Please let me see my mom again*, I thought to myself. The doctor kept his head down, fixated on his paperwork, his hands trembling. He began to stammer out, "Uh . . . could you . . . could you . . . tell me who her primary doctor is?" He looked up at everyone and no one. My dad, a type-A personality like I am, started with: "Well, she has been—" But the alpha male in him cut himself off something fierce. "Can you just tell us what the fuck is going on?"

Dead silence.

The doctor put his head back down. "I'm sorry," he said. "She didn't make it. We did everything we could."

Someone screamed. The cries began. As my dad started crying, I kept my composure, knowing someone would need to keep a straight head and figure out what exactly you do when the mother of the groom dies at the wedding. "Can we say goodbye?" I asked.

We slowly walked in and surrounded her bedside. My dad began sobbing, loudly repeating over and over, "You look so beautiful tonight. You look so beautiful." I gripped Amy's hand. While my dad cried and the family sat there in shock, I felt relieved in some small way. It's hard for me to admit this, but I felt *at peace* because for the first time my mother was finally *at peace*. No more struggling with her demons. No more having to worry about letting people down or having to answer for being inebriated the night before. No more struggles. No more pain. Just peace.

That sense of calm quickly turned into a void. When a parent dies, a part of you fades away. I would never hear that warm voice anymore on the other end of the phone or see her face light up when I came to visit.

Only an hour before, my mom and I had had our traditional mother-son wedding dance. Now she was gone. Forever.

In the emergency room, we said our good-byes and began to leave. As we were walking out, a young guy in the ER, unaware of what had happened, gleefully asked, "Hey! Aren't you the weather dude?"

This was my life long before I stood on the national stage in the United States Congress. A life in a giant spotlight with some discreetly managed dark places.

★ 13 ★
SHUT 'EM DOWN

While I was going a little crazy, so was Congress. A shutdown was looming.

As we descend into the depths of the 2013 government shutdown as well as into my own shortcomings, I hope this book has given you some perspective on the way government works (and doesn't) for you. Sure, it only scratches the surface, but this is not a lesson in political science or history.

It's my hope that this book has also refrained from being overly partisan; I've stayed away from regurgitated talking points and pandering punditry. I'm an equal opportunity shot taker. I also don't want to drone on about the positives or negatives of the Affordable Care Act, but Obamacare was *undoubtedly* at the center of the shutdown and the battle over how Republicans wanted to appropriate—or not appropriate—money. The debt ceiling was also a part of this mess. The debt ceiling sets the maximum limit on the sum that a government is allowed to borrow. Compare it to your credit card. Mastercard or Visa tell you the maximum you can spend each month. Congress sets limits for the country as well.

At this time, in 2013, we were sitting at $17 trillion in debt, along with deficits that—no matter what rosy picture someone paints—have no end in sight. And now the only plan or plans with a shot of getting passed are those that do nothing to address our debt, decrease our deficits, or fix the shortcomings of the Affordable Care Act.

While I have taken plenty of shots at Republicans in this book, here's a reality check for most Democrats and some so-called moderate Republicans: Our country is screwed unless someone wakes up, steps up, and actually puts our spending in check, specifically our mandatory spending. Let's take a quick look.

The most basic way to lay out our situation is this: About 60 percent of the federal government's budget is on autopilot, an overwhelming portion of which is dedicated to Medicare, Medicaid, and Social Security. That 60 percent grows every single year and is now threatening to become 70 percent of the budget, maybe more someday. And few people in Congress debate it or even question it.

If left unchecked, the budget threatens programs like Social Security, which you are paying into right now in hopes of having your own safety net when you get older. Furthermore, mandatory spending crowds out all sorts of other things you want from the federal government—money for the military, infrastructure, education, and on and on. *And you can forget about a new post office, Paducah!*

You may hear, and even be frightened by, some Republicans saying, "Cut spending, cut programs, cut everything." But instead of saying, "Cut, cut, cut," they should be saying, "Save, save, save." After all, this is not about cutting at all. Adjustments and tweaks are all about *saving* what you have worked hard for and paid into all of your life—*saving* our Social Security, *saving* our Medicare, and, ultimately, saving our economy.

Almost a year before the shutdown, Texas Senator John Cornyn wrote a piece in the *Houston Chronicle* titled "Obama Must Engage Congress." In it, he argued, "It may be necessary to partially shut down the government in order to secure the long-term fiscal well-being of our country, rather than plod along the path of Greece, Italy, and Spain."

In the simplest terms, Greece *had to take away* their versions of social safety nets from people who had worked and paid into those programs their entire damn lives.

If we don't make even the smallest tweaks now, we're heading down the same path. It's one thing to say "Let's bump up the retirement age" to younger people like me. That's a good tweak for Medicare and Social Security. It's an entirely different situation when you go Greek and tell a sixty-five-year-old who has been working and paying into Social Security and Medicare their entire career, "Sorry, you're just not gonna get everything you were promised and worked for *your whole damn life*."

I believe our country's debt situation is a lot like the housing bubble that decimated our economy years ago: It's right in front of everyone's face, but no one talks about it or even recognizes that it exists.

In Southwest Florida, I witnessed the insanity firsthand.

Almost overnight, bartenders who barely got through high school suddenly became mortgage brokers making hundreds of thousands of dollars. The prototype was a dude in his midtwenties with a faux-hawk haircut (super stylish at that time!), a rock-solid body from hitting the gym every day and taking "supplements" (okay, steroids), and a tribal tattoo on at least one massive biceps that is always visible because his shirts are four sizes too small. This guy could talk your ear off for hours about what a great "deal" you're getting. How big is the home he owns? He doesn't. He never has. But he does drive an all-white Mercedes-AMG convertible with a white interior, oversize rims, and a boomin' system. It's classy enough to be taken seriously but sporty enough to let you know that those 'roids might have had a side effect.

Guys like this made deals for people from all walks of life, from the educated, who knew *exactly* what they were doing, to the downright ignorant. They sold condos, small homes, medium-size ones, and, of course, the big McMansions that are all over Florida cities like Cape Coral, which was ground zero when the cards fell.

These guys would belly up to a bar or, better yet, get a table at the club, and I would listen in absolute amazement as they joked about how they were lending to people who had no business getting a loan *at all*. They'd say things like: "Yo, Trey-Dawg, brah! This guy comes to me with terrible credit and wants a loan. So I says, 'Dawg, yo, you gotta gimme some numbers here. What kind of cheddah you got in the bank, brah?' Then I says, 'Nah, you know what? Just write it down.' T Dawg, they call it 'stated income.' Haha!" Tosses back drink. Flexes biceps as he does. Uses fingertips to make sure the faux hawk is still standing.

Stated. Freaking. Income. People "stated" their income all right. "Okay, here's a one with several zeros behind it. Loan me $300,000." Done. That was called a NINJA loan, which meant no income, no job, and no assets.

How could we not see that the housing market would fail?

How long can we sustain our debt? How long can we keep our government on autopilot without any structural changes until it falls apart?

No one with tribal tats who was a bartender a week ago is running the country (none that I know of, at least, but give it time), but some turn a blind eye or keep perpetuating the system based on self-interest. All of the numbers are there, but not many politicians want to acknowledge or talk about them.

> **We got the bubble-headed-bleach-blonde who comes on at five. She can tell you 'bout the plane crash with a gleam in her eye. It's interesting when people die. Give us dirty laundry.**
>
> ★ Don Henley, "Dirty Laundry"

How often do you hear explanations of our debt and deficits from your local news? Not regularly. It isn't as sexy as a car chase or shark bites. Honestly, would you rather watch a fifteen-minute presentation on the debt-to-GDP ratio or a fifteen-second insane rant by Kanye West at the Grammys? Yeezy, of course!

Just like round-the-clock fund-raising has become a simultaneous full-time job for Congress, making the bottom line is an endless scramble for TV, newspapers, and digital news. For owners and shareholders, the bottom line is profit. For the journalist, the bottom line is producing as much content as fast as humanly possible. *Who cares if it's right or not? You can correct it later.*

Local news is a particularly amazing product to behold when you recognize that newscasts are basically a McDonald's or Target—the same cookie-cutter shapes whether you're in Manhattan, Madison, or Monahans, Texas.

Tune in tonight and you will find a local newscast that mirrors thousands of others across the United States. The "top story," labeled "breaking news," will be either a murder in some neighborhood you've never been to or a car wreck on a road you've never driven on. After that, you'll see some national story "localized," meaning they'll ask your local sheriff what he or she is doing to better prepare against a terror attack like the one in (insert European country here). It's like after 9/11, when library administrators in Des Moines were asked what they were doing to prevent terrorists from striking their building.

After the "localized" stories, you'll get what's called a tease. That's just before the commercial break when the news anchor tells you, "Something in your kitchen you touch every single day is slowly eating your flesh. We'll be right back with that!" Big smile here. Then the meteorologist asks, "Will you need to build the next Noah's ark to escape flooding tomorrow? I'll let you know whether or not you'll drown to death right after we make our salaries and profits for shareholders." And smile.

Then it's time for a commercial break. In between evil

corporations brainwashing you, PACs with unlimited corporate funds, along with the NRCC and DCCC, run ads for candidates, propositions, and referendums.

In order to make sure the commercials don't bump into one another, we get to the next segment of news, called the B block. This block features stuff that means absolutely nothing to you but has "great visuals." The visuals include wildfires out West, tornadoes in the Midwest, flooding in the East, and whatever just happened in the South that the rest of the nation can make fun of. Then you get that weather you're so desperate for.

But wait! There's more! To wrap up, you get what's called the "kicker." The kicker is the happy news the team leaves you with. Think squirrels on water skis or pugs dressed as people. *OMG! How can you not love seeing a pug in a top hat and tuxedo?!* Like the mind eraser Will Smith used in *Men in Black*, your head has just been cleared of all the terrible tragedies you witnessed over the past thirty minutes.

I know this well because it's what I used to do. *I have held some of the most despised, least trusted positions in American society—journalist and politician.*

The digital media outlets have learned they can make a ton of money by paying someone eleventeen years old to grift other news organizations' stories with either a limited number of direct quotes, legally deemed "fair use," or by paraphrasing and not giving credit. Who needs sources when you have the omnipresent, magical Google?

For those consuming news, there's a fascinating catch with the Internet search engines, too. As if the natural inclination to shut out information we don't like isn't bad enough, they do it for us automatically. We are generally averse to digging, re-searching, or learning about things that don't fit what we want to hear. So search engines and apps tailor news and search re-sults to our beliefs and philosophies. Simple calculations of clicks, history, and your preferences determine what news is dished up to you that day.

We end up in echo chambers we have created, surrounded by voices telling us the same narrative over and over, often with no context. When you have a public with no depth, no perspec-tive, and no context, a huge power vacuum is created for polit-ical or corporate interests to fill by stepping in and shifting the conversation as they see fit.

News outlets, online and on cable, have become as polarized as our hyperpartisan Congress. If you lean right, you're not go-ing to tune into Chris Hayes or Rachel Maddow on MSNBC. Lean left? It's highly unlikely you'll watch *Special Report with Bret Baier* on Fox. Politics has boiled down to: From the right, it's "Democrats hate America." From the left, it's "Republicans are a bunch of racists."

Enough of that crap. Let's get back to the good times. The government is close to a shutdown!

Maybe my humor, votes, and actions have given you the impression that I am a "moderate" Republican. I don't think so. In fact, the things I believe in are quintessentially conservative, even if they appear moderate or liberal. I am a Republican who believes that anyone who wants to get married should be able to do so. I think the death penalty should be abolished. I talk about race issues with no qualms and feel the justice system dis-proportionately discriminates against men and women of color.

And even though my taste in music, TV, and film is quintessential liberal shit, I feel it's important to see all sides to a story, all perspectives.

Let there be no question, though. When it comes to fiscal issues, I was absolutely ready and willing to shut the government down.

Remember the "crazies" I talked about? I am one of the "crazies" on fiscal issues.

Whether you agree with the tactic to force, at minimum, a simple *conversation* about the irresponsible, insane spending culture of Washington or want to define me as a Republican "part of the problem," I ask you to consider this: *What some call obstructionism, others call checks, balances, and constituency representation.*

To continue my attack on both sides of the aisle, when it comes to spending, many Democrats won't even recognize the problem, and many Republicans won't budge on the problem. Democrats look at finances with their eyes closed, rarely willing to engage in a conversation. Republicans will talk about it all day long, but it's their way or the highway; there's no compromise, not even among members of the same party.

With little room to negotiate, the only available "compromise" is to kick the can down the road. Washington passes some BS continuing resolution that hands off the problem to the next group of politicians. Or worse, they pass the problem to the same career politicians who have been there for decades, like Collin Peterson, who calls $1 million of your money "modest."

Really, there's no compromise at all. It's not about working out issues; it certainly isn't about solving problems. It's just handing the problems off. It's like passing around mouth herpes:

one Congress has it and then they mouth kiss the incoming Congress while inflamed.

More than like passing around an STD, though, it's like a slow death for our country, which reminds me of a fantastically poetic line from Martin Luther King Jr.'s "I Have a Dream" speech: "This is no time to engage in the luxury of cooling off or to take the tranquilizing drug of gradualism."

We are *gradually* watching our influence and power abroad wane. At home, we are decimating our chances of having a consistently revitalized, reinvented, strong, and vibrant economy. *Tranquilized*, we do nothing as we watch out-of-control spending gradually chip away at investment in our country's infrastructure, actual roads and bridges, and also the infrastructure of our social safety nets.

This is what I was a part of in Congress, and it was disheartening.

The House Republican Conference was in our one thousandth meeting during mid-September in the basement of the Capitol. Leadership is at the front of the room. Rank-and-file members sit in a bunch of seats up front or stand in the back munching on bagels, fruit, or Chick-fil-A, all served with bad coffee.

We had a plan.

Leadership was so excited about the plan that when Eric Cantor and Kevin McCarthy got up to speak each one looked even less psyched than the other. Boehner sat in a chair in front, smoking, his drags even longer than usual. Inhale. McCarthy speaks. Exhale. Cigarette out. *Did he just kill that in one drag?* Cantor speaks.

Their plan—or at least the idea, the semblance, the concept of the plan—was that the House would send to Harry Reid, the Nevada senator and majority leader, a bill to keep the government up and running through the end of the year with a small catch. Seriously, just a tiny provision: to defund the Affordable Care Act. "Hey, maybe Reid won't notice when he signs off on it . . . or the president when it goes to his desk," said no one, as if President Obama, the Democratic president with veto power, was going to allow Republicans to destroy his signature legislation. Oh, and as if Harry Reid would send it to him no questions asked.

Tactically, the idea was to go big and start negotiating from the far right. Harry Reid had other plans.

Reid grew up in Searchlight, Nevada, in a shack with no phone, no indoor toilet, and no hot water. He was an amateur boxer, and his dad, who was a miner, committed suicide when Reid was in his thirties. Harry Reid is a hardened man and plays ball just as hard. Unlike a dice or poker game in his home state's city of Las Vegas, this was more like roulette, a simple bet on black or red, the Republicans or Democrats. Reid bet big on the Democrats.

Before the shutdown, members were tense. Boehner was frustrated. But now I saw for the first time a John Boehner who was beaten down. He had spent the past year dealing with ugly spats between different factions of the Republican Party; and to get a bill passed, he'd have to rely on a majority of the minority—in other words, he'd have to strike a deal with Minority Leader Nancy Pelosi to get enough Democrats on board with a bare minimum of Republicans. That is a no-no for the party in charge. The Speaker first had to do this just days before my group was sworn into Congress. On January 1, 2013, he brought to the floor what was called the American Taxpayer Relief Act of 2012, also known as the fiscal cliff bill. That involved the debt ceiling, too.

The "cliff" is one that members walk themselves up to almost every year. Some even threaten to jump off. The huge hypocritical catch is that the only people who threaten to *not* raise the debt ceiling and jump off the fiscal cliff are the members of the party who do *not* have control of the White House. So, during President George W. Bush's term, Republicans raised the debt ceiling like it was nothing more than a technicality, as easy as naming a post office in Paducah. As for Democrats, look no further than President Obama, who, as a U.S. senator during Bush's tenure, said the debt ceiling was "a sign of leadership failure" and that "Washington is shifting the burden of bad choices today onto the backs of our children and grandchildren."

Yet, somehow, a deal is usually worked out under Democratic and Republican presidents alike. Everyone rejoices! The members are saved; so is the country! Saved for at least another few months until Congress once again peers over the edge of the cliff they created.

Even though that last fiscal cliff bill had passed at the beginning of 2013, here we were at the end of September approaching an October deadline. And President Obama, along with almost every other Democrat, demanded the debt ceiling be raised with no questions asked and no political games attached.

Many House Republicans thought the debt ceiling was

leverage they could use to dismantle or delay Obamacare. And John Boehner and the rest of leadership told members that they were there to stick it out.

Deep into our 2,128th meeting about how we'd finally get rid of Obamacare once and for all, the gatherings felt more and more like the church scene out of Mel Brooks's *Blazing Saddles.* "Defunding Obamacare is the right thing to do!" "Yeah, Olson Johnson is right. What kind of people are we anyhow? I say defund!" "*Ag guh blah blurb burb,*" says the frontier congressman from some mountain state out West. Eyebrows are raised. Heads are cocked. Someone chimes in, "Dr. Samuel Johnson's right about Olson Johnson being right. And I'm not giving up my ice cream parlor that I built with these two hands for nothing or nobody. Let's defund Obamacare!" Everyone cheers and shoots into the air with their guns they bought with NRA contributions to their campaign!

But like the characters Cleavon Little and Gene Wilder played, President Obama and Senator Reid would *own the town* and *win over* the hearts and minds of the American public on this issue.

We passed that bill defunding Obamacare. Reid got it. And he accepted it! *Nice!* Except he crossed out that little part defunding Obamacare and sent it right back to the House. *Oh, not nice!*

Call another meeting!

In the last weeks of September 2013, meeting number 31,522 takes place. Now we have a really brilliant idea: We'll change our demands from defunding Obamacare, and we'll delay the implementation of the ACA for a year and—interesting catch here—we'll repeal the tax on medical devices.

Once again, while I paint the silliness of the House Republican Conference meetings, allow me to show you some of the Democratic members' positions.

Republicans picked the medical device tax issue because some Democrats were also adamant about repealing it. Take the liberal—some would say far-left—Senator Elizabeth Warren of Massachusetts. She supports Obamacare. However, she does not support the punitive—and, by the way, seemingly random—tax on medical devices. It just so happens that Massachusetts has quite a few medical device manufacturers. This tax was not received well by those companies, their employees, or CEOs (who maybe, possibly, were also campaign donors).

Everyone has their "thing." Some could call Warren a hypocrite for picking and choosing what she supports, but the reality is that she is a senator *representing* a state and doing what the people elected her to do—*represent* their interests. And taxing the hell out of an industry based in Massachusetts, which provides solid, high-paying jobs, is not in the interest of her state. This is Congress. In some ways, it is, in fact, compromise.

With October drawing near, House Republicans passed the bill to delay ACA for a year and repeal the tax on medical devices.

Reid didn't budge. Didn't do a thing.

More *Blazing Saddles* meetings. "Okay, boys, now we've got it. Let's delay the individual mandate for a year!" Then members were sent out with marching orders to sell this next move to the press and the people.

The bills, the messaging, the attempted negotiations were all thought out by leadership, staff, and advisors to implement a winning strategy and make Harry Reid and the Senate come to the table. But how can you negotiate with someone who won't even talk to you? Thinking we would make Harry look bad, the messaging among House Republicans was: "It's the Harry Reid Senate that's not compromising! It's them!" Point finger really hard!

While House Republicans kept pointing the finger at the Senate, the public pointed the finger (first the pointer, then the middle) at one party—the Republicans, specifically in the House, who were "holding the country hostage!"

Why? Blame the mainstream media. Blame an out-of-touch public. Blame an in-touch public. Blame the messaging. Blame Republicans. Blame Democrats. Reid stood firm. The man didn't budge. He placed his bet and stuck to it.

When October 1 hits, we're at the cliff, staring down into an abyss.

The government goes into a partial shutdown. Most of the country wouldn't have even noticed except that the twenty-four-hour cable news networks talked about it every minute of the day, complete with big clocks adorning their screens like a New Year's Eve countdown clock. The only thing missing on CNN was Kathy Griffin, but you bet Anderson Cooper was there! Once the shutdown hit, the clocks were replaced with ones that ticked down every second the government remained closed.

In our 1,240,105th meeting, Speaker Boehner wrapped up a few final details on where we were and where we were heading, which is to say in every direction and nowhere. The Speaker finished by saying, "I will ride this out to the end with you. But just know, it may not be pretty." A visual memory I still carry with me from all of these meetings is of Matt Salmon, a hard-core conservative from Arizona, standing up, looking out at everyone, and saying, "Speaker Boehner, I know I speak for many here when I say thank you. Thank you for sticking with us through this." They shook hands, and Boehner looked visibly uncomfortable. Cantor and McCarthy stood nearby like assistants to Dr. Kevorkian ready to administer the final drugs.

When the shutdown hit, everyone was ordered to stay in D.C. and be ready at a moment's notice for votes. We had no idea when we would have to report back to the Capitol to get back to work. We were told day after day that we might have votes.

Caught in the middle of this were the more than 800,000 federal workers who were put on furlough. Only so-called essential workers stayed. The rest were told to "pack up and go home, you nonessential schlubs!"

Things got eerily quiet on the Hill. Republicans began putting together random pieces of legislation. We approved things like opening national parks and museums, funding FEMA, and even trying to get the Head Start program back up and running, which funds and helps low-income children and their families with everything from education to health and nutrition.

Reid ignored everything.

Meetings with us rank-and-file members dropped off. We sat in limbo while high-profile meetings between House leadership and the president were underway.

Just like at orientation, Congress became college again, although under the radar. The weekend rolled around. No spouses

were in town because the schedule was so unpredictable. Everyone headed to a bar to watch Sunday football, but not Democrats and Republicans together.

I now found myself away from my wife and child for even
longer stretches. I certainly wasn't out at the clubs, but I was
out—a lot. Two years of stress was coming to a head—the campaign, the time in Congress, the shutdown, a long-distance relationship, and a newborn. I was drowning it all out by
socializing, drinking, working insane hours, and not thinking
about anything or, unfortunately, anyone . . . except myself.

As Speaker Boehner and his team headed to the White House
for more meetings, the rank-and-file members headed out to
people's homes and, occasionally, bars. If people were out, they
were sporting ball caps and T-shirts, no suits or nifty pins identifying them as members of Congress. During the shutdown,
there were absolutely no fund-raisers or political events.

Boehner eventually relented. He did what he had to do. It was
again time to grab a minority of the majority, strike a deal, and
get enough votes to pass the bill to reopen the government. The
deal was essentially crafted the day before by Mitch McConnell,
the Senate minority leader from Kentucky, and Harry Reid.

Insert the *Price Is Right* loser horn here.

Earlier, I used the cliché "kicking the can down the road."
Senator Mitch McConnell and Reid's "deal" barely kicked the
can a few feet. The deal was this: Reid and McConnell said,
"Hey, let's get our butts home for the holidays and take this up
early next year when we get back. Good? Good! Deal? Deal!"
Shake hands and take a steamy dump on the taxpayer. *They
extended the exact same situation by a few months. What kind of a deal*

is that? Some in Congress, not I, voted to reopen the government and extend the debt limit to February. *That was the deal.*

The whole sloppy and exhausting process from September through October was coming to an end. But only after one last twist that almost had me fearing I was going to get shot on the House floor.

It was—*I have no idea*—o'clock at night. It was late. And Congress was all back in the Capitol on the House floor to take the final vote to reopen the government. I was right in the well just off the Speaker's rostrum, standing near the first row of seats. Adam Kinzinger was standing on my right. He had just finished casting his vote. I looked over, and said, "What a ride, man."

He shook his head in amazement. "I know. I know." We were both exhausted.

I was just about to ask, *What are you doing after this?* Because, of course, the only thing that made sense was to go out for a drink after this madness.

All of a sudden, I heard a woman's voice almost screaming, "He will not be mocked! He will not be mocked!" I looked up and saw this stranger talking into the microphone just below the Speaker's spot. The presiding member on the floor that night was Ileana Ros-Lehtinen, a friend, a fellow Floridian, and a fiery Cuban American. Ily, as friends called her, looked down in confusion. The seemingly crazy woman ranted on. "The greatest deception here is this is not one nation under God." I thought, *Oh, no, she's going to open fire!* Ily slammed down the gavel and yelled, "Order! Order!"

I quickly looked around to find a place to take cover. The woman was screaming, "It never was. Had it been, it would not have been!" I was certain she was going to pull out a gun and shoot into the sea of people on the floor. Just as I was about to bolt out, she was grabbed and dragged off the floor. "What the hell?" I asked Adam. "How can someone like that get past security? Any one of us could be attacked, even killed!"

Adam's mouth was wide open as he gazed at the woman, who continued shouting from the hallway as she was dragged out. Adam shook his head, as amazed by this as he was by the shutdown. He then looked me directly in the eyes, and said, "No. That woman works here!"

She was a government employee who worked on the House Floor. Just like every member of Congress—she, too, had lost her mind.

It was the perfectly insane ending for this period of insanity.

★14★
BEEN DOWN TOO LONG

The government was open again. Things were getting back to normal—as in Congress was still barely functioning and I was still going out too often and too late.

The afternoon of October 29, 2013, I was on the House floor. I have no idea what we were doing or voting on, but Kevin McCarthy invited me out to a dinner he was hosting.

"Yeah, man. I would love to!"

"Let's meet in my office later."

During the past several months, Kevin had taken me under his wing and offered to mentor me. I would check in with him from time to time, and we'd meet for coffee, grab a beer, or just talk on the floor. An athlete, he'd also invited me to go on the early-morning bike rides he took with a few members. I went on those as often as I visited Paul Ryan's P90X workouts. Never. Kevin laughed it off.

I sometimes found that the unbridled aspirations of some people in leadership roles warped their personalities. They rarely talked about anything except policy, politics, and fundraising. Kevin was not that way at all. I could bounce around conversations with him on sports, music, and more. He was a down-to-earth guy who always had a smile and was always there with helpful advice and thoughts.

The evening's dinner was set for a couple of hours after votes. After wrapping my day at the office, instead of heading home to Dupont, where a fridge full of empty random condiment bottles and a days-old pizza box awaited me, I headed over to a favorite spot on the Hill, Bullfeathers, where I had a few beers with friends.

Two or so hours later, I met Kevin at his office in the Capitol. While he was working the phone, I cracked open a beer someone had left in one of the office refrigerators.

Kevin hung up. I grabbed a football he had in the office and began tossing it back and forth with him. "Where we headed?" I asked.

"Ruth's Chris," he replied, as he tossed the ball back. "There should be about twenty or so people, all good connections, all helpful."

Kevin's rise to the whip position, the number three spot within leadership, was one of the fastest in Congress. From his time in the California state legislature to his stint in Washington, Kevin's ability to connect with people set him apart. With a touch of Paul Ryan's wonkiness and a dash of Eric Cantor's intense focus, Kevin had a personality that was uniquely his. He may have been a Californian, but he struck me as a Chicagoan—

hard enough to know, soft enough to be a midwesterner, and a genuinely nice guy.

Like hanging out with John Boehner, rolling with McCarthy meant we would be shuttled around in an armored SUV. He had a smaller security detail than Cantor and Boehner, but a detail nonetheless. We wouldn't be ripping down roads at one hundred miles an hour with anyone inhaling massive drags off of cigarettes, but we'd roll up in style with at least one guy armed to the teeth.

We exited out of the east side of the Capitol and quickly shuffled down the steps into the waiting car.

Kevin hopped in the back with me. We were situated in the exact same seats that John Boehner and I had sat in on our way to the Naples fund-raiser we held exactly one year and twenty-seven days earlier. I was behind the driver; Kevin was behind the passenger's seat. As we rolled out of the Capitol parking lot, I asked, "Anything I need to know before tonight?" in case I'd be called on to give an impromptu speech.

"No," he said, peering out the window, his mind somewhere else. Then he looked over at me with a smile and shrugged his shoulders, saying, "At these things, I just like to get to know people."

From past events, I knew the always-playful McCarthy would do an "around the room" question. For example: "What was the first concert you ever went to?" It was cheesy but fun. Unlike members who held people hostage with lectures about "the punitive damage of Obama's executive actions," Kevin always said, "Trey, it's not always about the policy or their ask. Most of the time, whether it's a mayor of a city in your district or a Washington lobbyist, they just want to get to know you and know you'll listen."

When we got to Ruth's Chris, a red flag popped up in my head; it was one, like so many others, I would ignore. The server brought me my choice of poison before I had to ask. "Sir, your Ketel One, soda, two limes." Having done a few events at Ruth's Chris, I had gotten to know a few guys on the waitstaff. Many were from Latin America, and with a few cocktails in me, I loved to talk with them *en español*. We'd talk about home, whether it was Costa Rica or Puerto Rico, and always about food, from *gallo pinto* to *arroz con gandules*. They'd formally address me in English and Spanish, "Congressman" or "Señor." I'd always stop them. But since "Trey" is nearly impossible to pronounce for a native Spanish speaker, I told them to just call me "TropiGringo." They obliged with a laugh.

While I talked with Kevin and the others, the waiters would bring me another cocktail without asking. I blatantly ignored the fact I was basically being fed vodka through an IV and passed it off as "networking," you know, just being out and "getting to know people."

McCarthy's group assembled in a private dining area. The large table was arranged as a square so everyone faced one another. In a standard operating procedure, Kevin sat in one section and I sat in another to give more "exposure" to the two members in attendance. God, we're cheesy.

Kevin first went around the room, asking, "What was your first concert?" and "What is your most embarrassing moment?" Almost a dozen people shared stories; so did I.

After beers on the Hill and a few cocktails at the restaurant, I was in an exceptionally gregarious mood. I let loose with the most embarrassing moment of my life (for the next few hours, at least). Here we go.

"So I'm in the second grade, Mrs. Berninger's class at Our Lady of Lourdes school in Cincinnati, Ohio. This was a Catholic school, so pretty prim and proper. We were in the middle of some sort of test. I'm sure it was something critical like handwriting or whatever you do at seven years old. I had to go to the bathroom, and so I raised my hand." I paused.

"But Mrs. Berninger had her head down. She was reading and deep into whatever it was. Now, even though I was only a kid, I was thinking some profound thoughts to myself, like 'Try the clear-your-throat move.' So I did. 'A-hem!' I let out in my deepest, loudest, most booming prepubescent voice. Then I started freaking out. *Oh no, I'm gonna pee. No. Don't do it.* 'A-HEM!' I tried even louder.

"Then I had the most brilliant, thoroughly logical thought, *I'll just let out a little bit of pee to feel better.* My logic went even a step further. I thought, *Just a* little, little bit *will soak into my underwear, I'll be fine. No one will see it.* I let it unleash, still keeping my hand in the air. 'Ahhh!' It felt *soooo* good, but then I looked down.

"*Oh no!* A small puddle underneath me was turning into a huge lake. *No, this can't be happening!* Then, *still* looking down, with my hand *still* raised in the air, I heard, 'Trey?' I jerked my head up. In a total panic, all I could get out was 'Um, um, I had an accident.' Mrs. Berninger stood up from behind her desk to walk toward me, and even though I was in the back of the room, she could see that a brand-new Great Lake had just been created underneath me. Her eyes got huge as she slowed her pace toward me. But then things got worse! The girl in front of me, Carrie, turned around and screamed like she had just seen someone murdered with a blunt object. 'Ahhhhh!' She then started crying. Carrie was screaming and bawling with her tears dropping into my puddle of piss. Mrs. Berninger walked over quickly and tried to calm us both, 'It's okay. We have these accidents sometimes, Trey.'"

The crowd at Ruth's Chris was laughing hard. So was I. I hadn't thought of or told that story in a long time. Then I added, "But that wasn't it!"

"Mrs. Berninger and I left the classroom and went to a nearby office. By this time, I was crying, I was so upset. She called my mom and asked her to bring in new clothes. I aggressively reached for the phone and piped up, 'Can I speak to my mom?' As an embarrassed little seven-year-old, I begged my mom, 'Mom, just please don't bring my Hulk Underoos!'"

We had a lot of laughs that night. I was also in rare form. I had been drinking fairly heavily the past few months, but this was exceptional—beers after work, several nearly straight vodkas before and after dinner, and some wine with my steak drowned in Ruth's Chris butter. While dinner was fun and I made great "connections" who would be "helpful," I was the member of Congress who had just told a story about pissing himself. Even if I was only seven at the time, maybe, just maybe, it was a little much.

We wrapped up. Everyone left. Not me. I went back into

Ruth's Chris bar to have another drink and call John. We hadn't hung out since before the shutdown. He talked up everything from a "new friend" to a bizarre event he said was "a high-heel drag queen race near Dupont."

"Uh, okay," I said, almost in the form of a question.

He said, "Drag queens get together before Halloween and run down Seventeenth Street in high heels. It's a traditional race. It is hilarious, and it's a huge party!" This event is apparently very popular in the diverse neighborhoods of Washington.

"All right, man! When the going gets weird, the weird turn pro!"

I finished my drink and had another for good measure. I texted John, "Let's meet at Circa." Circa was my go-to meeting spot that had great food, drinks, and friendly bartenders. I called an Uber and headed north.

At Circa I spotted a few open seats at the bar, which was rare even on a Tuesday. "Ketel One, soda, two limes." Killed it. Just as I ordered another, John came in and ordered a Johnnie Walker Black, rocks. While we chatted, he kept saying, "You've got to meet my friend; he has the best shit." He seemed wired; maybe he'd already met his "friend" and gotten his "shit." But John often had "friends" who were always carrying, so this didn't strike me as odd.

His friend rolled in. Deep into multiple drinks with my logic and sound judgment long gone, I lost every street smart I had ever picked up in Chicago or the roughest parts of Cambodia.

As we made typical "guy talk" about sports, things veered off into the strange. We made off-color jokes, and the friend pushed hard to hang out with us and bring his friends. I chalked it up to "This dude is a dealer, must be lonely and have issues." *Certainly not me! I don't have issues!* I kept it informal. "Hey, John and I might head back to my place. If you want to swing by for a cocktail with friends, cool."

Then, as the conversation continued, I bought cocaine from him for some reason. Me. Not John. Me, the United States congressman sometimes referred to as Representative Radel and occasionally called the Honorable on paper. I bought it.

To this day I have no idea why. Sober Trey has a million questions for drunk Trey. *Why were you even doing this? Why did you buy it? How did you get that out of control?*

All those words I had heard throughout my life came back to haunt me: "Total disregard. Cavalier. What the hell were you thinking?"

I don't have answers because there are no answers. I was out of control, deep in a behavior and pattern of *total disregard*. I was *cavalier*. I was *not thinking*.

We headed north on Connecticut Avenue. The "friend" split to "go meet his friends." John and I walked away. As we took a right on R Street, I heard, "Trey! Hey, Trey!" They probably knew better than to say the word "Congressman." I would not have responded to that. I turned around with a smile on my face, as if to say, *Hey, more friends to hang with!*

Then came the horrifying words "Trey, FBI, stay calm." Several men, though it felt like thousands, swiftly swarmed me from the back and flashed their IDs.

Hilariously, I tossed the bag, as if the thousands of men next to me and the millions of others now approaching from the other side of the street wouldn't anticipate that awesomely smooth move. "This yours?" an agent asked, picking it up. The agent who had called out my name was now at my right. He stepped directly in front of me, looked me in the eyes, and said, "Trey, your life is about to change."

Understatement of a lifetime.

My world began collapsing. I felt my legs get weak, and I noticed dozens of pedestrians staring at me. I looked at the FBI agents, and said, almost as if they were my drinking buddies, "Let's just head to my apartment." With my heart racing and my breathing getting faster and lighter, I said, "My place is right around the corner." But, uh, I'm pretty certain they knew where I lived.

We went to my apartment. As my world continued imploding and a few tears streamed down my face, an agent asked, "Are you going to be okay?" I knew what he meant. He was asking if I was going to hurt myself. I assured them that I was okay, adding, "I have been living recklessly. I knew what I was doing was illegal. I just didn't care." That was true. Regardless of my libertarian opinion on the ill-fated War on Drugs, my bullshit was just that: a load of crap. What I was doing was breaking the law, and I was—of all things—a lawmaker.

I've been to all sorts of rough places, even been held up at gunpoint, yet I've never had a scratch. My street smarts always kept me safe, whether it was knowing what kind of a stern look to keep on my face while walking through a dangerous neighborhood or knowing who and who *not* to talk to. But I had let John and his "friends" into my inner circle. And just as I let my guard down, the FBI got to John.

John was the one who had set me up.

The reason, as the FBI agents explained, was very simple: "We heard a congressman was buying drugs, and we were compelled to investigate." Understandable. However, I do not know how they got to John or what they had on him. I don't care. We never spoke again. I don't blame him or carry any feelings of anger or hatred. I was the idiot. Not John.

★ 15 ★
RIVER OF DECEIT

Here's what should have happened the next day: First thing that morning I should have called Amy and my father and confessed everything. I should have then walked directly into Speaker Boehner's office and handed in my resignation. But that would have required clear thinking, which was not part of the equation.

In the thickest haze imaginable, I got up and, *unbelievably*, I went to work. I walked into 1123 Longworth without greeting anyone and sat in my office without turning on a computer or the TV. I didn't even check news or e-mail on my phone, which I usually did incessantly. Noises from the adjoining offices only temporarily snapped me out of my mental fog. If I was a robot before, I was now some sort of a hollowed-out machine that had only a few directives: avoid human contact when possible; if in a serious conversation, nod head and smile only if appropriate.

For two days I shuffled from one point to another and carried out my regular responsibilities as a congressman, but physically and mentally, I was not all there. Forty-eight dreamlike hours later, I followed my schedule and flew back to Fort Myers. The plane touched down. I went home. I talked to my wife. She knew something was up. She kept asking, "What's wrong?" Like an ass, I pulled back instead of opening up. I remained in robot mode. I asked about Jude's second Halloween and what costumes we would wear. I smiled. I floated. We talked about some issue with our cable bill. The robot in me recalculated. *Serious. Don't smile. Nod head.* I then told Amy that I had to "head to some meetings soon." I had no meetings; I had to make a call.

An hour later I was sitting in my car on a side street in Fort Myers, away from my family, away from my house, talking to my longtime friend and attorney, Laird Lile. As I barely held back tears, my first words to him were "I screwed up, man. I really screwed up."

In a calm tone, he asked, "Trey, are you okay? What's going on?"

"In the last few months, I got out of control."

As I explained what happened, Laird kept his cool. "Okay. Have you contacted an attorney in D.C.?"

"No. You're the first person I'm calling." The tears were getting harder to fight back.

"Okay. Give me a day to make a few calls and ask my colleagues who would be the best criminal defense attorney there."

When I heard the words "criminal defense," the tears and emotion suddenly shut off and an entirely new level of panic hit me. My mind started racing with thoughts and questions about my family, my job, what was going to happen publicly. As Laird started talking about "checking with other attorneys," I checked completely out of the conversation, overloaded with thoughts of getting beat up in prison because I was a congressman. A Republican one at that! *My God, I'm gonna get killed. I need to get tatted up before I go in. I need to join a gang and get protection. I need to learn how to make a shank out of a toothbrush. I need to—*

"Trey? Trey?" Laird interrupted my thoughts. I snapped out of it. "Yeah, make the calls. I'll be at home practicing how to smuggle razorblades in my mouth."

I celebrated Halloween with my family, smiling when appropriate and limiting my words to "trick or treat." That weekend I also had the distinct pleasure of celebrating my cousin's wedding. Ever so slightly sliding out of robot mode, I made a pact with myself: *I'm going to drink my ass off and dance my ass off at that wedding and then, that's it! I am done. I quit drinking!*

I made good on my promise, drinking enough at the wedding to eliminate my pending thoughts of doom. I also tore up the dance floor. I got "low" to Lil Jon with my wife and was *caliente* as hell dancing salsa to Sonora Carruseles's "Micaela" with my cousin's new Colombian in-laws. No one had a clue what was happening or any idea of just how close I was to imploding. *Classy.*

The next morning I woke up with a bit of a hangover, but I was prepared to face a harsh future without IPAs or Ketel Ones. Laird called. I left the house to "run errands" and take his call.

"David Schertler is your guy," he told me. "We have a call set up with him on Monday."

I hung up and immediately called Pusateri. It was the first

time I had spoken to him since my arrest, but, of course, I didn't share a thing. "Matt," I said. I didn't even use "man." "Clear my entire schedule Monday. I have some personal issues I have to deal with."

On Monday I went to Laird's office in Naples. He hugged me, then pulled back, locked eyes with me, and asked, "Are you okay?" I could see sadness in his eyes. While Laird was a close friend and an attorney, he was also my constituent.

"Yeah, yeah, I'm good. I just want to know what happens next," I said, in a soft whisper.

"Trey, you're going to be okay. David will be on the phone with us soon."

A few minutes later the speakerphone rang. It was David. Firm but compassionate, he said, "Hi, Trey. I know this is incredibly difficult for you, but it's good to meet you by phone. I want you to know that I'm here to help. We will be able to walk you through this step by step. And before we even start, I also want you to know that we have some good news for you."

Trying to sound cheerful, I said, "I'll take it where I can get it."

"Well, what you've been arrested for is a misdemeanor in Washington, D.C. The maximum penalty is jail time, but you have no record. You've never been arrested. I have dealt with these kinds of cases often. They're quite common, and the common resolution is probation."

Images of shanks, gang tattoos, and other crazy things started fading slightly in my mind.

"There are a few things I would suggest. Get help. We'll let the court know you have a problem. You have a disease and need help. You can seek treatment. I think the court will look favorably on your beginning a treatment program right now. Plus, we will work out a longer recovery program once you plea."

My numb shell of being an unemotional machine started to get pierced with sadness. As David said words like "disease" and "treatment," I thought about my mom. *My God, am I an alcoholic? Am I a drug addict?* I started to feel nauseous. My mind was all over the place. I thought, *You need to get ahold of yourself. You have been out of control, a cavalier jerk not thinking at all, ever. And whether or not you're an alcoholic, the only way you'll get through this is by letting the world know just that. Trey, you are an alcoholic. This is a disease.*

As the word "disease" echoed in my head, survival mode kicked in. I took over the situation and approached the crisis as if it were another political campaign. *Boom!* Back in robot mode. I paced back and forth as I formed "a plan," except I wasn't in my living room running a bootstrap operation, I was in my attorney's office handling my arrest—*as a sitting U.S. congressman.* I began ranting, "Okay, we'll need to figure out how to handle this publicly. We'll need a press release, statements, all of the things that come along with this."

David stopped me. "Trey?"

"Yes?"

"You're not going to resign?" His tone suggested that what he really wanted to say was *What the hell are you thinking, man? You should seriously consider stepping down.*

I stopped pacing. Once again I had an opportunity to think straight for a second. That second passed.

"No. I'm going to stick this out. I love what I do. I never let my faults or vices get in the way of work. I made a terrible, terrible mistake, but I"—I paused as a slight touch of panic hit me—"I have a disease. I'll get the help I need. Maybe I can draw attention to this and be some sort of a positive role model."

I have no idea what I was thinking while I said this. Whoever the hell I thought I was to talk about being a role model is beyond me. But I was grasping at every possibility to keep my career and myself afloat.

Then my more devious side spoke up. "David, my name is Trey Radel. Everyone knows me by that. But my legal name is Henry Radel, which will appear on all the records, right? Is there a chance the press might not pick this up?" David paused, and for two seconds I felt a ray of sunshine beam down on me and heard a choir of angels sing in unison, "Ahhhh!" I thought, *Whoa! Is that possible? Everyone will miss this because no one will read a court docket and know who Henry is! Ha! Yes! Thank you, Mom and Dad, for naming me a third and calling me Trey! Thank you!*

David interrupted the angel choir in my head. "Well, it's possible, Trey, but highly unlikely. The people in the courts are always on the lookout, and they are always talking to the press. You're a high-profile figure. They're gonna know. Someone is bound to leak it."

I still prayed for it to fly under the radar.

"Trey, at this point I'll make some calls and see where we stand. This may take days, even weeks, before we get to a hearing. In the meantime, don't talk to any press or colleagues. If you decide to, talk to me first. But for now allow me to see where things stand before anything goes public."

Like an absolute ass, like a complete moron, I kept everything to myself. I don't know what I was thinking. I didn't tell Amy or anyone in my family. Sometimes I prayed the whole episode would miraculously disappear, or I hoped some sort of deal or plea would be struck and it would stay out of the press. All of these notions, in retrospect, were incredibly naïve. No, worse. They were willfully ignorant.

Robot mode kicked in once again. I went back to being a congressman. "Aaaand we're back." *Insert smile.* I worked social media. I went to political meetings. I gave speeches and even held fund-raisers! *Serious face.* "Here to fight for our country . . . fight for your children and your grandchildren!" Every time I spoke, I was in this weird dreamlike, automated state. *Be compelling.* "Must make the right choices, not the easy ones, the right ones!" I took questions. I asked questions. *Nod head in interest.* "Oh really? You have a solution to our debt crisis?"

I'd go from feeling numb to being overcome by intense bouts of depression. When the darkest of dark thoughts crossed my mind, I'd zone out by playing with my son, feeling both incredibly blessed and damned to hell at the same time as we rolled Hot Wheels across the floor.

The next Monday rolled around. Matt and I drove up to Tampa for a briefing with local officials on the city's port. I have no idea what we talked about in the two-hour car ride. Robot: "Yes." *Smile.* "No." *Tilt head in concern.* "Hmmm." *Act as if you care.*

Our schedule included a tour from the water, and just as the boat was pulling up, my phone rang. It was David Schertler.

I got nauseous.

I walked quickly away from our group and answered.

"Trey, I have bad news." As David said those words, I heard a touch of panic in his voice for the first time. *More nausea.*

My knees got weak. I let out a breath and put my head down. My mouth dried up. "Okay," I said, my voice cracking. My knees got weaker. I felt numb.

David spoke firmly and clearly. "They're ready to do this now, and it's on their schedule and their terms. They're agreeing to the plea deal we talked about—probation." His words were no longer compassionate, they were firm. He was in legal mode and had to get these details to sink into my thick head. "Ultimately, it will be up to the judge to decide the sentence. But they want you here in D.C. to go to court Wednesday morning. Two days." Then he paused. "Trey," he said, in a hushed voice. *May vomit.* "Trey, if you haven't already told them, you need to let your family and staff know now."

With Matt and the rest of the group standing nearby, I walked farther away in case I puked. I hung up, took a deep breath, walked back over to our group, and said, "Family emergency, I have to leave right now."

The waiting phase was over. It was time to face the proverbial music. So cue up *Donnie Darko*'s depressing "Mad World" because all I wanted was to "drown my sorrow" and "pray for no tomorrow."

I spent the next twelve hours breaking the news to Amy and her parents, my father, my uncles and aunts, cousins, and close friends. I cried. Then I cried more, thinking about the crisis I was about to send crashing down on my family.

The storm was just beginning. I thought I knew how much of a circus this would be.

I did not.

Once again, enter John Boehner.

=★16★=
UNFINISHED SYMPATHY

'm sitting across from Boehner in the Speaker's private office in
the Capitol. He's staring at me, suit jacket off, one leg crossed
over the other. He is not taking drags from a cigarette. He's not
smoking at all. He's just looking at me with his piercing blue eyes.

I start. "Mr. Speaker, I'm so sorry." A tear began to stream
down my face. I put my head in my hands. I didn't need to say
anything. He knew it all.

Fifteen minutes before this meeting, I was sitting in a car
outside the Capitol with Dave, my chief of staff. He'd been in
the job for only a few months, but he'd become a friend, and
now I had handed him a mountain of crap to deal with. *Good
call on joining our team, Dave!* His reaction was measured. "You
need to tell the Speaker in person—now. I'll call his office.
We'll set up an emergency meeting. No details. Just get you in
there with him right away."

As I was about to head up to the Speaker's office, Dave's

phone started buzzing while we were sitting in his car. Jake Sherman from *Politico*, a reporter I had grown to respect as thorough and aggressive, was blowing up Dave's phone. A rarity for reporters, Jake actually picked up the phone, sent texts, and e-mailed us looking for a response to what he had just learned. A source had apparently leaked to him the news that I was heading to court the next day to face charges, and he was offering us a chance to respond before he ran the story.

We did not.

Determined to have the Speaker hear it from me first, I bolted out of the car in a full sprint for his office to tell him the news before it broke.

Ready. Set. Go!

I broke quickly for the Capitol steps as if I were running the forty-yard dash for high school football. I hit the first steps and shot up them, leaping two and three at a time with my suit jacket blowing like Superman's cape behind me. When I was inside, I turned a corner so fast my shoes slipped on the floor. My feet caught back up under me. I hit full stride in an all-out sprint for the Speaker's office.

In the mad dash through the Capitol, my phone vibrated. Breathing hard, I pulled it out and looked down. It was a text from Dave. "Speaker's office knows."

"Noooo!" I said out loud. I slowed down as another text came through. It was a screenshot of *Politico*'s webpage. The headline read, "Rep. Trey Radel Faces Cocaine Charge." And under my picture, the caption read, "Radel, a tea party favorite in Florida, was sworn into Congress in January." Another damn tea party wacko!

When I got to the doorway of the Speaker's office, his staff turned to look at me. Some of their eyes lit up. *Oh, God, there he is!* Others tilted their heads and blinked like sad puppies.

I couldn't help but reflect on what a special place his office was for me; I was desperate to grasp at any sense of comfort. Many things that adorned the walls reminded me of where I grew up. The Cincinnati Bengals pictures brought back memories of football games with my family. The Reds paraphernalia reminded me of watching TV with my mom and dad when Pete Rose broke Ty Cobb's record for hits.

The Speaker and I had grown closer over the previous months. I occasionally visited his office with other members to talk strategy and policy. Sometimes I'd head to his office before an event to catch up and then grab a ride with him.

Hanging with Boehner was quite the experience. I would wait in the hallway outside of his office checking my e-mail and making calls. Boehner would swing around the corner, full entourage in tow, a cigarette blazing in his mouth with smoke blowing past his face, which made him look like one of those long dragster race cars. It was a scene straight out of a movie. All he needed to do was walk in slo mo. "Radel!" he would yell in his raspy, cigarette-stained voice as he gave me a nod. Then the best part: Like a handoff in the NFL from a quarterback to a running back, a young assistant would pop up from behind a desk and hand Boehner his glass of wine as the Speaker turned left to swing into his office. Never breaking stride, he'd smoothly take it out of her hand and give her a wink. I wanted to yell, "Da-yum!"

When I was sworn in, there were two other members from

Cincinnati who also went to Catholic high schools: Steve Chabot, who went to La Salle, and Brad Wenstrup, who graduated from St. Xavier. We were all part of what's called the Greater Catholic League, or GCL, and were rivals in sports.

One day all four of us took pictures together on the Speaker's balcony, which overlooked the Washington Monument. All four of us wore ties with our alma maters' colors. Speaker Boehner broke out his blue and gold. I pulled out my purple. Wenstrup had his royal blue and white. Chabot sported his scarlet and white. It was a touching moment. The *Cincinnati Enquirer* printed it—*in black-and-freakin'-white.*

As I walked into the Speaker's office, I thought to myself, *This is it. Those are the last fun memories I'll have of John Boehner or this office.*

Our meeting was quick, neither cold nor warm, neither compassionate nor sympathetic. I apologized and put my head in my hands, and the Speaker made it painless. His words were simple. "Go home, check into a program, and get well." I was shocked at how quick and easy it was, and that is the last time I'll use the word "easy" to describe anything in this process.

As I walked out, I glanced at the Ohio decorations again and thought about my dad in Cincinnati. I had tried my best to prepare him for the media onslaught, saying, "Dad, the phone will ring, reporters will show up at work and at your home, just please avoid them and don't talk to them."

If you want to know just how fast media outlets pick up a story, allow me to be the test case. Less than ten minutes after Jake Sherman at *Politico* broke the story, it had spread around the world. Political reporters from Florida, D.C., and New York, some of whom I knew personally, were bombarding my personal phone with calls and texts. "Is this true? Can you talk? Confirm? You need to comment!"

Even the famous Savannah Guthrie from NBC was hounding me. She texted: "Hi, there. It's Savannah Guthrie of the TODAY show. I just left you a voice mail. I'm sure it has been a long day . . . I just wanted you to know you have an open invitation to come on our show." She even capitalized the word "today" to maintain brand continuity! Jack Donaghy would have been proud.

Calls and texts came from friends, family, and a few select members. "What happened? Are you okay? Can I help?"

Then it was time for court.

> But everybody respects the dead. They love the
> friendly ghost.
> ★ Daniel Johnston, "Casper the Friendly Ghost"

"Congressman! Congressman!" Barking dogs. Reporters. Microphones. Knives. Photographers. Cameras. Shoulder-fired missiles.

After the insanity of the courtroom, complete with TMZ in my face and the girl getting run over by the pack of rabid reporters, David Shertler and I headed to his office, where I met with Dave, my chief of staff, and planned our escape from D.C. We also finalized the details for the press conference I would give in Fort Myers that night.

D.C. was usually Dave's territory, and Florida was Matt's,

but we needed all hands on deck for the press conference, so Dave and I would fly to Florida that night. Leaving Schertler's office, Dave said, "We're heading to Baltimore because the press is expecting us at Reagan."

The long ride to Baltimore was miserable, cold, rainy, and quiet. Boarding the plane in Baltimore, I put on an old all-black Chicago Cubs hat I'd had for years, pulled it way low over my eyes, and thanked God for a few things. The first was Dave's height. As we walked down the aisle, I hid from the other passengers by putting my head down and standing so closely behind him that he might have questioned my sexuality. I also thanked God for answering some of my prayers in the past . . . because I was about to ask quite a bit from Him.

Just as the plane leveled off at cruising altitude, I crossed my hands, bowed my head down, and I prayed.

I prayed hard.

I mean really, really hard.

I prayed the plane would crash.

I prayed to go down in flames in a wild ride spinning toward the earth, with me yee-hawing like Major Kong in *Dr. Strangelove*, until—*boom!*—I'd smash into the ground! And right then and there, buried deep below the earth, I would die a martyr.

I'd die a martyr because as long as I'm alive I'm the jackass tea party Republican who bought blow and got busted. But if I was dead, even liberals would rally around my memory. Nancy Pelosi's words came to mind in that cold, calculated, monotone voice of hers. "He was a good man. He did his best for our country. He will be missed."

After all, society rallies around—better yet, *affectionately praises*—dead people. But never people who are alive and could use positive support. Aw, hell no!

Think about Rob Ford, the former mayor of Toronto, who just before my bust had blown up his own life when he got caught on video doing drugs and saying outlandish things. When he died in 2016, social media and newscasts across North America exploded with condolences, wonderful memories, and kind words. But when the guy was alive and obviously struggling, he was assassinated and smacked around while he was at the lowest depths of his life.

The formula seems to be: Alive? *Die!* Dead? *Wish you were here!*

Without even a hint of turbulence to give me hope, the plane began its descent into beautiful Southwest Florida.

Flying at night is always so peaceful. The passengers are quiet, and the peaceful hum of the airplane is like the calming sound of white noise. I gazed out the window, catching a glimpse of my own reflection. My face had thinned out. I'd lost weight, but not in a good way. I was eating maybe one meal a day. I also hadn't had a drink for weeks. The bags under my eyes told my story: years of an insane work ethic plus no exercise, plus eating terribly and drinking, had slowly chipped away at me. It hit me: I would soon have to give a press conference to my former colleagues in the news industry. Disgusted with myself, I stopped looking at the sad face in the window. Beyond my reflection was pure beauty. In the glow of the streetlights, I could see Sanibel and Fort Myers Beach dotted with the illuminated palm trees that as a midwesterner I had come to adore. I could see the outlines of the beaches. This was home. It was my district, and I loved it.

In the next second, I threw my head back, closed my eyes, and thought, *I hate this place. I hate those palm trees. I despise how beautiful and serene this place is. I hate everyone.* With every second the plane descended, my anger built up more. *I have the most beautiful district in the entire United States, and I probably just threw it away.*

In between my sick prayers and thoughts of crashing, I managed to put the finishing touches on my press conference speech. I was ready to talk, to take questions, to defend, and to admit. Well, sort of.

Dave and I knew there would be loads of cameras at the airport so our plan was to try to blend in with the crowds of passengers. We didn't want to speak to the press until it was on our terms at our district office.

Right outside of the gate were three cops. My thoughts turned dark. *What? They can't arrest me again! What do these guys want?*

To my delighted surprise, they were there to help. "Congressman," said the officer who appeared to be in charge. "We can get you past these media guys." I laughed, and thought to myself, *We have a common enemy: TV news reporters!* But what I said out loud came from my heart. I felt compelled to apologize to them. "That'd be great, but first, guys, I'm sorry. I am sorry I let you down." They were men of the law, and I sure as heck had broken the law that they put their lives on the line for every day. One of them answered, "We all make mistakes." A pleasant surprise, but not that surprising. Men and women in law enforcement, like journalists and even undertakers, have a front-row seat to some of the harshest realities in life. They tend to be forgiving.

The officers quickly shuttled us toward the exit. As we turned a corner, the lights of cameras that were about fifty feet away hit us. At the same time, more than a dozen reporters yelled, "Congressman!" like they were chanting a college cheer. "Gimme a C!"

We turned the corner, then . . . *bang!* We slammed through a set of doors, continued through a small room, and then the officers popped open two more doors and we stepped out onto the sidewalk. My trusty district director, Matt Pusateri, was waiting in a car at the curb. Dave shoved me into the car as if I were the president being thrown into his limo by the Secret Service.

Matt laid on the gas. Through the window, we watched the group of TV reporters and photographers run out of the main doors trying to get a shot of us. As we headed toward I-75, I broke the awkward silence. "I'm ready to do this press conference." Sounding like I was prepping to go to war, I added, "I'm ready." Dave looked back at me from the passenger's seat with a dismissive stare. In the rearview mirror I could see Matt raise his eyebrow as if to say, *Uh . . . Okay, man. You're ready.*

As my voice got bolder, so did the deranged thoughts in my mind. *How am I going to handle this press conference? What will I say? Gotta be big . . . gotta be bold . . . gotta make a statement.*

I could keep it ridiculously short and stun even the most seasoned veteran journalists. I'd walk up to the podium and say, "I drank too much and made a bad decision. I'll be back to work on Monday. Questions?"

Hmmm . . . that could work. But I need something really big.

Crazier voices continued. *Ima go hip-hop,* a low baritone

voice said in my head. I'd walk up to the mic with my black ball cap down over my eyes, rip the mic off the podium, say, "YOLO," in a smooth low voice, then drop the mic and strut out. My family would probably have stuck me in a mental institution, but it sounded good.

(We now pause for a public service announcement for anyone potentially lost by the generational slang: "YOLO" is a term coined by the hip-hop artist Drake that means "You only live once." Feel free to use it. It's as spectacularly awesome as soccer moms putting their hands in the air palms up and saying, "Raise the roof!" or my dad saying, "That's da bomb!")

In the end, I did what any good politician would do: I relied on my carefully rehearsed talking points. That night, I went before the press and said, "I'm an alcoholic. I'm an alcoholic, and I will be seeking treatment. I'm taking responsibility and accountability for my actions."

By now, you may judge me the worst person in the world. Sure, I "took responsibility," but I was really just doing what I needed to do to survive. That night, when I said, "I'm an alcoholic," I wouldn't have bought those words with your money. That is the raw truth, and I get a sick feeling in the pit of my stomach writing it and reading it.

When someone has an issue with alcohol or drugs, they often go through the twelve-step process. The first step is to "admit" you are "powerless," that you are, unquestionably, a full-blown alcoholic or drug addict. You often don't fully and honestly accept this until long after you've sought treatment. I certainly wasn't there yet. I was dealing with a mix of feelings, including profound sadness about the mess I'd created, as well as nearly uncontrollable anger.

Shortly after my press conference, I would have the blessing and curse of time—*lots and lots of time*. Whether I wanted to or not, I would fully and completely reevaluate my life—my wonderful, sad, fun, awful, incredible, pathetic life.

=★17★=
HANDS OF TIME

After the press conference, Amy, Jude, and I had to leave our home and escape to Amy's sister's place. Within forty-eight hours, our house had become ground zero for every TV news reporter in the market, who used it as the background for live shots. Reporters were banging on our door day and night, sometimes as late as midnight. Try to imagine someone pounding on your door, screaming, "Let's talk," while your two-year-old shrieks in terror.

In the refuge at Amy's sister's, Dave and Matt pressed me to enter rehab and both came to the same conclusion. "You have to do this long-term, thirty days."

"Five days, and I'm out!" I insisted, hoping to convince them that performing less than a week of the "rehab show" would be enough. I asked myself, *What the hell did I need rehab for?* I didn't have a problem. Dave shot me down. "No way. Thirty." Matt, my ever-present calming figure, took a more reassuring approach. "Man, you'll be fine. This'll be good."

During this awful time, it felt like every political pundit on the planet; every TV newscast, newspaper, and online publication; and every comedian in the world was coming after me. Although, after all those years of dreaming I'd be on *SNL*, I made it. Seth Meyers ripped me often on "Weekend Update." Every pundit and comedian seemed to take particular glee in my vote on the provision in the farm bill regarding food stamps and drug testing. Remember when I said that this vote would come back to bite me in the ass?

It all started when the *Huffington Post* ran an article with the headline: "Trey Radel, Busted on Cocaine Charge, Voted for Drug Testing Food Stamp Recipients." The irony is the *HuffPo* reporter, in at least one of the articles, actually expounded on my view on the failed War on Drugs and my past votes focused on criminal justice reform. *But, c'mon, who reads articles?* At the lowest moment of my life, I was being savaged on national television for getting busted for drugs after voting to *drug test* food stamp recipients.

After the press broke the massive farm bill down to a headline, the public boiled my vote down to one meme—a picture of me with white powder Photoshopped all over my face saying: "Republican votes to drug test food stamp recipients, gets busted for cocaine."

The truth was that it had not been a single vote to "drug test these dirty dogs getting handouts!" It was part of the thousand-plus-page farm bill loaded with other provisions, and it gave states more power over how they wanted to administer their food stamps. I believe in "to each state its own," especially when it comes to addressing local issues and concerns. I thought that Washington's constant "one size fits all" mandates were doomed to fail.

So while I am a Republican who is *so libertarian* that I could have been labeled a *liberal* because of my determination to end the War on Drugs and work with Democrats, it didn't matter. I was just another tea party asswipe who got busted for drugs and voted to drug test food stamp recipients.

This was especially tough for me to take because I had empathy for people facing addiction issues, had struggled in my own life, and had my own family history. Plus, I had always been a staunch opponent of the War on Drugs.

The War on Drugs is misguided at best, intentionally blind at worst.

Our drug policies in the United States should be focusing on *rehabilitation, not incarceration.* There's a fiscally conservative argument for this because we throw away billions of dollars a year locking people up and turning our backs on them. Many times nonviolent drug offenders return to society lacking skills to get a job, or they're turned away from jobs because of their record. Worse, they come out as hardened criminals, which places an even greater economic burden on society.

Ironically, shortly before my bust, I worked with Democrats to cosponsor the Justice Safety Valve Act. In fact, I was one of only a few Republicans to do so. The goal: Get rid of mandatory minimums and allow judges to impose penalties below the statutory sentences. We often see cases of nonviolent drug offenders who get locked up for years only to come out with little to offer society and a society with little to offer them. It's a catch-22 with terrible results for both the individual and society. Furthermore, young Hispanics and African American men are disproportionately locked up, making life that much harder for those who have had the deck stacked against them from birth.

And there's another group of men and women who are *really, really* screwed over by the War on Drugs because they are caught in the middle of violence and hatred due to our inept laws. Liberals won't talk about this group because it's not politically expedient, and conservatives won't because it reveals their hypocrisy and exposes the very problems they've created through their ignorant "just say no" bumper-sticker policies.

The group? The men and women of law enforcement. I'm talking about cops.

The War on Drugs is one of the main sources of anger and resentment between communities and law enforcement in the United States today. Sure, there are heavy-handed rogue cops who use drug laws to unnecessarily surveil or outright harass individuals. But there are loads of good men and women in law enforcement who privately rail against the system that puts them and others into dangerous situations. "Hey, coppers, did you think breaking up that domestic disturbance sucked when the drunk guy pulled a gun on you right after he knocked out his wife? Yeah, well, now we're sending you, a couple of white cops, into a minority neighborhood where you are utterly despised. If you 'smell something funny,' the law will compel you to drag some young adults out of their car in front of their families and friends, frisk them, embarrass them, and undoubtedly make them angry." Good luck.

Ask yourself: Would you rather have the FBI, DEA, and local law enforcement arresting people who are using recreational drugs in *their home* or tracking down fanatics about to *walk out of their home* strapped with AK-47s and suicide vests?

Do you think that example is too extreme? Go ask law enforcement how much time they waste dealing with low-level drug offenders. And after officers throw away taxpayer dollars and time to keep you safe from someone who made *what is essentially a private transaction for their own private use,* Juan or Devon goes to jail, crowding our prisons with these not-so-grave threats to society. And, mind you, you're paying the bill— billions a year—to keep them locked up.

Oddly, when it comes to alcohol, society somehow looks at people who get busted for DUIs with a chuckle and shrug. "Haha! Did Uncle Billy get popped for driving after his twelfth Busch heavy?!" Yes, he did! And the difference between Uncle Billy, and millions of others like him who drink and drive, is the person behind the wheel after a few drinks might kill your entire family with their car while you're sharing the road with them.

As for drug testing food stamp recipients, the policy has been proven to be a failure economically and in terms of enforcement; the cost of the testing hasn't been outweighed by arrests because the states rarely catch anyone. There are very few of those evil people doing drugs and taking food stamps. States that enforce this kind of policy end up targeting the elderly, the disabled, or mothers and fathers working eight days a week to put food on their families' table. All an evil constituency! A test drags parents away from their jobs, or their multiple jobs, and their kids, who they see only late at night or early in the morning, if they're lucky.

The only context I can offer for voting for the provision is this: Every few months or years, thousand-plus-page bills are passed that are loaded with tons of garbage that keep the current status quo within our tax code and continue subsidies. Big Oil gets their tax break; green energy gets their money. But accusing a liberal of supporting oil or a conservative of supporting government handouts is a gross overgeneralization. It's just not true. But, damn, it sure sounds good politically.

But whether we like it or not, this is how the legislative process is built. The men and women in Congress face "damned if you do, damned if you don't" situations every day. As an eternal optimist, I call it compromise. *And, dammit, compromise is not a dirty word.*

The farm bill presented such a vote. If I voted for it, I'd be the jerk who approved the drug testing provision. If I voted against it, I'd be the jerk who stole food stamps from hungry children and destroyed the lives of family farmers. Democrats who voted yes with me did so because the good in the bill outweighed the bad: food stamps would continue, the ag industry would be assured stability, and your milk wouldn't shoot up to ten freaking bucks a gallon. Looks like we are all terrible people.

They tried to make me go to rehab but I said,
"No, no, no."

★ Amy Winehouse, "Rehab"

I finally agreed to a thirty-day rehab program and checked myself into a place in Naples. At the beginning, I was physically there. Mentally, not so much.

Incredibly, I was still focused on my career. I kept my phone on, reading news, social media, and texts. I was desperate for support, for someone to tell me everything was going to be okay. *I was pathetically desperate.*

Meanwhile, local county Republican groups were creating formal resolutions to get me to resign. Then—get this!—as I sat in rehab, I started getting e-mails asking me to consider supporting candidates running for Congress . . . in District 19 . . . my district! Two of the startup campaigns had recruited people who, a year before, had ties to my campaign. They had stolen my e-mail list! Some were addressed to my legal name, Henry, which I never use. They said uplifting things like "We need someone honorable to serve Southwest Florida in Congress." I was soon asked to donate to their campaigns!

Then a state representative, an ally of a state senator who would soon announce her run for my seat, started hounding me with texts telling me to resign. I'm in freakin' rehab and this Florida house member, who, by the way, had come to my D.C. office and solicited my support on legislative issues and messaging, was suggesting I call him in the morning because he did not see a "reality" for my reelection.

I was losing my mind and felt totally helpless. I could not do anything publicly, and I had to watch what I was texting and which people I was calling. Anything could be leaked to the press at any moment.

In this dark, dark time, something that sticks with me today is that when I see people going through their own crisis I remember how my political opposition and detractors seemed really, really loud. I had wished that my friends and political supporters who called me and offered up their undying support had been louder. Unfortunately, in business, and especially in politics, even some of your most ardent supporters stay far away when you become radioactive.

Once again, it was professional, not personal. I get it. But, wow, it hurt.

I texted the state representative, saying I wasn't "talking politics anymore," that I was going "to focus on my family and health" instead. Then, almost as *incredibly* as my working the phone from rehab, I shut the thing off.

My phone was shut off for the first time in years. *Years!*

It was so quiet. So, so quiet.

I was left with the thoughts in my head, which began to get quiet, too. I was done confronting the public. Now it was time to confront myself.

During group meetings, I began to pay attention to and reflect on what the other people were saying. I listened to men and women who had hit their bottom with nightmarish consequences. Some had almost killed their kids as they drove them to school at seven in the morning while being inebriated. One person was under the influence while driving when they killed another person.

Was this me? Had I been close to killing anyone? Was I so physically dependent on alcohol that I started drinking in the morning? No. *Could I have gotten that bad?* Maybe.

There are addictions, there are patterns of behavior, and

there are moments in life. I believe that individuals cross the line into addiction and addictive behavior when they compromise their family, their friends, their career, and/or their health.

What had I compromised?

Physically, I was a little overweight but healthy.

Professionally, I had been at the peak of my career when my choices landed me at the bottom.

When it came to family, I was a sad shell of a husband and father. I was losing touch with my wife and barely saw my son. I reflected on how many times I had chosen to stay out and continue "networking" instead of going home, how many days I'd stayed in D.C. instead of returning to Florida, or how many months it had been since I made a genuine emotional connection with either my wife or my son.

As meetings in rehab continued, I learned about the twelve steps. In the first one, you admit and accept that you are powerless over alcohol and that your life is unmanageable. Could I "give in," as was being asked of me? "Trey," a counselor told me, "being an alcoholic is like being pregnant. You either are or you aren't."

That was difficult for me to accept, especially after what I had seen in life, including my mother. She undoubtedly had been physically dependent on alcohol and had stopped during my childhood and teens by, I suppose, "white-knuckling it," a phrase I heard often in rehab. Later it was pills. However, I had loads of friends and relatives who had also slipped into patterns that would definitely be labeled as alcoholism. And they slipped right out of them. They were successful entrepreneurs, loving mothers and fathers, who now rarely drank. Should they have quit long before and gone to AA meetings? Were they flirting with danger when they enjoyed a few glasses of wine?

I was not only asking myself, "Who am I?" but also "What am I?" *An alcoholic?* The counselor said, "Absolutely." *A drug addict?* "No," the counselor said, adding, "Trey, you abused drugs. You're a drug abuser, maybe not an addict."

In and out of self-reflection, I plunged deeper into depression as I thought about everyone I had let down: the people who had supported me from the beginning, blindly putting their faith in me; the people who had cut checks to me, some of whom had no business sending money to a candidate when they had financial problems at home; the entire Nineteenth District of Florida with its hundreds of thousands of people who, even though they may not have voted for me, had relied on me; close friends from childhood and college, many of whom donated thousands of dollars; my son, who would now grow up with the stigma that his dad was the one who got busted in Congress and became a massive failure who blew up in a most public way; and, of course, my wife and my dad.

Oh, yeah, and I also let down the entire damn country. With Congress's approval ratings hovering around those of a root canal's, I single-handedly brought them down to a colonoscopy's.

Rehab went on.

Amy visited on Sundays, and I'd occasionally leave to spend time with her and Jude. I worked on connecting with them again while fighting deep, painful feelings of regret, remorse, and shame.

In particular, I began to come to grips with the pain I had caused Amy. She had stood by my side through everything, and

I had completely failed her and destroyed all credibility and trust. Whether or not I wanted to label myself an alcoholic, it began to sink in: I was out of control. I had a problem. I was a problem. My behavior, my lifestyle, was a problem. I was a cavalier asshole. I abused alcohol, and when I did, I occasionally abused drugs.

To come to grips with what I had done, I needed to find a way to push back on the dark, depressing thoughts in my head. I couldn't grab a couple of beers anymore, so I took up my old method of blowing off steam, the one I had relied on long before the insanity of the campaign and the year in Congress. I started exercising.

I picked up a jump rope, something Marcus, my boxing trainer, had me use consistently at every practice before we ever stepped in the ring. I also started running regularly, something I missed so much, especially in the saltwater air of Naples under the palm trees. Slowly, my anger and hate began to fade away, almost as if they were being melted by the Florida sun.

Approaching thirty days in rehab, I felt better. It would soon be time to go back to a cold, wintery Washington. I knew there was a chance I might have to resign. However, I had come this far. I wanted to serve out my term and finish some of the things I had started. And, of course, I also entertained thoughts of a brilliant reelection campaign, becoming the comeback story of the year!

Ha! What an ass!

=★18★=
NEVER GOIN' BACK

eading back to Washington, I was in a different state of mind. I was in a better place but not at peace. Happy but not content. I was in survival mode, but I was no longer a robot. I had a lot of explaining to do and serious business to attend to.

The feared House Committee on Ethics had officially launched an investigation. The only time I had ever heard of the ethics committee was from the few cases that had made headlines, like Tom DeLay's and Charlie Rangel's. I had no clue what an ethics investigation meant or what it entailed, but being either naïve, willfully ignorant, or eternally optimistic, I believed I could get through it. David Schertler helped me retain a lawyer to handle the probe. *Yes, you need an attorney just to deal with the Committee on Ethics.* I gave Rob Walker of Wiley Rein a call.

Ring, ring.

"Hello?"

"Hi, Rob, you may have seen me on CNN, MSNBC, Fox, BBC, Al Jazeera, Comedy Central, or any one of the late-night comedy shows, allow me to introduce myself, I'm—"

"Hello, Congressman Radel, thanks for calling."

Rob was optimistic. The way he saw it was that everything had been taken care of. The incident, the arrest, and the circumstances around it were all on my own personal time, involved no staff and no other members of Congress, and I had taken steps to show I was getting the necessary help in rehab. He believed the committee would recognize these factors and would not want to drag my personal issues into their investigation. I loved his optimism! Like Schertler had, Rob asked me to wait while he made calls to see where things stood. I hoped he'd come back with better news than David had. *Let's see where this goes*, I thought to myself.

While Rob did his thing, Dave and I worked out a plan. Being an infamous member of Congress, I had to do everything possible to avoid the media. No one had figured out where I lived in D.C., so I wasn't fighting off reporters at my apartment like I was in Florida. But cameras hounded my office doorway. I could barely get in or out.

Dave and I organized face-to-face meetings with members. First, I would meet with and apologize to leadership: Speaker Boehner, Majority Leader Cantor, and Whip McCarthy. Then I would meet with every single Republican member of the Florida delegation, every single Republican freshman I was sworn in with, and then meet with Democratic members of the Florida delegation and the entire Democratic freshman class.

My first meeting was with the Speaker. The last time I had seen him, Boehner had told me to go home and get well. That meeting was easy. This one, not so much.

I walked into his office and once again looked at the Cincinnati and Ohio decorations. Within seconds, I heard, "Radel." It was not the old affectionate shout-out delivered with a smile. For the first time I experienced the cold side of John Boehner. In the jaded world of Washington, I cannot stress strongly enough how warm and kind John Boehner is. He has a big heart among savages, and I broke it. While he and Eric Cantor and Kevin McCarthy had worked tirelessly to improve the terrible, awful image and brand of the Republican Party, I took a giant crap all over their hard work.

As he and I sat down, I prepared myself to hear him get to the point immediately and say, "You need to resign." But he lit up a cigarette, took a big ol' drag, and sat back in his chair. In a blunt, cold tone, he said, "My advice to you is to announce you will not seek reelection. You should do this as soon as possible." He took another Boehner drag. "Now you have this ethics thing going on, too." He shifted in the chair, exhaled, and in the brief pause, I thought, *Oh, no, where is he going next? What are they doing?* He went on. "I have nothing to do with the Ethics Committee. I can't speak with any of them or learn about their investigations or procedures. I also have no idea whether or not they will back off *when you announce you are not seeking reelection.*" He paused to allow that to sink in. "When you do, it will be much easier for everyone." He put out his cigarette and lit another. "Trey, I know this is difficult, but this is my advice to you." He then walked me out of the office.

Any real possibility of running for office again that I had sort of, kind of still entertained had now been shut down. As you know by now, I'm not the first to jump at the answer no or rule out trivial details like impossibilities, even after I'd been given my marching orders from the Speaker.

For days and some sleepless nights, my mind raced. *Maybe. Maybe not. Fight. Resign. Ride it out. Quit. No way! Fib! Say you won't seek reelection then decide to run later! Now* that's *a devious plan! Muwhaha!*

My face-to-face apology tour continued.

Shit's about to get weird.

I met with Representative Steve Southerland. Steve and I had something in common: We both grew up in the funeral industry. Southerland's office was also in Longworth. Most of the cameras outside my office door had left, but at least one young guy, either a tourist or staffer, snapped a picture of me with his phone. I thought to myself, *Maybe someone is going to get shanked near the Capitol after all.* I made my way to Steve's office without even brandishing a weapon. Steve's chief of staff escorted me into his private office. "Come in, Trey," Steve said, with the big smile he often carried between slightly chubby cheeks. Maybe it was because of his background in the funeral industry, but I felt comforted right away. I sat on his couch. He pulled up a chair. I began my speech-slash-apology.

"Steve, I wanted to come by to look you in the eyes and apologize. I'm sorry I let you down. I have no excuse for what I did, and I want you to know, I'm going to make this better. I have learned from this and want to be a stronger person."

You might label someone like Steve Southerland a "social

conservative" or "Bible thumper." What happened next was incredibly touching, and for me, a half-ass Catholic who hasn't been to church in years, *incredibly weird.*

"Trey, you have a hole in your heart," he told me, and put his hand on my shoulder. "Say a prayer with me, Trey." He bowed his head. I followed.

"Jesus, we kneel before you," he started, as we remained seated. "We ask for your guidance. We know that without you we are nothing. You fill our hearts and guide us with your infinite wisdom." I ever so slightly opened one eye to take a peek. His head was down, with his chin touching his chest. He swayed a little side to side and then really turned it up. "Trey," he said, with some more volume.

As he called my name, I shut my eye quickly. *Hope he didn't see me!*

Nope. Steve was just getting started.

"Trey, I want to know. Do you feel Jesus in your heart?"

"Yes," I said softly, my voice cracking as if I were just hitting puberty.

"No, Trey," he barked, sounding like my high school football coach. "I need to know, do you feel Jesus in your heart?"

"Yes," I said, this time more firmly.

"You need Jesus in your heart, Trey!" He paused.

I thought, *Uh, is this my part?*

But then he went into an all-out frenzy. *"Trey, you tell me right now! Is Jesus here?! Is Jesus present here with us right now?"*

I stepped it up a notch, too. "Yes, he is."

Not satisfied, Southerland fired back. "I need to hear you!"

I thought, *Is this a rock concert or pep rally?*

He gripped my shoulder tighter. "Trey! Tell me Jesus is in your heart!"

And then, dammit, I went off.

"Jesus, I feel you in my heart!" I nearly shouted. "I feel you!" I was yelling, hoping the people in the next room couldn't hear. "Jesus, I need you in my heart! Jesus, I am empty without you! Jesus, I am nothing without you!" I continued shouting as if I had been the son of a Baptist preacher all my life.

Then silence.

Steve uttered a quick, soft-spoken prayer. "Thank you, dear Lord, amen." And as if he had done this a thousand times before, he stood up and hugged me. "I'm here for you, Trey." And that was it. Done.

I didn't feel Jesus in my heart, but I was both sad and amazed. *Sad* because I was *amazed* at how at peace Steve was in his life. Tiny fragments of peace had come my way more often lately but not because of religion. It happened because I was focusing on what was—*and was not*—important in life.

Organized religion, specifically Catholicism, lost me long ago. It started at the epicenter of the Roman Catholic Church—the Vatican. All those years ago, when I visited St. Peter's Basilica, I was in awe of the art, the architecture, and the overwhelming beauty. It was amazing. It was also disheartening.

I wondered, *If Jesus was angry with people buying and selling in the temple, as described in the Bible, how would he have felt about this monstrous structure or the church itself, given its politics, business dealings, and net worth?* I bet that if Jesus came back today he would take one look at the Catholic Church and be so disgusted with what people did with his simple teachings that he'd shake his head and start practicing Buddhism. Or go *South Park* and "lock and load."

I heard a lot about Jesus on my apology tour. I had often passed judgment and stereotyped people who are sometimes dismissively called holy rollers. But as my colleagues shared their own personal issues, from drinking to abusing drugs in the past, I was amazed at how at peace they were with themselves, and with my shortcomings as well. They were forgiving; they were gentle. *They had their faith and were in a better place because of it.*

Suddenly becoming devoutly religious *was not* going to come to me like an order from Amazon. But I wanted what they had— peace and serenity.

> You've got to know when to hold 'em. Know when to fold 'em.
>
> ★ Kenny Rogers, "The Gambler"

My attorney Rob called, catching me just as I was getting off the Metro at Dupont. It was about seven at night, cold and dark. "Hey, Rob," I said, as I began a frantic pace around the Circle so no one would recognize me or listen in.

Rob was dumbfounded. I could hear it in his voice. "Trey, I have the official investigation, which includes the questions from Ethics. In my decades of working in this field, I have never, ever seen anything like this."

I stopped walking. All I could say was a long "Ooohhhkay."

"First, they want you to list every single illegal or controlled substance you have ever tried . . . ever . . . *in your whole life*. That means, even if you tried pot in college, you need to cite it. Names and dates and details. Another big request here . . . they're demanding you hand over documents and travel logs from the moment you were elected to Congress, meaning back in November, which is now well over a year ago. This would take hours, days, even weeks for you to round up and for us to properly document."

I started up my mad pace around Dupont Circle, exhaling clouds of breath in the cold.

The frustration in Rob's voice hit a slightly higher pitch as he went on. "They even have this ambiguous part that asks for 'any and all documents that relate or pertain to your schedule while you were physically present in the Washington, D.C., metropolitan area, including but not limited to any official, campaign, or personal events or activities, the time and date and location' and et cetera, et cetera, blah, blah, blah. Trey, I don't even know how you'd pin all this down. And remember, this is sworn testimony. They will call in your staff and have them testify. They can subpoena everyone!"

He paused. I could hear him flipping pages and sighing. I thought of my staff, many of them like brothers and sisters at this point, being dragged into this for questioning when they genuinely knew nothing. More guilt and shame came crashing down on me.

Rob went on, sounding more subdued, even confused. "I . . . I don't even know what they're looking for . . . or *why*. Some of this is nonsense. It's like they want to bury you with questions."

He stopped and took another deep breath, and I suddenly felt both sadness and relief. I said calmly, "Rob, they don't want answers. They want me out."

After a long pause, Rob quietly said, "Yeah, Trey. I'm sorry, but it appears that way."

"I get it," I said, as softly as he had.

There was a long pause.

We talked through what was likely to happen next. Still pacing around Dupont and aware of the people around me, I whispered, "Rob, I got my first death threat just a day ago. I had to go to Capitol Police. That's one thing. Another, I can't walk in or out my office door without either a print reporter or TV news photographer getting in my face. My staff is freaked out and going through hell. And I do not want to drag them through any more of this. It's all adding up to be too much. I gotta go."

Once again, Rob leveled with me in that tone that only attorneys can pull off. "Trey, whatever you want to do, I will stand by your side and fight with you the whole way through. But I will be up front with you. This will cost a lot of money, and it will be painful. The Ethics Committee will demand specific answers from you, subpoena your staff, and grill them. This whole situation will get worse as you try to move forward with your life and put this behind you. I don't want to encourage you to resign. But do know this: As soon as you do, the Ethics Committee loses all jurisdiction over you. *Everything is over.* Again, I will fight for you through it all, but you need to know your options. Sleep on it. Think about it for a day and give me a call."

Having the slightest notion of hanging on and fighting back, I couldn't help but ask, "Rob, could you e-mail me that document from the Ethics Committee? I want to read over the questions they're asking."

Despite the cold, I sat down on a park bench next to the Dupont Circle fountain—now shut off for the winter. Rob's e-mail showed up on my phone minutes later, and with my numb fingers, I opened the attachments.

The Ethics Committee's letterhead lists the chair and the members.

Guess who was the chair of the House Committee on Ethics?

Who was in charge of the committee that was about to probe every inch of my life, drag my staff in by their ears to testify, and sacrifice my firstborn child?

Figured it out yet?

The sheep-shearing "fiscal conservative" accountant and member of the Ag Committee, Mike freakin' Conaway.

The *only* person in Congress I had ever had a testy exchange with was the chairman of the Ethics Committee. Right there in Dupont Circle, next to a few homeless people and tourists, I laughed out loud "Ha!" and yelled, "No way!"

At that moment I knew I was done. I was done with attorneys, done with the press, done with Congress; I was done with it all. It was all over. I resigned a few days later.

Home is where the heart is.

★ Proverb

I cleaned out my office late one night, hopped on the Metro for the last time, and trekked through the January snow to my apartment. (Our landlord was incredibly kind and allowed us to break our lease as soon as she found someone else to rent to.)

Amy and Jude were waiting for me. They had come up from Florida to stay for a few weeks because no reporters had figured out where we lived. It felt like home again, not a bachelor's pad. The three of us went out to dinner like a family, and during the day, I built snowmen with my son. While still depressed, I began to smile a little more.

At this time we had just started allowing Jude to watch a little bit of TV here and there. He was beginning to talk, and after we watched a few parts of *Kung Fu Panda 2*, he picked up the two words that Jack Black utters as he fights off evil. Walking around the house and playing with his toys, he'd say, over and over, "Inner peace."

Even with the stress hanging over us, time would heal, and with my family, I did begin to feel a tiny bit of inner peace.

Wasted away again in Margaritaville, searching for
my lost shaker of salt.
★ Jimmy Buffett, "Margaritaville"

Wait. That's inappropriate.

Sun is shining, the weather is sweet, yeah.
★ Bob Marley, "Sun Is Shining"

Much better.

A few weeks later we were back in Florida. It was eighty degrees, the sun was shining, and the palm trees I loved so much swayed in the wind.

It was peaceful.

But then another crazy surprise.

"You have the right to remain silent."

Oh, no!

★19★
THE END, PHOENIX

Y ou have the right to remain silent. Anything you say can and will be used against you in the court of law. You have the right to an attorney. If you cannot afford one, one will be appointed to you."

I'm in a small, stuffy police station in a rough Miami neighborhood called Overtown. But get this: I'm the one dictating the Miranda warning to someone else. I'm nervous, pouring sweat, but I'm reciting it with authority, as if I've done it a million times.

It's 1978, the same year Gloria Gaynor released, "I Will Survive." Check out my poop-brown pants and vomit-beige shirt, two sizes too big; and, oh, that awful tie! My beard is just thick enough not to be scruff, and my aviator shades are stuck in my pocket. It's a perfect late-'70s look!

I know you're asking: *Trey, what the hell is going on?*

I'm an actor in a TV show! I'm no Don Johnson, but I am a

detective in Miami. But how did I go from the disgraced, terrible, awful, food-stamp-recipient-hating, disgraced congressman to actor?

Well, with my impressive résumé of never acting a day in my life and having had a few classes at Second City in Chicago almost twenty years ago, I auditioned for a part in an Investigation Discovery documentary and landed the lead role in a murder documentary. You know the type: The writers intersperse interviews with real people, like detectives, and then cut to a range of decent to bad actors. I was the bad actor!

For more than a year, I'd hidden in my home, and I'd hidden in my music. Whenever I was forced to go out, I hid below my Cubs hat. I quit drinking—not a beer, cocktail, glass of wine, and certainly not a Ketel One, soda, two limes. Nothing.

As I worked to get back on my feet, some of the dark, painful moments of reflection and regret that I had had during rehab stuck with me, coming in waves for days and weeks at a time. There were periods when I was paralyzed and didn't want to leave the house or talk with anyone. And as my son grew, I dwelled on how my every action would live on the Internet forever, and I spun into even darker places.

Goddammit, move on, man! I'd scream loudly in my head. I wanted to be happy again. I wanted so bad to be the eternal optimist I used to be. I didn't want to be depressed, angry, bitter, full of hate, or an empty void.

I realized that I couldn't allow myself to be consumed or overwhelmed with what was out of my control. I also held close something I learned in AA, the Serenity Prayer. Its brilliant phrases apply to so much in life, whether you are religious or not, struggling or not.

God grant me the serenity to accept the things I cannot change; courage to change the things I can; and wisdom to know the difference.

Instead of allowing my past decisions and actions to weigh me down, I chose to use my understanding of them to help me grow as a man, a husband, and a father.

While there was no coming to Jesus, as many of my colleagues would have wanted me to shout and testify about, I began to crawl out of some of my darkness and spend more and more time with my family and the few close friends I felt comfortable with.

I was a stay-at-home dad for a year. As I had in my twenties and early thirties, I had the precious resource of time. I wasn't about to go off and shoot AK-47s in any jungles, but I grew a beard again, and I spent time—*incredibly rewarding time*—with my young son, who could now walk, talk, run, and toss a ball with me. Amy and I began to heal after the chaos and destruction I'd inflicted on our marriage.

Instead of struggling with life-and-death decisions over Syria, stressing over the national debt, and shutting down the entire government, my daily question was: Should I take my kid to the park or the pool?

Don't call it a comeback. I've been here for years.
★ LL Cool J, "Mama Said Knock You Out"

It took me a year to do anything even remotely public. The first place I went was the "hood" to see my friend Marcus. I needed to hit the gym and work off some stress. What better way than to beat the hell out of a bag?

I walked into his dimly lit gym on a bright summer afternoon. Loud hip-hop was blaring out of his old stereo, and I heard, "What's up, Trey?" Marcus greeted me with a big grin and hug.

"You smiling cuz you're that happy to see me?" I asked.

"Naw, I'm just ready to give you shit," he said, giggling.

"Yeah, yeah, lemme have it."

"Looks like you really are hip-hop! Haha!"

Once again, the moniker bit me in the ass. "All right, you done?" I asked, smiling.

"Jump some rope and let's get in the ring."

With Marcus and the others at the gym, there was no judgment. Many people there had been through their own tough times. For those with criminal records, I felt a new sense of compassion, even kinship. I helped some of them with their résumés as they struggled to find employment, and I walked a few of them through job interviews.

At home, my creative juices were flowing. I started strumming my acoustic guitar again and returned to making terrible to semitolerable electronic music. I also began to think about what I'd do next professionally.

Over the next year, I wrote down hundreds and hundreds of business ideas, from advertising campaigns for different industries to concepts for nonprofits.

I didn't do a thing with them.

What was I going to do? Go raise capital?

"Hi, I know we haven't spoken since I got busted buying blow, but I was wondering if you would like to invest in a new startup company I plan to helm?"

I didn't even apply for jobs. *Who the hell would hire me?*

Eventually, I had to return to the beaten-down, controversial, tarnished "brand" of Trey Radel. I knew it would be difficult to get a job with the kind of baggage I was dragging around. I also knew I was not going to take a nine-to-five job sitting in a cubicle; I'd lose my mind. I brainstormed ideas with Dave Natonski, who remained a good friend, and ended up returning to what I knew best—media. I started a company with Matt Pusateri doing media training and speech coaching, working with CEOs, athletes, and attorneys. I also helped people through crisis situations. It was rewarding work.

Then, about a year and a half after my bust, I considered a move back into what I loved, TV and radio. I went to New York and met with two people: Pete Dominick, who has a show on SiriusXM, and Chris Hayes of MSNBC, both flaming-red communist liberals. Just terrible human beings!

Pete and I had known each other for a few years. He had occasionally interviewed me while I was in Congress and more recently had encouraged me to get back into radio. He even had me on as a guest from time to time.

Chris Hayes had occasionally made fun of me during my term on the Hill for my "out of the box" work on social media. But when my arrest hit the news, Chris gave a supportive monologue on his show that someone shared with me. As I was just starting to get on social media again, Chris sent me a short note. "Nice to see you here on Twitter. Hope you're doing well." I thanked him and suggested lunch next time I was in New York. We met and hit it off.

Then another set of dominos began to fall and connect in a great way. Chris had me on his show in a segment on Jeb Bush and Marco Rubio, both longtime Florida politicians and one-time rivals for the Republican nomination for president. No longer worried about votes, voters, positions, policies, or political correctness, I lightened up a bit and suggested that "Jeb to Marco wasn't so much Obi-Wan to Luke, more Dre to Snoop Dogg." I have no idea what that meant, but it got some good laughs!

It also led to a big call.

I was sitting on the same couch where I'd taken the call from Connie Mack encouraging me to run for Congress years before. Once again, my wife was watching some *Real House-wives* show. As two women beer-bonged bottles of chardonnay and then began stabbing each other with nail files, my phone rang.

Before I answered the phone, I leaned forward, looked directly at Andy Cohen on the TV, and said, "Andy, after all I've been through, thank you for producing these kinds of shows, which make me feel so sane and so normal. Thank you." I hugged the TV and then began pacing around the room. The call was from a Los Angeles area code. "Trey?" the voice on the other end asked.

"Who's this?"

"My name is Vanessa. I work on HBO's *Real Time with Bill Maher*. We'd love to have you on as a panel member."

A month later, as I was walking through the CBS lot where Maher shoots, I snuck into one of the back lots and spun the famous *Price Is Right* wheel. I even took a cheesy selfie. Soon I was having makeup applied and sitting in a dark studio with two other panelists. The next thing I know, Bill freakin' Maher, who I have been a fan of since I was a kid, is sitting next to me, playfully giving me crap for voting to drug test food stamp recipients!

"Ah, yes, that, Bill . . ."

I don't feel "back" or "rebranded" or "reinvented." I've learned a few things and applied them to my life, but when all is said and done, I did what I had to do—stand back up, dust myself off, and get back to living. And living for me is and *has always been* about passion and love—a passion for people, an insatiable curiosity for culture, and an undying love of life.

Shortly after my resignation, I heard the same line repeatedly from friends and even strangers: "Things happen for a reason." I don't believe that. *Things do not happen for a reason; you make the reason.*

I don't let the past weigh me down or let the future stress me out. While carpe diem had meant many different things to me, after I left Congress, it was about creating moments. I worked hard to create a balance in my life between work and family. That may sound simple, but it takes a lot of effort and patience for me.

Have I achieved "inner peace"? Some days are better than others. Following my resignation, I often asked myself, *Am I an alcoholic or an asshole?* Maybe both. Maybe tomorrow things will change. Maybe they won't. While I occasionally enjoy a beer and do not go to AA meetings now, I attended many for more than a year and listened to people's struggles and applied their cautionary tales to my own life. Most of all, I learned "one day at a time."

All of this might come across as *cavalier*. Maybe you're even asking, *What the hell are you thinking?*

Well, there are gray areas in life.

The gray areas of my life, and the ones in yours, also exist in Congress.

The American public may demand purity and litmus tests from their elected representatives, but the reality is that they live in gray areas, too. Some call it compromise; some call it concession; some call it weak; some call it strength. Some may disparagingly refer to it as moral ambiguity. I call it life.

From specific votes to overall policy, very little is black-and-white. Whether it's Congressman Mike Conaway calling himself a fiscal conservative while fighting to make sure millions are appropriated to sheep shearers, or Senator Elizabeth Warren supporting Obamacare while arguing for the repeal of parts of it, they are both doing what their constituents elected them to do—fight for them. I don't know either of them personally, but I'd bet Mike and Elizabeth are both good people who do fight like hell for the cities, states, and people they represent.

My experience in Congress taught me that most people serving in our country's capital are good men and women from all walks of life who share the same goals—to make our country a better place filled with opportunity for all. But remember, they're regular people no different from you or anyone else, and some, including me, are vulnerable to bad choices. What I realized in the institution, *inside the belly of the beast,* is that it's not so much Democrats against Republicans or vice versa; it's Americans against the institution.

The institution of Congress is like society itself. As individuals, we know that sometimes *we could have and should have* made some better choices in life. We recognize some of the corners we've boxed ourselves into—the crappy job we've worked at for too long, a failing marriage we've helped create, or an intolerable family we can barely talk to. But most of us are good people who mean well. Sure, we could have made some better choices in the past, and our current situation may be tough to change, but finding a new job or fixing your broken relationship takes a ton of work and includes getting involved with others on a deeper level by constantly communicating with family, friends, coworkers, your spouse, and even yourself. *It requires bonds and relationships.* Sometimes it requires getting outside help.

Similarly, Congress, as an institution, has drawn itself into corners that will be extremely difficult to get out of—impossible promises, huge giveaways, failed oversight, unsustainable spending, and more.

We, as voters, as people, and as participants in our democracy, are ultimately responsible for the institution. We created it *intentionally with a vote or unintentionally by not voting.*

For more than two hundred years, we have been fighting over how much government or how little government we need in our lives. Liberals demand "more here, but not there," and conservatives say "some here, but not there." And both of them are operating in gray areas.

Perhaps the answer exists within the context of time. Maybe

more government is better at times. And as little government as possible might be best at other times. As a conservative, I lean toward the latter, but that's not to say I am always right. *Gray, I know.*

I don't have all the answers. But while the system may be broken, the people are not—not the representatives, not the senators, not the presidents, and certainly not Americans.

Patience is a virtue.

★ Proverb

In these hyperpartisan times, as groups, we are so damn quick to yell at one another instead of talking to one another. We approach people from different walks of life with suspicion instead of an open mind. But *as individuals* we are much more understanding and empathetic. Outside of D.C., in "real life," as couples, as friends, and as coworkers, we form bonds and relationships to better one another and ourselves. We also compromise. It's how we get things done.

We could also use more patience with those evil politicians in Washington we despise so much. When we are quick to shout down members for even talking to someone from the other party or, God forbid, using that filthy word "compromise," a little patience would go a long way.

Members should spend more time together, visiting one another's districts, having drinks and dinner together, even getting their families together. Will it lead to a landslide of solutions for immigration, the tax code, or foreign policy? Not right away. However, with bonds and personal relationships, members can start talking *with* one another again instead of *at* one another.

Democracy is ugly, it is tough, and sometimes it's a little crazy. But only through unity, both as a society and a government, can we form a more perfect Union. Congress is a lot like you and me. It is a reflection of our society, all the good, bad, and questionable. When we look at Washington, we're looking in a mirror.

While my deepest personal weaknesses cut short my dreams and work in Congress, I picked myself up. As individuals and a country, we can do the same.

Life has ups. Life has downs. Hang on tight, especially to your sense of humor.

ACKNOWLEDGMENTS

First, to the most important people in my life, my wife, son, father, and brother, thank you for your patience, your understanding, your unwavering support, and your love. I owe you more than I could ever give back in a lifetime.

To my extended family and friends, even though we may be separated by time and geography, you remain close to my heart. I think about you every day and hope to see you soon.

To my staff I worked with in D.C., any small feat I may have accomplished during my short time in office was because of you. More than being staff, you were *and are* family. Thank you for your support through everything.

To the current, past, and future members of the U.S. Senate and House, I hope many of you have read this entire book, not just listened to the critical parts in the news. I refrained from riding on any moral high horse in this book and am not about to begin doling out more clichéd advice on what you should be doing. The only thing I will say is this: In these hyperpartisan times, with social media and traditional media breathing down your neck 24/7, do not put all of your faith in the loudest voices.

Flip Brophy, my agent, and David Rosenthal, my publisher, mentor, and friend, thank you for your leap of faith. As a first-time writer, I could never have gotten through this without your guidance and patience. David, your confidence was a huge inspiration.

Ruth Fecych, Katie Zaborsky, and David Hough, while I may have sounded frustrated when receiving your edits and suggestions (and privately yelled things like "What the hell? Is this high school English class?!"), thank you for your help in creating a tighter and much more fluid book.

To my few close friends and mentors in the media, who I have never publicly recognized or mentioned in this book, thank you for your friendship and for being there for me. In our many years of friendship, I have always appreciated your guidance and words of wisdom.

My random shout-outs: Thank you Square One and Kabab Village in Fort Myers, my offices away from home, where I wrote most of *Democrazy*. By the way, what a great combo—a burger and beer joint from Oklahoma and a local Muslim-owned restaurant and hookah lounge, with a Palestinian who speaks Spanish. *I love America!*

And finally, to you reading this, thank you. Thank you for taking time to read my story. Even if we don't agree on everything, I hope someday we can sit down for a civil conversation or, better yet, a laugh or two.

ABOUT THE AUTHOR

Trey Radel is an author, an actor, a journalist, a TV and radio show host, and a former member of Congress.

In his twenties, Radel built a successful career in media, doing TV, radio, digital, and print. Radel worked as a journalist, reporting and anchoring television news. He built and sold a community newspaper to the E. W. Scripps Company. Soon after, Radel was hosting one of Florida's premier talk radio shows, doing four hours of live talk every weekday.

Passionate about our country and politics, Radel ran for the United States Congress in his thirties. The underdog won big, building a massive coalition of people cutting across generational, ethnic, and cultural lines.

Fluent in English, Spanish, and Italian, Radel has lived in, worked in, or backpacked through nearly fifty countries around the world, sometimes living off just ten dollars a day. His love for people, places, and especially foreign cultures has taken him from South America to Southeast Asia and about everywhere in between.

Currently, as an occasional actor, Radel has had roles in Sony's Crackle app and the Discovery Network. Radel studied improv comedy at Second City in Chicago. While in Chicago, he also played guitar in a band.

Radel resides in Florida with his family, where he owns a business doing media training, communications consulting, and crisis management.